THE GUILD®

The Designer's Reference Book of Artists

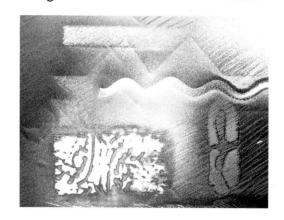

Kraus Sikes Inc.
Madison, Wisconsin

Published by:
Kraus Sikes Inc.
228 State Street
Madison, WI 53703
800-969-1556
608-256-1990
FAX 608-256-1938

Administration:
Toni Fountain Sikes, President
James F. Black, Jr., Vice President
Susan K. Evans, Associate Publisher
Darin J. Edington, Business Manager
Yvonne Cooley, Secretary

Production, Design, Editorial:
Kristine Firchow, Production Manager
Liz Stephens, Copy Editor
Scott Fields, Copy Editor
Jorge Arango, Writer
Gerri Nixon, Writer
Leslie Ferrin, Writer
Logan Fry, Interviewer

Toppan Printing Co.,
Separations, Printing and Binding

Regional Representatives:
Susan K. Evans
Sharon Marquis
Andrea Moriarty
Cynthia Snook

THE GUILD REGISTER:
Scott Fields, Coordinator
Sharon Marquis, Fiber Art Representative

Distribution:
This book is exclusively distributed
by Rockport Publishers, Inc.
Rockport, Massachusetts

ISBN (softback) 1-880140-05-5
ISBN (hardback) 1-880140-04-7
ISSN 0885-3975

Printed in Japan

Cover Art: *Sculptural Design Series,* © 1991, bowl
15", vase 12", fluted vase 8", perfume vial 5 ½",
tapered vase 10", created by **Jonathan Winfisky**
(see page 197). Photo: Tommy Elder

Cover Art (Background): detail, mixed-media
painting on textured aluminum, 1992, created by
Bruce R. Bleach (see page 95). This piece, from
the *Performance Series,* is now in a permanent
corporate collection. The detail shown also
appears throughout the book. Photo: Nick Saraco

INTRODUCTION

Welcome...to our eighth annual publication of THE GUILD, the definitive resource of top artists. All are juried into the book on the basis of their experience, the quality of their work, and their reputation for working with design professionals.

This volume features artists who create work for the wall, and artists who make furniture and accessories. The book is divided into those three major sections, and then subdivided according to the medium used within those sections.

This volume also introduces THE GUILD REGISTER of Fiber Art. It runs from pages 55 to 75 and provides the names and addresses of hundreds of artists who produce fiber-related art for the wall. THE GUILD REGISTER is the latest manifestation of our effort to be the most comprehensive source of artists who are enhancing our public places and private spaces.

For years our users have been asking for more details on the pricing of work they see in THE GUILD. We have responded with a new feature, The Price Index, which you will find on pages 252 to 255.

And since galleries and showrooms that specialize in hand-crafted work are an important link in finding artists and seeing what they produce, we have included a state-by-state list of over 1,200 North American galleries. This list, on pages 225 to 249, highlights those galleries that carry the work of artists in THE GUILD–in case you want to see in person what you have seen in print on these pages.

The work of artists in THE GUILD gets better and better every year in every way. It is our goal to make sure that THE GUILD does as well.

But, this book is not just a professional sourcebook. If it really works, it should stimulate the senses, inspire the imagination, and expand creative horizons. We feel it does all that and more.

And so, with pleasure and pride, we present THE GUILD 8.

Toni Fountain Sikes
Publisher

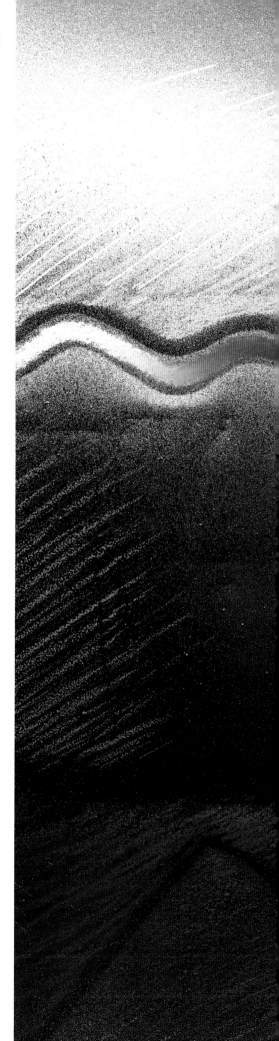

Special thanks to our
1993 Review Committee:

Peter Mistretta
Mistretta Designs
Charles Morris Mount
Silver & Ziskind/Mount
Mark Simon
Centerbrook
Sue Wiggins
ArtSouth, Inc.

TABLE OF CONTENTS

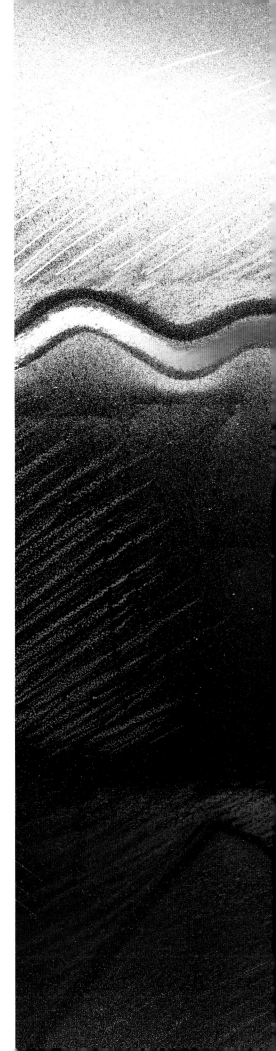

NEW FEATURE:

THE GUILD REGISTER
of Fiber Art pages 55-75

WORK FOR THE WALL

The artists who create work for the wall have grown increasingly imaginative and expansive in their choice of media, in the aesthetic sophistication and technical mastery. In this section one finds ceramics and glass, paper, tapestries, art quilts and wall sculptures in a variety of media. All are garnering new attention in art circles as a growing number of museums and galleries across the country have begun exhibiting an exciting array of new works.

An increase in visibility and status serve both artists and art buyers well—designers have never had more choices nor artists working in craft media more opportunities.

In the words of one of the fiber artists in THE GUILD, "the public's consciousness has been raised and along with it my own inspiration." As the corporate world's interest in acquiring unique works of art grows, she and other artists are enjoying new opportunities for creating commissioned, one-of-a-kind pieces.

Not surprisingly, these artists are as concerned with the endurance of their work as those who purchase it are. They have experimented with materials, dyes, adhesives and finishes and they have mastered these materials and their craft. They have studied the masters in their fields and they have formed associations among themselves to further improve the quality of their work.

They are not only professionals at their craft but in the entire process resulting in an inspirational new dialogue with their clients. One GUILD artist spoke of getting blueprints, samples of granite, carpeting, and photographs of furnishings from a potential client to acquaint her with the client's corporate environment. Later, when the client received sketches of the artist's proposed design, he sent photos of the intended wall space with brown paper models based on the dimensions. From then on, the artist included the client in the process by sending Polaroids of the work in process, including some buckets of dyed pulp!

In these pages, you'll find amazing choices. Ceramic artwork that adds a colorful spark, subtly woven pieces that bring richness and comfort to a space, whimsical mixed media sculpture that makes the environment friendly, and tapestry pictures that inspire dreaming.

Here are beautiful things to enrich the quality of our lives, and the artists who create work for the wall bring us all grand, new possibilities. We are all realizing that re-personalizing, beautifying our interior environments makes them far more inspiring places in which to live, do business and play.

See our article on pages 76-78 "The Care and Maintenance of Fiber Art," for more information on positioning , framing, installation and cleaning.

WORK FOR THE WALL

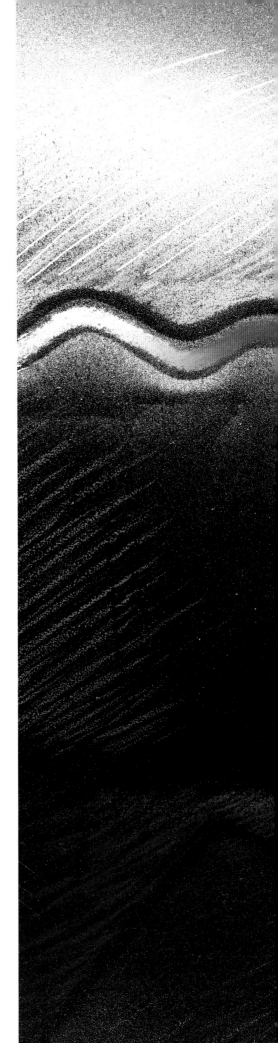

A Conversation with Martha Chatelain

Martha Chatelain creates sculptural work in paper.

How did you choose the medium of paper in which to work?

At UCLA I trained as ceramicist, but later worked in various media, including experimental photography. To obtain acid-free, textured paper for photographic prints, I taught myself the basics of paper making. I was intrigued with the visceral similarities between paper, pulp, and clay, and I immediately realized that I could use paper as a medium in its own right, rather than as merely a passive surface for other media. Working with paper pulp also allows me to have my whole body interact with the work, instead of just my fingers and hands.

How do you make your paper?

My paper is made entirely from non-acidic materials, principally cotton and abaca fiber. I make 20-gallon batches of pulp, which I transfer into five-gallon buckets. Fiber-reactive dyes are then added. I repeat the process until I have up to 20 pails of colored pulp. The pulp has the consistency of a runny oatmeal at this point. I pour it in a very gestural way to form sheets on the vacuum table. All of this needs to proceed very quickly, because it is important that some of the dye remain free in the pulp solution to migrate within the sheets. This flow of color in the creative process helps to explain the reason the color appears to flow visually in the finished piece. As the work proceeds, I can also emboss the sheets to create various textures and surfaces.

What is your procedure when dealing with clients?

Perhaps telling you about a recent commission will help you understand the entire process. An architect and art consultant, who was working on the American Airlines Admirals' Club in New York's Kennedy Airport, liked my work and commissioned a wall piece of mine for the entry lobby as well. There wasn't room in the budget to bring me to New York from San Diego, so they sent me photographs and a small color board. From this material, I prepared several pastel sketches to give an idea of size, shape, color interaction, and mood of the proposed piece.

After receiving design approval, I proceeded to execute the commission, "Unfolding Passages." Its final dimensions are 4' x 14', but it was created in three interlocking sections to facilitate shipment. Mounting the work required nothing special, so I sent mounting instructions with the work. I still haven't seen the installation in person, but the photographs look very good, and my clients say they are very happy with it.

Karen Adachi

702 Monarch Way
Santa Cruz, CA 95060
(408) 429-6192

Karen Adachi creates her three-dimensional handmade paper pieces by using layers of irregularly shaped vacuum-cast paper. She makes free-standing, two-sided sculptures and wall-pieces for corporate, private and residential interiors. Her work is shown nationally through major galleries and representatives.

The pieces are richly textured and embellished with dyes, acrylics, metallics and pearlescents. Painted bamboo and sticks are used to create a dramatic statement of pattern and line. Three-dimensional sculptures are mounted on painted metal bases for stability and strength.

Custom work in any size, shape and color is available. Contact the artist for further information and slides.

Martha Chatelain

Artfocus, Ltd.
P.O. Box 9855
San Diego, CA 92169
(619) 234-0749
FAX (619) 234-0821

Martha Chatelain creates richly textured, three-dimensional, handmade paper and mixed-media wall sculptures. Colored by fiber dyes, accented with iridescent mica powders or patined copper, works can be framed in plexiglas or unframed with a protective spray. Chatelain's artwork complements the architectural and design features of the interior spaces for which it is created.

Please call to discuss design specifications, client environment, and/or site-specific commissions. Allow 6 to 8 weeks following design approval. Works are shipped FOB San Diego.

Prices depend on size and complexity of work.

Selected Collections: American Airlines, Bank of America, Champion Paper, IBM, International Paper, Potlatch Corporation, Sheraton Hotels, Upjohn Corporation, Xerox Corporation.

Right: *Kasumigumo (Misty Cloud),*
   86" x 33" x 4"

Karen Davidson

P.O. Box 637
Hana, HI 96713
(808) 248-7094

Collaborating with nature, Hana-Maui artist Karen Davidson's work begins with the actual fibers themselves.

"I am guided by the rythymic play of light and shadow I see developing as I work with each sculpture," Karen Davidson says.

Gathering materials from the abundance of the tropical jungle surrounding her studio, she draws from her classical European and East Coast art training to create unique imagery. Davidson's work embodies the qualities of aged metallic surfaces with the colors and textures of antique leather and parchment.

Paradis, detail

Paradis, 1991, private collection, Napili, HI, collaged handformed paper, 54" x 48" x 6"

Susana England

P.O. Box 20601
Oakland, CA 94620
(510) 261-5646

Susana England uses a wide range of techniques to enhance the textural qualities in the abstract images of her dimensional wallpieces and free-standing sculpture. These fiber collage "paintings" of cloth and handmade paper are embellished with stitching and painted forms.

Her work is included in private and corporate collections including Kaiser Permanente, Moody's Investor Service, North Bay Medical Center and the USDA. Slides and information regarding commissions are available.

Right: *Unquilted*, wallpiece, paper, fiber, 46" x 31"
Left: *Azul*, sculpture, paper, fiber, 35" x 15" x 12"

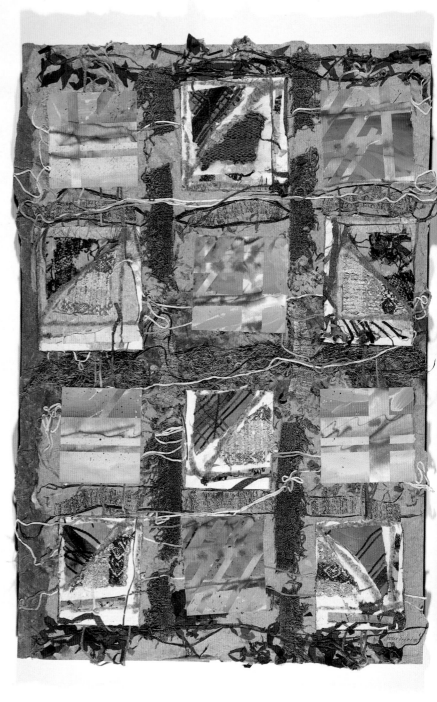

Joseph Gallo

Editions in Cast Paper
1101 N. High Cross Road
Urbana, IL 61801
(217) 328-0118
FAX (217) 328-4864

Years of collaborative production in handmade paper with such artists as Victor Vasarely, Peter Max, Hanna Barbera and Agam have left Joseph Gallo well-versed in papermaking's vast array of applications.

Sheet formation is the basis for all of Gallo's work. Figurative images are created by templates, multiple pulls and drawing with water. Other works involve wet collage and air brushing. Mono casts and low-relief floral prints (not shown) are also available. Sizes range from 11" x 12" to 4' x 8'. All works consist of pigmented cotton rag, linen and abaca. Colors are lightfast and site-specific color poses no problem.

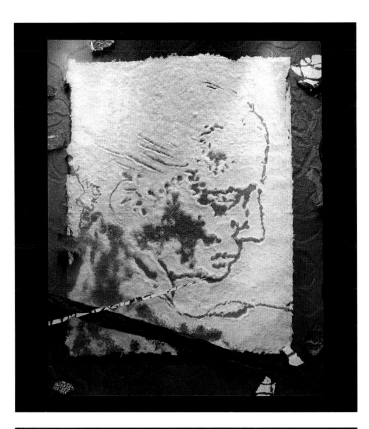

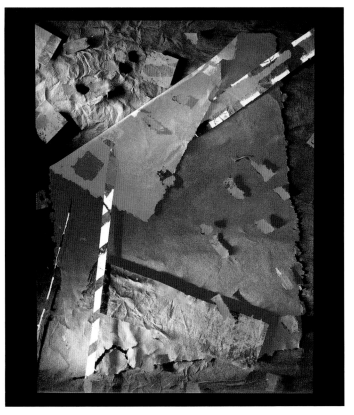

Susan Gardels

1316 Arthur Avenue
Des Moines, IA 50316
(515) 265-2361

Susan Gardels has created archival-quality paper pieces for corporate and private clients for the last 15 years. Pieces are constructed of acid-free rag, mulberry, and esparto grass papers, are painted with acrylic glazes, and machine sewn for texture and durability. Large pieces are backed with cotton canvas for additional strength. After framing, the works require no further care.

Please contact the artist for information regarding commissions, prices and slides.

Top: *Malawi Dream: Outside the window maize flour was spread as if to dry, glowing white as powdered stars,* 24" x 26"
Bottom: *Night Boats from Msaka Village,* 36" x 39"

Lenore Hughes

P.O. Box 1862
La Jolla, CA 92038-1862
(619) 456-1144
FAX (619) 291-8362

Lenore Hughes' innovative and exquisite watercolor tapestries are beautiful and exciting blends of color, sparkle and dimension. She hand cuts and weaves her original paintings into unique abstracts that hint of landscape or still life.

Hughes especially enjoys personalizing her art to perfectly accentuate your specific environment. Whether you seek pure, bright, summer colors, soft spring tones, decorator colors or sophisticated greys and tans, Lenore Hughes' pallette provides colors to evoke any mood. Her scale is equally diverse: she produces top-quality pieces from as large as a full-scale mural to as small as a wine label (Carey Cellars' *Arabesque*).

Lenore Hughes' work is exhibited across the country and around the world, and is hailed by some of America's preeminent modern art collectors.

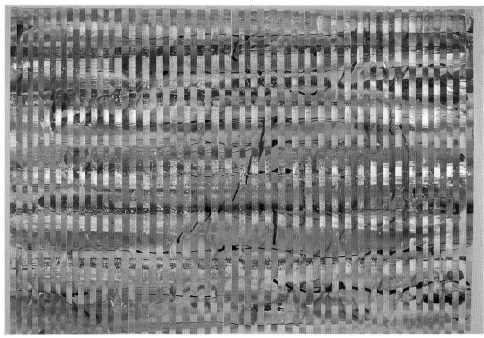

Woven Streams of Light, 1991, private residence, watercolor, metallic, india ink collage, 29" x 43"

Peace Rose, 1991, private residence, watercolor, mixed-media collage, 60" x 42"

Joan Kopchik

1335 Stephen Way
Southampton, PA 18966-4349
(215) 322-1862

Joan Kopchik folds and layers sheets of archival quality handmade papers and incorporates textural elements and objects to create works of distinction. Her elegant designs are nature inspired and are suitable for many environments. She holds a BFA from Carnegie Mellon University and has worked with design professionals to develop site-specific works for private and corporate spaces.

Selected commissions/collections: DuPont, Hercules Incorporated, Johnson & Higgins, McNeil Consumer Products, Chemical Bank, Fidelity Bank, Wilmington Trust, CoreStates First Pennsylvania Bank.

Top: *Cascade*, 24"H x 30"W x 2 ½"D
Bottom: *Hanging Garden*, 24"H x 32"W x 2 ½"D

Cal Ling

Cal Ling Paperworks
441 Cherry Street
Chico, CA 95928
(916) 893-0882

Cal Ling mixes the idea of paper and clay by producing paper tiles that are durable as well as aesthetically pleasing. Treated with a waterproofing agent and grouted with masonry grout, these paper tiles may register as murals, wall papers, architectural accents or formal artworks.

The combination of smooth and textured papers adds depth and dimension to the painterly surface. Cal Ling is experienced at both small- and large-scale works.

Prices, samples and slides are available upon request.

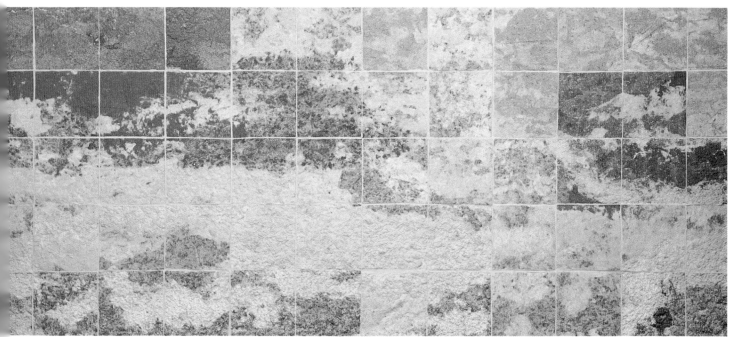

Marjorie Tomchuk

M. Tomchuk
44 Horton Lane
New Canaan, CT 06840
(203) 972-0137
FAX (203) 972-3182

As a professional for 30 years, Marjorie Tomchuk has art placed in more than 50 major corporations, including IBM, Xerox, Citicorp, AT&T, GE and also museums including the Library of Congress. She specializes in paintings and embossings on artist-made paper, the style is semi-abstract.

A 20-page color brochure packet can be obtained for reference, price: $5.ppd. Commissioned art: sizes up to 4' x 6'. Maquettes available. Delivery: 4 to 6 weeks. Also available: a hard cover book *M. Tomchuk Graphic Work 1962-1989*, 143 pages, $32, ppd.

Top: *Red Lake*, painting, marbling and embossing on artist-made paper, 34"x 26"
Below: *Sunrise Valley*, painting, marbling and embossing on artist-made paper, 26"x 34"

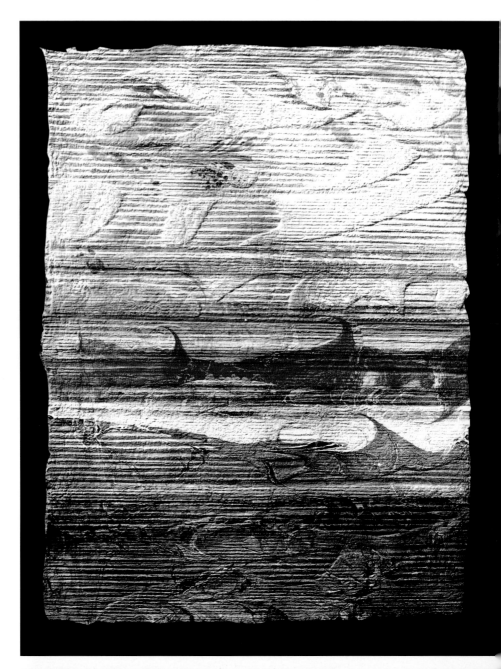

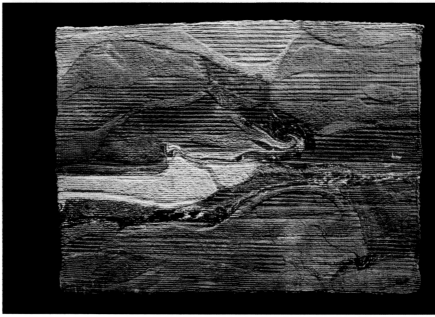

Ellen Zahorec

Island Ford Studio
1418 Country Club Road
Brevard, NC 28712
(704) 883-2254

Southern Highland Handicraft Guild
P.O. Box 9545
Asheville, NC 28815
(704) 298-7928

Ellen Zahorec creates one-of-a-kind, contemporary, mixed-media, canvas constructions and handmade-paper collages. Zahorec fuses fine-art media and craft processes resulting in rich patterned surfaces of color and texture.

This internationally recognized artist and instructor holds an MFA from the University of Tennessee and a BFA from Kent State University. Her work is represented in numerous corporate and private collections including IBM, TVA, Asheville Art Museum, Mint Museum, Fez Museum and Taidekeskus Maltinranta, Finland.

Collages and canvas constructions are available for private and corporate collections and are designed for specific dimensions and color range.

Top: *The Triangular Edge*, 1992, Artsource Indianapolis, IN, handmade paper, acrylic paint, 76" x 36"
Bottom Left: *Sixty Year Shroud #2*, 1991, stitched canvas, acrylic paint 45" x 92"
Bottom Right: *Guardians of the Holy Virgins*, 1992, mixed-media collage, handmade paper, 28" x 34"

A Conversation with
Janis Kanter

Janis Kanter combines traditional tapestry with neon lighting to make work for the wall.

How did you come to combine neon and tapestry in your work?

I consider myself a fiber artist, but several years ago I decided to introduce lighting into my work. I found that interesting effects could be achieved by combining the warmth and texture of fiber with the glow and definition of neon tubing. In collaboration with neon artists, I worked out the technical aspects of using neon with fiber. I learned, for example, that by keeping the diameter of neon to a certain size, the tubing would remain cool. That eliminated a potential heat source that could damage the fiber. We also worked out mounting methods that were very attractive, yet would conceal the wiring and small electrical transformer needed to make the installation work.

Has the use of neon changed the way you conceive of your art?

At first I used neon as an added decorative feature to bring emphasis to elements in my tapestry, or to outline images. Now that I am thoroughly comfortable with neon, I am beginning to let it stand on its own. A Chicago developer, for example, wanted me to create a work that would say something about his business. Before, I might have created the whole image in fiber first. Now I can weave a dark background of sky, and use neon to define the skyline. In another weaving, I used the neon to simulate the sparks of energy coming from a radio tower.

Are there any special installation considerations to your work?

The team of artists that I use to actually bend the neon tubing also builds the mounting frame for me. Shipping is a factor I must consider. Pieces are usually packed by professional packers and carried by art forwarders. Occasionally, to eliminate the shipping problem, I have a piece assembled in the client's city.

Once installed, maintenance is not a major problem. Sometimes a transformer may require replacement, but that is not difficult. Also, the neon elements are replaceable if broken. I retain all my original plans and specifications to assist the glass professionals who may be called on to repair an installation.

The usual design factors of size, shape, color, and traffic patterns come into play. Because glass is used, the piece should not be in an area where it could be easily brushed by passing office traffic or things like mail carts. The only other major characterization of work is that I need a standard wall receptacle to plug it into.

Rebecca Bluestone

P.O. Box 1704
Santa Fe, NM 87504
(505) 989-9599
FAX (505) 989-9599

Rebecca Bluestone's unique textiles are hand-woven and hand-dyed with lightfast silk, wool and metallic threads. By applying her skills as a colorist and designer, Bluestone creates an unlimited palette of colors, allowing her to work closely with other Professionals in planning and executing site-specific commissions. Each piece leaves the studio ready for installation and requires very little maintenance.

Bluestone's work is shown nationally in galleries, museums and juried exhibitions. Her work hangs in settings as diverse as the Lovelace Medical Center and the U.S. Embassy in Jakarta, Indonesia.

Slide portfolios available upon request.

Top: *New Sounds/1*, silk, wool, dyes, metallic thread, 56" x 48"
Bottom Left: *Hexagram/4*, silk, wool, dyes, 56" x 43"
Bottom Right: *Silk Journey/1*, silk, wool, dyes, 60" x 45"

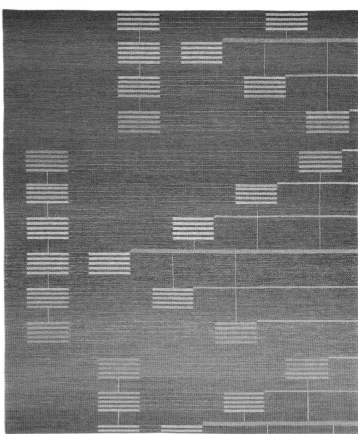

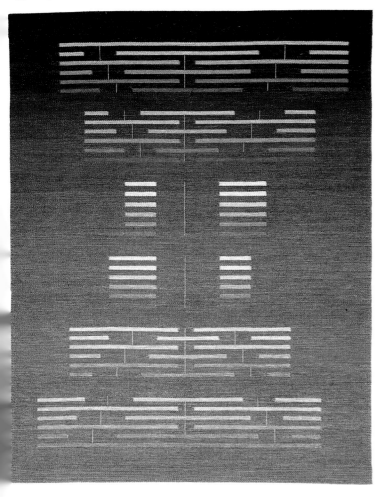

Linda Denier

Denier Tapestry Studio
745 Edenwood Drive
Roselle, IL 60172
(708) 893-5854

Dynamic colors bring detailed imagery to life in the tapestries of Linda Denier. While colors create depth, fiber adds warmth to these durable, low-maintenance works of art. Beautifully crafted, primarily of wool, all work is hand finished in the studio.

Commissions are welcomed for residential and commercial spaces, as Denier enjoys the challenge of designing to meet the client's vision. Completed tapestries are also available; all work is installation ready.Slides and prices furnished upon request.

Top: *Do You Know the Way*
Bottom: *Oz*

Alexandra Friedman

56 Arbor Street
Hartford, CT 06106
(203) 236-3311

Alexandra Friedman approaches the traditional art form of tapestry weaving with refreshing contemporary imagery. The award-winning tapestries have been exhibited and collected by corporate and residential clients both nationally and internationally.

She enjoys working on commissions and will collaborate with the client to design a tapestry that best suits a specific site.

There is a selection of completed tapestries available. Further inquiries are welcome.

Left: *Wicker Chair*, 1990, Aetna Life and Casualty, Co., wool tapestry, 96" x 54"
Right: *Beach Stairs,* 1990, wool tapestry, 72" x 49"

Irene R. de Gair Tapestries

2260 Teel Drive
Vienna, VA 22182-5154
(703) 698-9281
FAX (703) 698-9208

The intricate and diverse patterns of Irene de Gairs' tapestries provide warmth and dimension to complement a wide range of interior spaces. The pattern of each sheep's-wool tapestry is hand woven and maintenance free.

International commissions by Kemper Life Insurance, Marriott Hotels and Embassies worldwide include floral designs, contemporary abstracts, landscapes and corporate logos.

A preliminary color pencil sketch and elevation of the space will be provided at no cost.

Irene de Gair works closely with art consultants, architects and interior designers to create unique, site-specific tapestries of any size, ready for delivery in 8 to 12 weeks.

A large selection from her collection is available immediately and will be sent on approval.

Please call for visuals. Prices quoted per foot or per tapestry.

24 Work for the Wall: Tapestries

Victor Jacoby

1086 17th Street
Eureka, CA 95501
(707) 442-3809

Victor Jacoby has been creating woven tapestries and exhibiting them nationally for more than 20 years. Since 1975 he has also woven numerous commissions for both corporate and residential spaces. Land-scape, floral and figurative themes have been explored as well as other themes appropriate to individual client's needs. Clients include AT&T, Kaiser-Permanente, Marriott Corporation, SEIU, and Sherson, Lehman, Hutton.

Further information, slides and price list are available on request.

Top: *On the Road Again*, 1991, 36" x 37"
Bottom: *Warner Mountains Landscape*, 1991, 24" x 37"

Libby Kowalski

41 Union Square West, Suite 502
New York, NY 10003
(212) 627-5770
FAX (212) 989-9702

Libby Kowalski's black-and-white woven and painted pieces are delicate, yet bold, highly-patterned and hard-edged images. Although her earlier work was more constructivist in style, recent compositions reveal an exploration into symbolism. She used computers and computer imagery to design these compositions.

A professional of many years, Kowalski's work is found in the collections of IBM Corporation, UNISYS, General Motors, Kresge Corporation, Automobile Association of America and North American Communications. Her work has been exhibited in galleries and museums nationally and internationally.

Production time varies depending on size and complexity. Commissions are accepted. Price list and slides of currently available work upon request.

Top: *Characters to Shape the Composition Players in Their World,* 1990, cotton, linen, wood and acrylic, 41 ½" x 25"
Bottom: *Dancers Who Know the Tune Speak Little of Its Content, Dancers Who Know the Rune Silently Sway to the Music* ,1990, cotton, linen, wood and acrylic, 35" x 49"

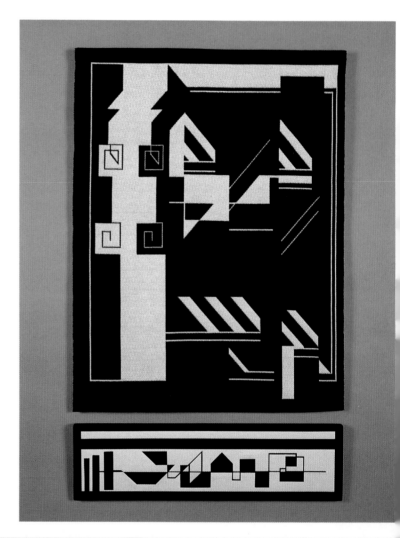

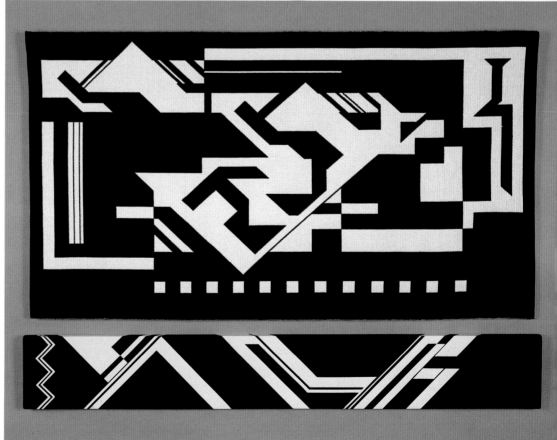

Ulrika Leander

Contemporary Tapestry Weaving
107 Westoverlook Drive
Oak Ridge, TN 37830
(615) 482-6849

Ulrika Leander completed her degree in fiber arts at the College of Fiberarts in Stockholm, Sweden in 1971; this was followed by a four-year appointment as Head of the Department of Fiberarts at the University of Lund. Ulrika Leander has installed more than 150 tapestries commissioned for public, private and commercial settings in Scandinavia and the U.S. Inspired by her native country's traditions, Leander has established a reputation for superb craftsmanship and a remarkable range of creative and imaginative designs. Using 100 percent natural fibers, she produces single pieces measuring up to 12' by 30'.

Resume, slides and a videotape are available on request.

Top: *Gennesaret*, 1986, Norwegian Seaman's
   Church, Houston, TX, 4 ½' x 9'
Bottom Left/Right: *Dancing with the Birds*,
   1990, private collection, 5 ½' x 7 ½'

Sharon Marcus

4145 S.W. Corbett
Portland, OR 97201
(503) 796-1234
FAX (503) 796-1234

Sharon Marcus' woven tapestries combine classical technique with expressive, innovative style. Premium quality wool, linen and cotton are utilized to create designs that are dramatic and "readable" at a distance, yet increasingly complex in detail when viewed more closely.

An internationally recognized artist, her work has appeared in publications around the world, has received frequent awards and is represented in corporate, public and private collections.

Further information is available upon request.

Top: *Dreams of Passage*, 1992, 36"H x 56"W
Bottom: *Departure*, 1992, 36"H x 60"W

Loretta Mossman

2416 Aspen Street
Philadelphia, PA 19130
(215) 765-3248
FAX (215) 483-4864

Loretta Mossman's tapestries are artworks conceived and developed for individual spaces and design concepts. A colorist, she creates moods with her rich palette. Using traditional techniques, pure wools are colored with luxurious natural pigments and woven to form single panels or multi-dimensional constructions. Designs and textures are created and enhanced with ecclectic accents such as appliquéd fabrics, buttons and found objects.

The artist welcomes the opportunity to collaborate with architects, designers and consultants and will scale designs to meet the specifications of private, corporate or architectural settings. Design portfolios are available for a fee, refundable with first commission.

Loretta Mossman's work has been exhibited widely and she is represented in public and private collections.

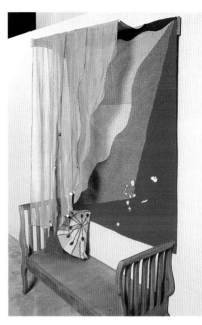

Deann Rubin

Deann Joy Studios
990-A La Mesa Terrace
Sunnyvale, CA 94086
(408) 739-9609

Incorporating the finest yarns available, Deann Rubin weaves her powerful graphic designs into contemporary gobelin-style tapestries. Her work ranges from pieces based on photorealism to more graphic abstractions. Many of her works reflect urban themes that use human imagery.

Rubin holds a B.F.A. Degree and has been producing handwoven tapestries for 12 years. She has designed and woven commissions for site-related areas and clients' interests. Her tapestries require little care and are made to last. Works by Deann Rubin have been exhibited and publicized nationally and are included in private and public collections.

Further information is available on request.

Top: *Alleged*, wool, cotton, cowhair, 32" x 95"
Bottom: *Sweet Shoppe*, wool, cotton, cowhair, 49" x 54"

Efrem Weitzman

Efrem Weitzman Art Works, Inc.
P.O. Drawer 1092
South Fallsburg, NY 12779
(914) 434-2408
(914) 434-7956

Shown here are hand-tufted wool tapestries created by Efrem Weitzman for corporate clients. These tapestries are thematic and the themes chosen are the result of a dialogue between the artist and the CEO. The choice of color and the scale of the design are also the result of a dialogue. In this case, between Efrem Weitzman and the architect or interior designer.

Because he is interested in creating art works that are uniquely suited to their setting, Efrem Weitzman employs other media for his walls such as metal, fiber, mosaic, etc. He invites inquiries.

Top Left: *Arkansas Tapestry,* Worthen Bank, Little Rock, AR
Top Right: *Land Rush Tapestry,* Liberty Bank, Oklahoma City, OK
Bottom: *Battery Tapestry,* detail, General Battery, Reading, PA

A Conversation with
Joan Schulze

Joan Schulze makes art quilts
in northern California.

What's involved in your design process?

Like contemporary jazz, my work is
constantly evolving. In that sense, it is
like the music of Miles Davis, who is
one of my cultural heroes. He could
take a musical phrase, reverse it, turn
it upside down and inside out, or
repeat it with constant variations.
Over his lifetime, his music continued
to evolve and grow. I want my own
work to have this same attribute of
evolution and growth. I approach a
new piece in terms of the idea or
mood or memory I want to evoke, but
I avoid making exacting drafts before
beginning. In this way, the placement
of images and colors and lines of
movement in the work can trigger new
responses and ideas as the work
progresses. The stability in the work is
that I am talking about my own life,
the people I have met, my travels and
experiences.

How have your travels influenced your work?

I have traveled throughout Japan and
have shown my work there as well.
More recently, I served as a cultural
specialist in the "Arts America"
program in The Netherlands. There
were a few embassy receptions, but
more importantly, I had the chance to
meet and share ideas with textile
artists there. When I travel, people
give me photographs, calendars and
all types of pictures that I later incorporate in my work through photo
transfer methods. I still correspond
with my many new friends, and even
though I have been back in America
for two years, I find that the images of
my trip to Europe keep coming back
into my work.

Where do you show your work in this country?

My best showrooms are the offices
and living spaces of the people who
already have my work. Because my
work is in about ten corporate/public
collections, I receive a good number of
direct inquiries. Another method that
has worked very well for me is placing
work in selected corporate spaces on a
loan basis. The building owner gets
the work at no cost, but doesn't
receive a commission for any work
sold. The advantage is that the
building owner maintains a complete
portfolio of my work at the reception
desk, and refers interested people to
me. This type of informal gallery
setting allows the potential client to
see the work in a non-threatening
environment, and it helps the client to
visualize the work in a corporate or
living space.

B.J. Adams

Art in Fiber
2821 Arizona Terrace, NW
Washington, DC 20016
(202) 364-8404 (S)
(202) 686-1042 (H)

B.J. Adams creates mixed-media art for commercial and residential interiors. Collaborating with clients, art consultants and interior designers, commissioned designs can be colorful, or subdued, textured or flat, illustrative or abstract.

Work has been commissioned by collectors as well as business, medical, banking and hotel facilities.

Brochure available upon written request.

Top: *Isolated Permanence*, 24" x 32", manipulated and stitched fabrics
Bottom: *Ten Views of Milford Sound (N.Z.)*, 32" x 27", machine embroidery over painted canvas
Below: *The Blooming of an Idea*, 21" x 13", fabric with machine sketching

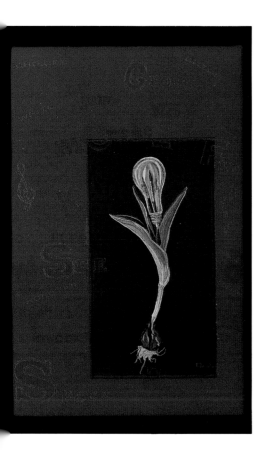

Barbara Cade

262 Hideaway Hills Drive
Hot Springs, AR 71901
(501) 262-4065

Luscious Vegetation.
One flower or a whole bouquet.
For people who are not afraid of getting
  back to nature
For people who like making dramatic
  statements.
For people who like being different.

Working in age-old primitive methods, Barbara Cade creates one-of-a-kind, hand-felted wool flowers. Her work has been exhibited in museum juried shows for 20 years, is represented in many corporate collections and is part of the permanent collection at the Tacoma Art Museum.

Easy to install. Arrangeable.

Care: dust with hose-type spray vacuum; to protect against insects, use insect spray labeled for fabrics. No weeding required.

For slides of other species and varieties, send $5.00 (refundable).

Top: *Pansy*, 60" x 40" x 12"
Bottom: *Lily*, 72" x 40" x 36"

Joyce Marquess Carey

913 Harrison Street
Madison, WI 53711
(608) 256-1537

Joyce Marquess Carey's sewn fiber wall pieces bring spirit and warmth to public, professional and residential interiors all over the United States. Her works, characterized by rich color and texture, visual illusion and playfulness, range in size from ten to 300 square feet. Carey's fiberworks are durable, easy to install and maintain.

Clients include the Shriner Children's Hospital, Salvation Army Headquarters, the Ralston Purina Corporation and state arts agencies in Wisconsin, Minnesota, Florida and Alaska. Additional information available on request.

Top: *Building Blocks,* University of Mankato, Mankato MN, 5.5' X 20'
Bottom: *Ribbon Candy,* Shriner Children's Hospital, Minneapolis, MN, 30" X 115"

Gloria E. Crouse

Fiber Art
4325 John Luhr Road NE
Olympia, WA 98516-2320
(206) 491-1980

Gloria Crouse creates highly textured art rugs and wall works, using unique variations of hand hooking and sculpting. Her work is included in many collections including: Weyerhaeuser; SAFECO Ins; Sea-Tac International Airport; Western State Hospital and the Tacoma Art Museum.

Additional works may be seen in her recently published book, *Hooked Rugs: New Materials/New Techniques* with accompanying video (Taunton Press).

Top: *Metro-Plex*, hooked/sculpted wools, 7' x 9 ½"
Bottom: *Diverse-Directions*, commissioned by Waste Management Inc., Chicago, IL,

Margaret Cusack

124 Hoyt Street in Boerum Hill
Brooklyn, NY 11217-2215
(718) 237-0145
FAX (718) 237-0145

Margaret Cusack's stitched hangings reflect her interest in representational imagery, her extensive drawing skills and a striking command of color. Since 1972, she has been creating stitched commissions for both public and private collections. Cusack's technique is sewing machine appliqué using a wide variety of fabrics and textures.

Commissioned works are in the collections of Yale New Haven Hospital, Seagram's, Aid to Lutheran Association and American Express.

© 1992 Margaret Cusack.

Top Left: *Lobster*, 36" x 36"
Bottom Left: *Watermelon*, 36" x 36"
Right: *Hands*, 1992, The Culinary Institute of
   America, Hyde Park, NY, 153" x 114"

Layne Goldsmith

Studio Textiles
P.O. Box 563
Snohomish, WA 98291-0563
(206) 334-5569
FAX (206) 334-5569

Layne Goldsmith specializes in contemporary textiles with a focus on color and content. A graduate of the Cranbrook Academy of Art and recipient of a National Endowment for the Arts Individual Artist's grant, her work is included in private, corporate and Percent for Art collections.

Goldsmith's dimensional, wall-mounted textiles maintain their form beautifully and use the relief possibilities of the non-woven medium to create a sense of depth and texture.

Top/Bottom: *Nightwatch/Asunder*, AT&T Gateway Tower Seattle, WA, dyed and felted wool, 8' x 6' x 3"
Below: *Salaam*, dyed and felted wool, Hartford Insurance Co., Hartford, CT, bronze armature, 10' x 7' x 3"

Ruth Gowell

7010 Aronow Drive
Falls Church, VA 22042
(703) 532-8645

Ruth Gowell creates shimmering weavings of rayon, hand-dyed in color progressions, and woven warp-face with up to four layers of warp. Since 1980 she has developed techniques that involve exploration of light and shadow, color interaction, texture and pattern. Three time winner of the Niche Award for Decorative Fibers, her work is in many private and corporate collections, including AT&T, IBM, Alabama Gas, and Warner Lambert.

Information on commissions, prices and slides is available on request.

Top: *Tropical Patterns: Mandarinfish*, 30" x 70"
Bottom: from *Series IV*, 1992, 14" x 16" to 16" x 20"

Barbara Grenell

1132 Hall's Chapel Road
Burnsville, NC 28714
(704) 675-4073

In Barbara Grenell's dimensional constructions, two separate tapestries are broken up and presented as sculptural relief that enhances the dimensional aspects of their content.

Grenell's works in fiber, in multiple tapestry panels or dimensional tapestry constructions, are internationally collected and commissioned. Grenell was awarded a National Endowment for the Arts Fellowship. Her landscapes are in installations for major corporations in technology, communication: financial services, hospitals and health care facilities, hotels, conference centers and in residential collections. Unrestricted in size, each work is created in response to the requirements of the specific site. Completed works are also available.

D. C. Idyll, Association of American Medical Colleges, Washington DC, 42" x 84" x 2"

Earthforms, 36" x 98" x 6"

Untitled, Casino, Jackpot, NV, 32" x 84" x 2"

Salinas River Valley, Mills Distributing Co., Inc., Salinas, CA 60" x 144" x 2, Barbara Grenell, 1132 Hall's Chapel Road, Burnsville, NC, 28714 (204) 675-4073

Marie-Laure Ilie

M-Laure Studio/Cocoon
1241 Kolle Avenue
South Pasedena, CA 91030
(213) 254-8073

Ilie's hand-painted silk wall hangings which depict the scenes of the ancient world, are painted in the styles of medieval Europe, the Middle East, the Orient and American Colonial. She uses a personal technique to capture the essence of her subjects and to give them an antique appearance. Since 1975, Ilie has achieved hundreds of successfull commissions, both private and corporate.

Commissions require one month after approval of sketches. Sizes range from 2' x 3' to 7' x 10'.

Colors are fade proof. Maintenance advice is available when required.

Please contact the artist for more information.

Marie-Laure Ilie

M-Laure Studio/Cocoon
1241 Kolle Avenue
South Pasadena, CA 91030
(213) 254-8073

Ilie creates large tapestry paintings by layering transparent organza on top of a hand-painted silk background. Her appliqué technique combines rich colors and distinctive texture with the inherent sophistication of silk. These paintings come ready to hang like tapestries. They can also be framed. Colors are fade proof.

For the past 20 years, Ilie has exhibited extensively in the United states and Europe. Patrons include private collectors, as well as major corporations.

Commissions are welcome. Additional photos, slides or samples are available on request.

Top: *Sailing Red and Blue*, 50" x 50"
Bottom: *Beyond Memories*, 63" x 81"

Janis Kanter

1923 W. Dickens
Chicago, IL 60614
(312) 252-2119

Tapestry artist Janis Kanter likes to think of her work as painting with yarn. Her woven images, whether narrative or abstract, are filled with an intriguing variety of rich texture and color, much like the impasto of a painter's palette. Sometimes Kanter will also use her trademark addition of colorful neon tubing, interlaced and floating over the textural imagery, creating work that is both two-dimensional and sculptural.

The subject matter for most of Kanter's work is sequential, with one finished piece suggesting the pathway into the next image. Kanter creates her tapestry paintings one at a time, and, as time permits, she is happy to discuss commissions or specially designed pieces.

Top: *Woolly Harvest*, commissioned piece for private collection, 5'W x 3'H
Bottom: *Every City Has Its Snake*, placed in private collection, 4'W x 4'H,

M.A. Klein

3840 Thorson Drive
Placerville, CA 95667
(916) 644-6396
FAX (916) 644-5411

M.A. Klein, a professional artist for more than 25 years, has a background in fine art. Her works, which hang in numerous public and private collections in the United States and Canada, are one-of-a-kind, mixed-media fiber collages.

Techniques include hand painting fabrics, collage and other applique techniques, fabric manipulation, hand and machine stitchery, patchwork and quilting. These combined techniques create unique, three-dimensional, heavily textured pieces. Sizes vary from large-scale installations to smaller, intimate focal points. Prices are based on complexity and size of work.

In addition to finished works, M.A. Klein welcomes collaborative projects with architects, designers and individuals to meet site-specific needs, scheduling and budget. Contact the artist for further information and slides of available work.

Top Left: *Twilight in the Hills*, 45" x 60"
Bottom Left: Detail, *Blue Grotto*
Right: *Blue Grotto*, 40" x 50"

Joyce P. Lopez

Joyce P. Lopez Studio
1147 W. Ohio Street - #304
Chicago, IL 60622
(312) 243-5033
FAX (312) 243-5033

Joyce Lopez is an internationally known sculptor who has successfully operated her studio for more than 18 years. Known for her innovative design solutions to site-specific requirements, she strictly adheres to the client's budget and deadline.

Commissioned work, for easily maintained mid-sized sculptures, usually takes two to four months. Exhibition opportunities are welcome.

A brochure is available upon request.

Selected collections:
Illinois State Museum
Burroughs Corporation
Sony Corp. of America
State of Illinois
Bank of America
Michael Reese Hospital
and private collections.

Sony Corp. of America, sculpture, chromed steel and thread, 7' x 4 ½' x 1 ½"

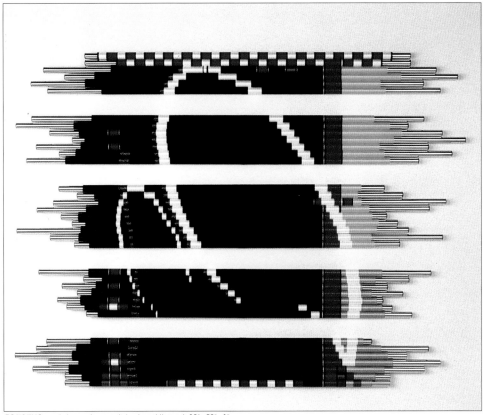

TO*KY*YO, sculpture, chromed steel and thread, 39"x 52"x 1"

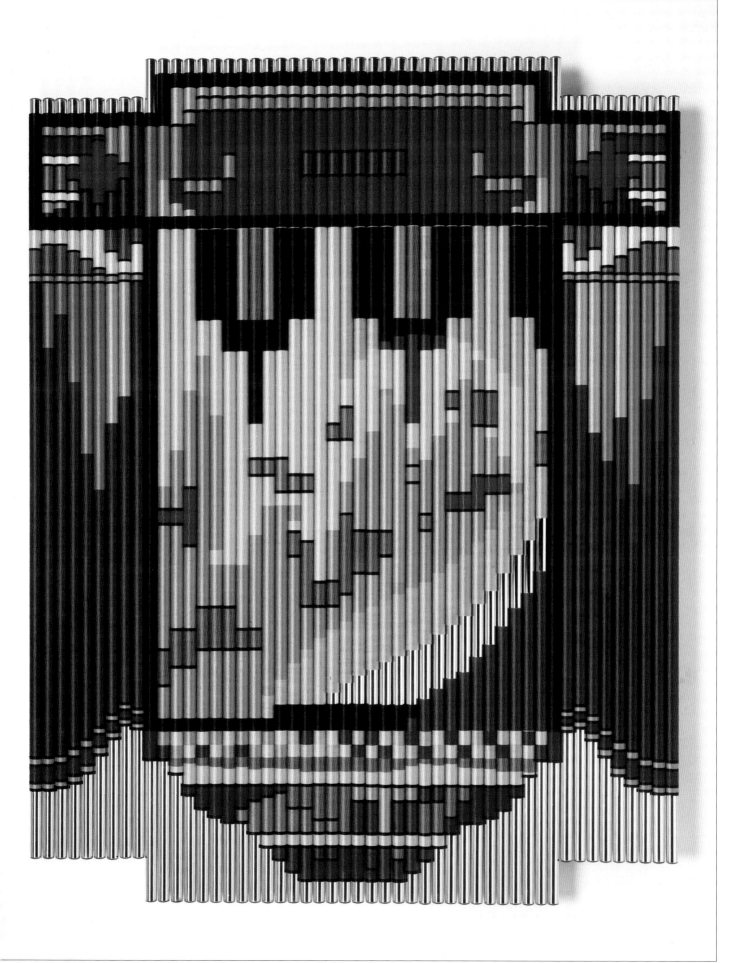

yce P. Lopez Studios, Chicago, IL, (312) 243-5033, *Trip-TK/S.A.*, sculpture, chromed steel and thread, 51" x 40" x 2"

Bonny Lhotka

5658 Cascade Place
Boulder, CO 80303
(303) 494-5631
FAX (303) 494-3472

These unique monographic transfer
tapestries are created on a tear-proof spun-
bonded fiber using sheets of acrylic paint.
They can be installed on curved walls, free
hung with images on both sides or hung as
traditional paintings. The work rolls for ease
of presentation and shipping.

Two decades of experience working to
specifications and meeting deadlines makes
her a professional who is appreciated by her
clients.

Recent commissions and purchases include
the U.S. Department of State, Jones
Intercable, PSI Energy, Random Access,
Hyatt Hotels, Public Service Company, AT&T,
National Conference of State Legislators
and others.

Call for quotes or slides. See page 272 *THE
GUILD 5*, page 205 *THE GUILD 6* and page 45
THE GUILD 7 for additional media.

Southwest Sign, Monographic transfer, 42" x 42", $900

Phone Home, Monographic transfer, 43"x135", $3,900

Dottie Moore

1134 Charlotte Avenue
Rock Hill, SC 29732
(803) 327-5088

Dottie Moore's art quilts are conversations with the earth and sky visually conveying quiet moments in nature. Each piece is one-of-a-kind, appliquéd, quilted and embellished with hand embroidery. Carefully selected cloth is sometimes hand-dyed or hand-painted then stitched intricately to produce a striking sculptural dimension.

Moore's work is collected, exhibited and published nationally. She has successfully completed projects for both individual and corporate clients since 1980.

Slides and prices are available upon request.

Top: *Dreams*, 38" x 47"
Bottom: detail

Photos: Michael Harrison

Karen Perrine

512 North K Street
Tacoma, WA 98403
(206) 627-0449

Nature inspires Karen Perrine's distinctive
fiber designs. A surface designer for 20 years,
she dyes and paints cotton, linen, rayon and
silk fabrics with layers of color, creating
unique yardage to cut and assemble into
evocative landscapes. She exhibits
nationally and internationally.

Finished work is presented as framed collage
or quilted textile. Slides and information
regarding prices and commissions are
available upon request.

Top: *Still Water*, 1991, 100"H x 62"W
Bottom: *Forest Flowing*, 1992, Waltron, Ltd.,
   75"H x 138"W

Joan Schulze

808 Piper Avenue
Sunnyvale, CA 94087
(408) 736-7833

Jazz-like improvisation, exploring the unexpected possibilities of invention, pushing traditional aspects of the quilt into new territory, all describe Joan Schulze's approach to the art quilt. Her work is the continuous dialogue between subject and materials leading to her unique, complex and rich expression.

Joan has pioneered the two-sided quilt which lends itself to unusual display treatments such as free-standing or hanging format. Smaller collages are often the forerunner of new possibilities in subject and media and invite grouping to fill unusual spaces. The work is easily installed.

Since 1970, Joan has exhibited internationally and placed numerous works in private and corporate spaces. Site-specific commissions are welcomed.

Top: *Detail, South Wall*
Bottom: *South Wall,* 1991, quilt, 38"H x 30"W

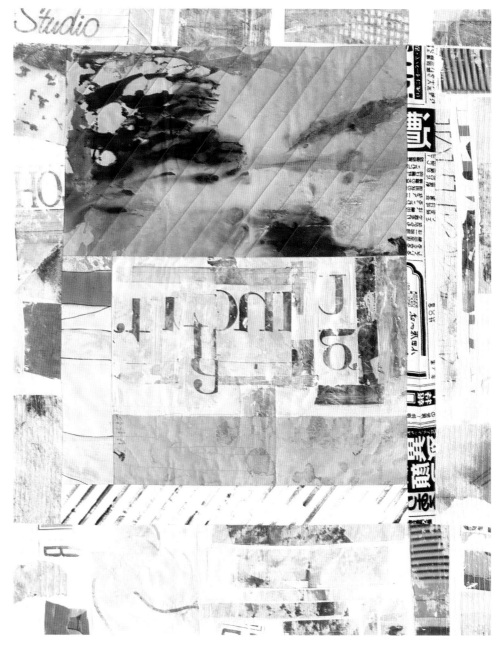

Amanda Richardson

Richardson Kirby
P.O. Box 2147
Friday Harbor, WA 98250
(206) 378-3224

The rich, light-reflective tapestries of Amanda Richardson respond to their environment, the image varying with the angle and intensity of light, allowing the viewer to become actively involved in the artistic experience. The artist developed the technique of Richardson-tapestry in which fabrics are hand-dyed, cut into intricate forms,and bonded together, layer on layer, to build up a rich and complex final image. These images give the impression of great spatial depth, with a visual impact few art mediums can equal.

A professional artist for 15 years, Richardson has had numerous shows in America and Europe. Recent clients include Embassy Suites Hotels, Marriott Hotels, Hilton Hotels, The Rouse Co., The Oliver Carr Co. and the University of Alaska.

Pricing, scheduling and commission details are available upon request.

Douglas Iris, Richardson Tapestry, 43" x 61.5"

Iris Garden, Richardson Tapestry, 60" x 81"

Pear Point, Richardson Tapestry, 84" x 60"

Joan Stubbins

2616 S. Mahoning Avenue
Alliance, OH 44601
(216) 823-7328

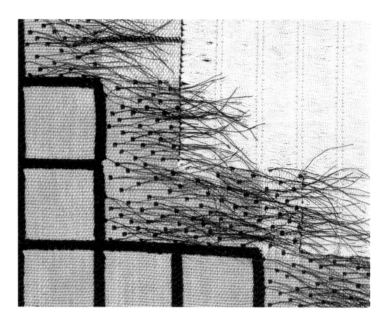

The art of Joan Stubbins is intuitive and personal, reflecting the unique structural and textural qualities of the woven textile. The one-of-a-kind pieces are crafted in natural fibers and colorfast, fiber-reactive dyes.

Ms. Stubbins exhibits nationally and is represented in private and corporate collections. A slide portfolio and price list are available on request. Commissioned work will be considered.

Top: Detail, *The Dawn Series: Revelations I*
Bottom: *The Dawn Series: Revelations I*,
  1992, 44" x 40"

Welcome to THE GUILD REGISTER of Fiber Art For The Wall.

THE GUILD REGISTER is a valuable tool to assist professionals (interior designers, art consultants, architects, hospitality designers, resource librarians and gallery owners) in contacting and commissioning experienced artists and artisans for projects they oversee.

The goal of THE GUILD REGISTER is to be a major source of relevant information about artists and artisans working in fiber art that is for the wall. The listing format includes basic contact information, as well as details on a broad range of products, techniques, services and pricing. *Please note size and price range are approximates.*

You will find THE GUILD REGISTER of Fiber Art For The Wall a valuable resource — the place to turn to for your Business in Art!

THE GUILD REGISTER currently lists experienced artists who were surveyed and recommended by industry experts. It's emphasis is quality. *All artists interested in next year's edition are invited to call 800-969-1556 for qualifying information.*

Name Address Phone FAX	LENORE HUGHES P.O. Box 1862 La Jolla, CA 92038 (619) 456-1144 FAX (619) 291-8362
Detailed information on the year their studio was established, the primary product,technique, size, price range and marketing material the artist can provide to prospective clients.	Established: 1987 Products: paper wall work Techniques: painting, stamping/printing Marketing Materials: brochure, photos, resume, slides Size Range: 3"x 2" to 108" x 156" Price Range: $150 - $6,000
Statement of additional biographical, technical or philosophical information. The listing is cross-referenced to the page on which the artists' work appears.	Lenore Hughes hand cuts and weaves her original watercolor paintings into unique abstracts that hint of landscape or still life. Hughes' palate includes pure, bright, summer colors, soft spring tones, decorator colors, or sophisticated grays and tans. She produces top-quality pieces as large as a full scale mural or as small as a wine label. See page 15 for photographs and additional information.

FIBER ART

KAREN ADACHI
702 Monarch Way
Santa Cruz, CA 95060
(408) 429-6192
Established: 1975
Products: paper wall work
Techniques: airbrush, casting, dyeing
Marketing Materials: brochure, photos, resume, slides
Size Range: 2' x 3' to 7' x 9'
Price Range: $200 - $7,000

Karen Adachi creates her three-dimensional handmade paper pieces by using layers of irregularly shaped vacuum-cast paper. The pieces are richly textured and embellished with dyes, acrylics, metallics and pearlescents. Painted bamboo and sticks are used to create a dramatic statement of pattern and line. Three-dimensional sculptures are mounted on painted metal bases for stability and strength. See page 9 for photographs and additional information.

B.J. ADAMS
Art In Fiber
2821 Arizona Terrace, NW
Washington, DC 20016
(202) 364-8404 (studio)
(202) 686-1042 (H)
Products: mixed media wall installations
Marketing Materials: brochure, photos, resume, slides
Size Range: 12" x 12" to 5' x 12'
Price Range: $100 - $400

B.J. Adams creates mixed-media art for commercial and residential interiors. Collaborating with clients, art consultants and interior designers, commissioned designs can be colorful, or subdued, textured or flat, illustrative or abstract. Work has been commissioned by collectors as well as business, medical, banking and hotel facilities. See page 33 for photographs and additional information.

DONNA ALBERT
PO Box 7743
Lancaster, PA 17604
(717) 393-7040
Established: 1969
Products: art quilts
Techniques: quilting, embroidery
Marketing Materials: photos, slides, resume, brochure
Size Range: 12" x 18" to 10' x 10'
Price Range: $400 - $8,000

SANDY ASKEW
50951 Expressway
Belleville, MI 48111
(313) 483-5529
Established: 1975
Products: Fiber installations
Techniques: weaving
Marketing Materials: photos, slides, resume, brochure
Size Range: 20" x 16" to 5'6" x 11'
Price Range: $50 - $2,000

ELLEN ATHENS
PO Box 1386
Mendocino, CA 95460
(707) 937-2642
Established: 1982
Products: tapestries
Techniques: weaving, dyeing, beading
Marketing Materials: photos, slides, resume, brochure
Size Range: 2' x 2' to 10' x 6'
Price Range: $700 - $15,000

CAROL ATLESON
465 Ruskin Rd.
Amherst, NY 14226
(716) 834-9384
Established: 1978
Products: tapestries
Techniques: weaving
Marketing Materials: photos, slides, resume, brochure
Size Range: 24" x 24" to 72" x 86"
Price Range: $800 - $8,000

MARJORIE ATWOOD
11 E. Brady
Tulsa, OK 74103
(918) 583-0886
(800) 484-9174 PIN # 5096
Established: 1987
Products: mixed media wall installations
Techniques: painting
Marketing Materials: brochure, photos, resume, slides
Size Range: 4' x 6' to 9' x 12'
Price Range: $1,000 - $7,000

Trained in faux finishes in New York and San Francisco, Marjorie Atwood creates distinctive floor and wall art meticulously crafted using high-quality paints and various metal finishes including gold and silver leaf. A protective sealer ensures easy cleaning, maintenance and durability. Designs in any size or shape can complement fabrics, wallpaper and artwork. See page 162 for photographs and additional information.

ILZE AVIKS
Durango Design Company
3306 Stover
Fort Collins, CO 80525
(303) 225-2577
Established: 1974
Products: tapestries
Techniques: dyeing, embroidery, weaving

Marketing Materials: slides, resume
Size Range: 3' x 3' to 8' x 5'
Price Range: $1,000 - $4,000

JOANN BACHELDER
4639 S. Elm Dr.
Bay City, MI 48706
(517) 684-6230
Established: 1978
Products: tapestries, fiber installations
Techniques: dyeing, weaving
Marketing Materials: slides, resume
Size Range: 21" x 20" to 9' x 12'
Price Range: $350 - $2,500

SHIRLEY ROESE BAHNSEN
PO Box 921
Clinton, IA 52733-0921
(319) 243-5863
Established: 1966
Products: paper wall work
Techniques: weaving, painting, laminating
Marketing Materials: photos, slides, resume
Size Range: 24" x 36" to 42" x 72"
Price Range: $600 - $2,000

See photograph on this page.

MARTIN K BAKER
Artesanos Tipicos/Coyote Designs
715 Cleveland St.
Missoula, MT 59801
(406) 728-2789
FAX (406) 721-4114
Established: 1974
Products: tapestries
Techniques: weaving, painting, silkscreen
Marketing Materials: slides, resume, brochure
Size Range: 24" x 24" to 36' x 22'
Price Range: $40 sq. ft.

DORIS BALLY
420 N. Craig St.
Pittsburgh, PA 15213
(412) 621-3709
FAX (412) 621-9030
Established: 1963
Products: tapestries
Techniques: weaving
Marketing Materials: slides, resume
Size Range: 20" x 20" to 94" x 20'
Price Range: $240 sq. ft.

TERESA BARKLEY
24-40 27 St.
Astoria, NY 11102
(718) 545-4281
Established: 1978
Products: art quilts
Techniques: quilting, painting
Marketing Materials: slides, resume
Size Range: 16" x 20" to 110" x 103"
Price Range: $500 - $15,000

BARBARA BARRON
Barron Custom Wallhangings
1943 New York Ave.
Huntington Station, NY 11746
(516) 549-4242
FAX (516) 549-9122
Products: fiber installations
Techniques: weaving, embroidery
Marketing Materials: photos,

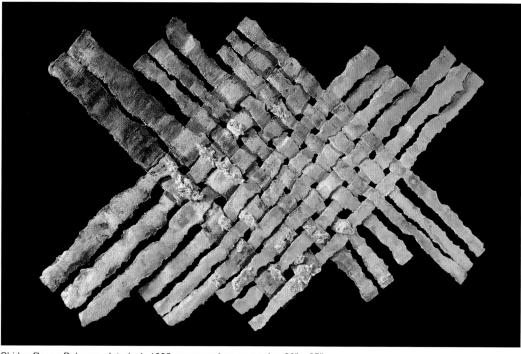

Shirley Roese Bahnsen, *Interlock*, 1992, paper and paper mache, 39" x 25"

slides, resume, brochure
Size Range: 24" x 24" to 24' x 24'
Price Range: $75 sq. ft. - $200 sq. ft.

SONYA LEE BARRINGTON
837 47th Ave.
San Francisco, CA 94121
(415) 221-6510
Established: 1970
Products: art quilts
Techniques: quilting, dyeing, appliqué
Marketing Materials: slides, resume
Size Range: 44" x 44" to 72" x 72"
Price Range: $1,500 - $3,500

DOREEN BECK
DINK SIEGEL
100 West 57th St #10G
New York, NY 10019
(212) 246-9757
Established: 1974
Products: art quilts
Techniques: appliqué, quilting
Marketing Materials: photos, slides, resume, brochure
Size Range: 3' x 2' to 4' x 5'
Price Range: $15,000 - $10,000

JUDY BECKER
27 Albion St.
Newton, MA 02159
(617) 332-6778
Established: 1982
Products: art quilts
Techniques: quilting, dyeing
Marketing Materials: photos, slides, resume
Size Range: 2' x 2' to 10' x 14'
Price Range: $500 - $10,000

PAMELA E. BECKER
3 Hendrick Rd.
Flemington, NJ 08822
(908) 806-4911
Established: 1981
Products: fiber installations
Techniques: painting, appliqué
Marketing Materials: slides, resume
Size Range: 40" x 25" to 8' x 8'
Price Range: $3,000 - $6,400

SUE BENNER
8517 San Fernando Way
Dallas, TX 75218
(214) 324-3550
Established: 1980
Products: art quilts
Techniques: painting, dyeing, quilting
Marketing Materials: slides, resume
Size Range: 12" x 12" to 10' x 15'
Price Range: $350 - $18,000

CHRISTINA BENSON-VOS
235 Washington St.
Hoboken, NJ 07030
(201) 656-7441
Established: 1986
Products: tapestries
Techniques: weaving
Marketing Materials: photos, slides, resume, brochure
Size Range: 4' x 6' to 6' x 8'
Price Range: $5,000 - $15,000

HARRIET BERKE
28 Marksman Ln.
Levittown, NY 11756
(516) 796-7280
Established: 1980
Products: fiber installations
Techniques: painting
Marketing Materials: photos, slides
Size Range: 18" x 48"
Price Range: $460

KAREN FELICITY BERKENFELD
150 West 79th St.
New York, NY 10024
(212) 799-3321
Established: 1979
Products: art quilts
Techniques: painting, quilting, stamping/printing
Marketing Materials: slides, resume
Size Range: 25" x 25" to 65" x 65"
Price Range: $300 - $3,000

LYNN BERKOWITZ
PO Box 121
Slatedale, PA 18079
(215) 767-8072
Established: 1978
Products: tapestries
Techniques: weaving, dyeing
Marketing Materials: photos, slides, resume, brochure
Size Range: 24" x 9" to 6' x 40"
Price Range: $400 - $1,200

JULIE BERNER
29953 Fox Hollow Rd.
Eugene, OR 97405
(503) 484-9220
Established: 1981
Products: art quilts
Techniques: silkscreen, quilting
Marketing Materials: photos, slides, resume
Size Range: 3' x 3' to 8' x 30'
Price Range: $2,000 - $15,000

ELIZABETH BILLINGS
Rt. 1 Box 7910
Underhill, VT 05489
(802) 899-4675
Established: 1987
Products: tapestries, fiber installations
Techniques: weaving, dyeing
Marketing Materials: photos, slides, resume
Size Range: 12" x 30" to 13' x 19'
Price Range: $350 - $10,000

THERESE BISCEGLIA
TOM MARTIN
Martin and Bisceglia, Handmade Paper
Rt. 19 Box 90-KS
Santa Fe, NM 87505
(505) 982-5914
FAX (505) 989-1937
Established: 1981
Products: mixed media wall installations, paper wall work
Techniques: painting, casting
Marketing Materials: photos, slides, resume, brochure
Size Range: 1' x 1' to 6' x 8'
Price Range: $120 - $2,500

REBECCA BLUESTONE
PO Box 1704
Santa Fe, NM 87504
(505) 989-9599
FAX (505) 989-9599
Established: 1984
Products: tapestries
Techniques: weaving, dyeing, embroidery
Marketing Materials: photos, slides, resume, brochure
Size Range: 4' x 2' to 10' x 6'
Price Range: $65 sq. ft. - $160 sq. ft.

Rebecca Bluestone's unique tapestries have been referred to as geometric landscapes. By using vibrant color, rich textural silks as a canvas, and the hard edge of metallic thread, she engages the senses in a quest to the unknown. Bluestone's work is shown nationally in galleries, museums, juries exhibitions and collections such as the Lovelance Medical Center in Jakarta, Indonesia. See page 21 for photographs and additional information.

CHRIS BOBIN
Fabric Effects
20 W. 20th St., Fifth Floor
New York, NY 10011
(212) 255-5225
FAX (212) 255-3077
Established: 1980
Products: art quilts
Techniques: appliqué, felting
Marketing Materials: slides, resume, brochure
Size Range: 4' x 3' to 7' x 9'
Price Range: $700 - $4,500

SUSAN BOHM
237 Edgemont Rd.
Scarsdale, NY 10583
(914) 723-4628
Established: 1987
Products: art quilts, mixed media wall installations, paper wall work
Techniques: casting, quilting, appliqué
Marketing Materials: photos, slides, resume
Size Range: 4' x 4" to 50' x 130"
Price Range: $200 - $1,400

NANCY BONEY
97 King St.
Fanwood, NJ 07023
(908) 889-8219
Established: 1970
Products: fiber installations
Techniques: appliqué
Marketing Materials: slides, resume
Size Range: 4' x 3' to 9' x 5'
Price Range: $850 - $3,200

DANA BOUSSARD
2 Heart Creek
Arlee, MT 59821
(406) 726-3357
Established: 1968
Products: fiber installations
Techniques: painting, appliqué, airbrush
Marketing Materials: photos, slides, resume, brochure, video
Size Range: 30" x 50" to 10' x 80'
Price Range: $3,000 - $75,000

KAREN BOVARD
Spectrum Quilts
102 Highland Ave.
Middletown, CT 06457
(203) 346-1116
Established: 1986
Products: art quilts
Techniques: quilting, appliqué, beading
Marketing Materials: photos, slides, resume, brochure
Size Range: 2' x 2' to 8' x 12'
Price Range: $400 - $10,000

ODETTE BRABEC
1107 Golf Ave.
Highland Park, IL 60035
(708) 432-2704
Established: 1977
Products: tapestries
Techniques: weaving
Marketing Materials: photos, resume
Size Range: 24" x 24" to 15' x 5'
Price Range: $200 sq. ft. - $250 sq. ft.

JEANNE BRAEN
4 Rockhouse Rd.
Wilton, CT 06897
(203) 834-9549
Established: 1978
Products: tapestries
Techniques: weaving, dyeing
Marketing Materials: photos, resume
Size Range: 2' x 3' to 15' x 4'
Price Range: $540 - $5,400

ANN BRAUER
126 Charlemont Rd.
Charlemont, MA 01339
(413) 625-2208
Established: 1981
Products: art quilts
Techniques: quilting, appliqué
Marketing Materials: slides, resume
Price Range: $70 - $5,000

LINDA BROTHERS
4592 Vista Del Valle
Moorpark, CA 93021
(805) 523-3101
Established: 1969
Products: tapestries
Techniques: weaving, painting
Marketing Materials: photos, slides, resume, brochure
Price Range: $35 sq. ft. - $250 sq. ft.

RACHEL BROWN
Weaving Southwest
216B Paseo del Pueblo Norte
Taos, NM 87571
(505) 758-0433
Established: 1962
Products: tapestries
Techniques: weaving
Marketing Materials: slides, resume, brochure
Size Range: 96" x 36" to 120" x 58"
Price Range: $1,800 - $10,000

TAFI BROWN
Ty Bryn Design Studio
PO Box 319
Pratt Rd.
Alstead, NH 03602
(603) 756-3412
Established: 1975

FIBER ART

Products: art quilts
Techniques: quilting, appliqué, embroidery
Marketing Materials: photos, slides, resume, brochure
Size Range: 1' x 1' to 9' x 12'
Price Range: $300 - $27,000

LAURA MILITZER BRYANT
2595 30th Ave. N
St. Petersburg, FL 33713
(813) 327-3100
FAX (813) 321-1905
Established: 1979
Products: tapestries
Techniques: weaving, dyeing, painting
Marketing Materials: photos, slides, resume
Size Range: 24" x 36" to 10' x 30'
Price Range: $1,200 - $20,000

LOIS BRYANT
503 S. 8th St.
Lindenhurst, NY 11757
(516) 226-7819
Established: 1979
Products: fiber installations
Techniques: weaving
Marketing Materials: photos, slides, resume
Size Range: 2' x 3' to 5' x 8'
Price Range: $750 - $6,000

STANLEY BULBACH, PHD.
328 W. 88th St.
New York, NY 10024
(212) 243-9010
FAX (213) 691-4991
Established: 1978
Products: tapestries
Techniques: weaving, dyeing
Marketing Materials: photos, slides, resume
Price Range: $6,500 - $9600

PATRICIA BURLING
Willoweave
17 Fresh Meadow Rd.
Weston, CT 06883
(203) 454-2742
Established: 1979
Products: mixed media wall installations
Techniques: weaving, dyeing
Marketing Materials: photos, slides, resume, brochure
Size Range: 3' x 5' to 8' x 12'
Price Range:$100 sq. ft.-$150 sq. ft.

NANCY ROWE BURROUGHS
Nancy Rowe Designs
PO Box 297
Kingston, RI 0288
(401) 789-0433
Products: art quilts
Techniques: quilting, appliqué, dyeing
Marketing Materials: photos, slides, resume
Size Range: 1' x 1' to 9' x 9'
Price Range: $200 - $15,000

MARY BALZER BUSKIRK
Buskirk Studios
53 via Ventura
Monterey, CA 93940
(408) 375-6165
Established: 1956
Products: tapestries

Techniques: weaving, painting, felting
Marketing Materials: photos, slides, resume
Size Range: 1' x 1' to 20' x 8'
Price Range: $175 - $25,000

ELIZABETH A. BUSCH
Rt. 1 Box 365
Hudson Rd.
Bangor, ME 04401
(207) 942-7820
Established: 1965
Products: art quilts
Techniques: painting, airbrush, quilting
Marketing Materials: photos, slides, resume
Size Range: 12" x 12" to 4' x 22'
Price Range: $300 sq. ft.

BARBARA CADE
262 Hideaway Hills Dr.
Hot Springs, AR 71901
(501) 262-4065
Established: 1978
Products: fiber installations
Techniques: felting, weaving
Marketing Materials: brochure, photos, resume, slides
Size Range: 24" x 18" to 78" x 40"
Price Range: $400 - $4,000

Working in age-old primitive methods, Barbara Cade creates one-of-a-kind, hand-felted wool flowers. Her work has been exhibited in museum juries shows for 20 years, is represented in many corporate collections and is part of the permanent collection at the Tacoma Art Museum. See page 34 for photographs and additional information.

MONECA CALVERT
3858 Baltic Circle
Rocklin, CA 95677
(916) 624-4671
Established: 1983
Products: art quilts
Techniques: quilting, appliqué, embroidery
Marketing Materials: photos, slides, resume, brochure
Size Range: 2' x 2' to 8' x 8'
Price Range: $800 - $20,000

JOYCE MARQUESS CAREY
913 Harrison St.
Madison, WI 53711
(608) 256-1537
Established: 1984
Products: art quilts
Techniques: quilting, embroidery
Marketing Materials: brochure, photos, resume, slides
Size Range: 24" x 40" to 11' x 25'
Price Range: $160 sq. ft. - $260 sq. ft.

Joyce Marquess Carey's sewn-fiber wall pieces bring spirit and warmth to public, professional and residential interiors through-out the United States. Her playful works, characterized by rich color and texture and visual illu-sion, range in size from ten to 300 square feet. Carey's fiber works are durable and are easy to install and maintain. See page 35 for photographs and additional information.

LUCINDA CARLSTROM
1075 Standard Dr.
Atlanta, GA 30319
(404) 231-0227
Established: 1970
Products: mixed media wall installations
Techniques: quilting
Marketing Materials: brochure, photos, resume, slides
Size Range: 18" x 18" to 60" x 100"
Price Range: $125 sq. ft.

Lucinda Carlstrom's mixed-media constructions and piece-work incorporate pure 23K gold leaf, imitation metal leaf, hand-made papers and new and sal-vaged silks. One series explores architectural themes of classical temples and contemporary pub-lic buildings. Another series examines the play of color and reflection of different shades of metals with colors. See page 96 for photographs and additional information.

ANN CARROLL
Beverley Hennessey, representa-tive
1017 Guerrero St.
San Francisco, CA 94110
(415) 550-1635
FAX (415) 285-8497
Established: 1973
Products: art quilts
Techniques: appliqué, quilting
Marketing Materials: photos, slides, resume, brochure
Size Range: 60" x 60" to 100" x 100"
Price Range: $2,300 - $6,300

ERIKA CARTER
2440 Killarney Way S.E.
Bellevue, WA 98004
(206) 451-9712
Established: 1984
Products: art quilts
Techniques: quilting, appliqué, painting
Marketing Materials: photos, slides, resume
Size Range: 26" x 36" to 66" x 60"
Price Range: $850 - $4,125

MARY ALLEN CHAISSON
Allen Point Studio
Allen Point Rd.
RR1 Box 285
South Harpswell, ME 04079
(207) 833-6842
FAX (207) 833-6820
Established: 1972
Products: art quilts
Techniques: painting, quilting, appliqué
Marketing Materials: slides, resume
Size Range: 2' x 2' to 3' x 5'
Price Range: $400 - $1,500

MARTHA CHATELAIN
PO Box 9855
San Diego, CA 92169-0855
(619) 234-0749
FAX (619) 234-0821
Established: 1982
Products: paper wall work
Techniques: dyeing
Marketing Materials: brochure, photos, resume, slides, video

Size Range: 1' x 1' to 4' x 15'
Price Range: $300 - $8,000

Martha Chatelain creates richly textured, three-dimensional, handmade-paper and mixed-media wall sculptures. Colored by fiber dyes, accented with iri-descent mica powders or patined copper, works can be framed in plexiglass or unframed with a protective spray. Chatelain's artwork comple-ments the architectural and design features of the interior spaces for which it is created. See page 10 for photographs and additional information.

ANNIE CURTIS CHITTENDEN
190 Neck Rd.
Madison, CT 06443
(203) 245-4925
Established: 1975
Products: paper wall work
Techniques: airbrush, painting
Marketing Materials: photos, slides, resume, brochure
Size Range: 3' x 3' to 5' x 15'
Price Range: $75 sq. ft. - $150 sq. ft.

JILL NORDFORS CLARK
Jill Nordfors Clark Fiber Art & Interior Design
3419 N. Adams St.
Tacoma, WA 98407
(206) 759-6158
Established: 1974
Products: mixed media wall installations
Techniques: embroidery, paint-ing, appliqué
Marketing Materials: photos, slides, resume
Size Range: 24" x 20" to 33" x 24"
Price Range: $750 - $1,200

SUSANNE CLAWSON
5093 Velda Dairy Rd.
Tallahassee, FL 32308
(904) 893-5656
Established: 1987
Products: paper wall work
Marketing Materials: photos, slides, resume, brochure
Size Range: 3' x 3' to 5' x 9'
Price Range: $1,000 - $15,000

JANE BURCH COCHRAN
6830 Rabbit Hash Hill Rd.
Rabbit Hash, KY 41005
(606) 586-9169
Established: 1972
Products: art quilts
Techniques: beading, appliqué, painting
Marketing Materials: photos, slides, resume
Size Range: 4 sq. ft. to 7' x 9'
Price Range: $2000 - $10,000

MARY KAY COLLING
Colling Contemporary Paper Art Salesroom
Village Gate Square
274 N. Goodman St.
Rochester, NY 14607
(716) 442-8946
Established: 1988
Products: paper wall work
Techniques: casting

Marketing Materials: photos,
slides, resume
Size Range: 5" x 7" to 4' x 4'
Price Range: $60 - $3,000

JUDITH CONTENT
Content Fabric and Design
827 Matadero Ave.
Palo Alto, CA 94306
(415) 857-0289
Established: 1979
Products: art quilts
Techniques: dyeing, quilting,
appliqué
Marketing Materials: photos,
slides, resume, brochure
Size Range: 45" x 12" to 15' x 20'
Price Range: $400 - $40,000

PILAR S. COOVER
P. Coover's Needle Art
690 Angell St.
Providence, RI 02906
(401) 274-2037
Established: 1979
Products: tapestries
Techniques: embroidery,
appliqué, painting
Marketing Materials: photos,
slides, resume, video
Size Range: 8" x 9" to 50" x 36"
Price Range: $250 - $4,000

BARBARA CORNETT
Fiberstructions
1101 Jefferson St.
Lynchburg, VA 24504
(804) 528-3136
Established: 1976
Products: mixed media wall
installations
Techniques: felting, dyeing
Marketing Materials: photos,
slides, resume, video
Size Range: 24" x 30" to 120" x 144"
Price Range: $600 - $10,000

JOYCE CRAIN
2018 Queen Ave. S
Minneapolis, MN 55405
(612) 377-0042
Established: 1970
Products: mixed media wall
installations
Marketing Materials: photos,
slides, resume
Size Range: 12" x 12" to 9' x 15'
Price Range: $500 - $40,000

BARBARA LYDECKER CRANE
18 Hill St.
Lexington, MA 02173
(617) 862-1579
Established: 1985
Products: art quilts
Techniques: dyeing, appliqué
Marketing Materials: photos,
slides, resume
Size Range: 36" x 36" to 72" x 72"
Price Range: $2,000 - $7,000

GLORIA E. CROUSE
Gloria E. Crouse Fiber
4325 John Luhr Rd. N.E.
Olympia, WA 98516-2320
(206) 491-1980
Established: 1965
Products: fiber installations

Marketing Materials: brochure,
photos, resume, slides, video
Size Range: 3' x 5' to 30' x 30'
Price Range: $3,000 - $25,000

Gloria Crouse creates highly textured art rugs and wall works, using unique variations of contemporary hooking and sculpting. Her work is included in many collections. Additional works may be seen in her recently published book, *Hooked Rugs: New Materials/New Techniques* with accompanying video. See page 36 for photographs and additional information.

NANCY CROW
10545 Snyder Church Rd.
Baltimore, OH 43105
(614) 862-6554
FAX (614) 862-6554
Established: 1969
Products: art quilts
Techniques: dyeing, quilting
Marketing Materials: slides
Size Range: 18" x 18" to 90" x 90"
Price Range: $2,200 - $20,000

BETH CUNNINGHAM
32 Sweetcake Mountain Rd.
New Fairfield, CT 06812
(203) 746-5160
Established: 1970
Products: mixed media wall
installations
Techniques: airbrush, painting
Marketing Materials: brochure,
resume, slides
Size Range: 2' x 3' to 6' x 12'
Price Range: $125 sq. ft.-$150 sq. ft.

Beth Cunningham creates elegant, ethereal, collaged paintings by airbrushing acrylic paint onto a rough, unprimed canvas background, and overlaying it with a smooth strip or grid surface of muslin, paint and silk tissue paper. Her one-of-a-kind wall pieces are sealed with an acrylic polymer that enables them to be exhibited without additional protection. See page 97 for photographs and additional information.

MARGARET CUSACK
124 Hoyt St. in Boerum Hill
Brooklyn, NY 11217-2215
(718) 237-0145
FAX (718) 237-0145
Established: 1972
Products: fiber installations
Techniques: appliqué, embroidery, quilting
Marketing Materials: brochure,
photos, resume, slides
Size Range: 14" x 17" to 5' x 9'
Price Range: $150 sq. ft.-$300 sq. ft.

Margaret Cusack's stitched hangings reflect her interest in representational imagery, her extensive drawing skills and a striking command of color. Since 1972 she has been creating stitched commissions for both public and private collections. Cusack's technique is sewing appliqué using a wide variety of fabric and textures. See page 37 for photographs and additional information.

EILEEN CUSTER
Eileen Custer Paperworks
870 Red Oak Ln.
Minnetrista, MN 55364
(612) 472-3189
Established: 1975
Products: mixed media wall
installations, paper wall work
Techniques: painting, airbrush
Marketing Materials: photos,
slides, resume, brochure
Size Range: 14" x 14" to 6' x 15'
Price Range: $100 sq. ft.-$200 sq. ft.

DIANA DABINETT
Box 254
Torbay, Newfoundland
Canada, A0A 3Z0
(709) 335-2637
Established: 1966
Products: fiber installations
Techniques: painting, dyeing,
quilting
Marketing Materials: photos,
slides, resume, brochure
Size Range: 6" x 4" to 9' x 21'
Price Range: $100 - $4,500

JUDY B. DALES
Judy Dales, Quiltmaker
129 Holly Ln.
Noonton Township, NJ 07005
(201) 334-1563
Established: 1980
Products: art quilts
Techniques: quilting
Marketing Materials: photos,
slides, resume
Size Range: 36" x 36" to 90" x 90"
Price Range: $800 - $6,000

JANET DANIEL
7459 Brigham Rd.
Gates Mills, OH 44040
(216) 423-0200
Established: 1973
Products: tapestries
Techniques: weaving
Marketing Materials: photos,
slides, resume, video
Size Range: 30" x 42" to 5' x 9'
Price Range: $500 - $2,500

NATALIE DARMOHRAJ
14 Imperial Pl. Unit 603
Providence, RI 02903
(401) 351-8841
Established: 1992
Products: tapestries
Techniques: weaving, dyeing
Marketing Materials: brochure,
photos, resume, slides
Price Range: $100 - $5,000

Using the finest fibers, including wool, silk and mohair, Natalie Darmohraj creates abstract images and patterns through the juxtaposition of textures and colors. Fabrics are suitable for both functional use or hanging on the wall. They are designed for both durability and aesthetic appeal and are appropriate for residential as well as commercial spaces. See page 165 for photographs and additional information.

KAREN DAVIDSON
PO Box 637
Hana Maui, HI 96713
(808) 248-7094
Established: 1980
Products: paper wall work
Techniques: painting, casting
Marketing Materials: photos,
slides, resume
Size Range: 2' x 3' to 12' x 10'
Price Range: $1,000 - $10,000

Hana-Maui artist Karen Davidson's work begins with the actual fibers, which she gathers from the abundance of the tropical jungle surrounding her studio. Davidson's work, guided by the rhythmic play of light and shadow, embodies the qualities of aged metallic surfaces with the colors and textures of antique leather and parchment. See page 11 for photographs and additional information.

ARDYTH DAVIS
Rt 2 Box 99F
Leesburg, VA 22075
(703) 777-9482
Established: 1975
Products: art quilts
Marketing Materials: photos,
slides, resume
Size Range: 12" x 12" to 80" x 80"
Price Range: $125 - $7,000

LENORE DAVIS
Soft Objects
655 Nelson Pl.
Newport, KY 41071
(606) 431-2353
FAX (606) 261-3780
Established: 1969
Products: art quilts
Techniques: painting, quilting,
stamping/printing
Marketing Materials: photos,
slides, resume
Size Range: 24" x 24" to 70" x 70"
Price Range: $800 - $5,000

NANETTE DAVIS-SHAKLHO
1289 E. Grand #318E
Escondido, CA 92027
(619) 745-6091
Established: 1984
Products: mixed media wall
installations
Techniques: dyeing, weaving
Marketing Materials: photos,
slides, resume
Size Range: 2'3" x 3'4" to 5'4" x 4'
Price Range: $950 - $2,400

JEANNE DAWSON
729 NE 17th Terrace
Fort Lauderdale, FL 33304
(305) 462-4347
Established: 1978
Products: fiber installations
Techniques: weaving, dyeing
Marketing Materials: photos,
slides, resume, brochure, video
Size Range: 1'6" x 1' to 10' x 20'
Price Range: $200 - $4,000

FIBER ART

JEAN DEEMER
1537 Briarwood Circle
Cuyahoga Falls, OH 44221
(216) 929-1995
Products: paper wall work
Techniques: painting
Marketing Materials: slides, resume
Size Range: 18" x 24" to 2' x 4'
Price Range: $375 - $3,500

IRENE R. DE GAIR
Irene R. de Gair Tapestries
2260 Teel Dr.
Vienna, VA 22182-5154
(703) 698-9281
(703) 698-9208
Established: 1980
Products: tapestries
Techniques: weaving
Marketing Materials: photos, resume, slides
Size Range: 2' x 2' to 7' x 20'
Price Range: $75 sq. ft. - $100 sq. ft.

The intricate and diverse patterns of Irene de Gairs' tapestries provide warmth and dimension to complement a wide range of nterior spaces. The pattern of each sheep's-wool tapestry is hand woven and maintenance free. Irene de Gair works closely with art consultants, architect's and interior designers to create unique, site-specific tapestries of any size. See page 24 for photographs and additional information.

LINDA DENIER
Denier Tapestry Studio
745 Edenwood Dr.
Roselle, IL 60172
(708) 893-5854
Established: 1988
Products: tapestries
Techniques: weaving
Marketing Materials: brochure, photos, resume, slides
Size Range: 12" x 12" to 5' x 6'
Price Range: $800 - $5,500

Dynamic colors bring detailed imagery to life in the tapestries of Linda Denier. While colors create depth, fiber adds warmth to these durable, low-maintenance works of art. Beautifully crafted, primarily of wool, all work is hand finished in the studio. Denier enjoys the challenge of designing to meet the client's vision. See page 22 for photographs and additional information.

SEENA DONNESON
Seena Donneson Studio
43-49 Tenth St
Long Island City, NY 11101
(718) 706-1342
Established: 1965
Products: tapestries
Techniques: casting, dyeing, painting
Marketing Materials: photos, slides, resume, brochure
Size Range: 20" x 20" to 96" x 64"
Price Range: $1,200 - $30,000

DRAWN THREAD DESIGNS
Julia A. Walsh
1905 Normal Park #201
PO Box 6503
Huntsville, TX 77342-6503
(409) 291-0195
Established: 1987
Products: tapestries
Marketing Materials: photos, slides, resume
Size Range: 16" x 20" to 6' x 5'
Price Range: $200 - $10,500

DONNA DURBIN
Donna Durbin, Artist
4034 Woodcraft
Houston, TX 77025
(713) 667-8129
Established: 1987
Products: tapestries
Techniques: weaving, painting
Marketing Materials: photos, slides, resume, brochure
Size Range: 8" x 8" to 6' x 20'
Price Range: $900 - $25,000

MARGIT ECHOLS
Rowhouse Press
PO Box 20531
New York, NY 10025
(212) 662-9604
Established: 1972
Products: art quilts
Techniques: quilting, applique
Marketing Materials: slides
Size Range: 24" x 36" to 100" x 110"
Price Range: $1,000 - $25,000

EDITIONS IN CAST PAPER
Joseph Gallo
1101 N. High Cross Rd.
Urbana, IL 61801
(217) 328-0118
FAX (217) 328-4864
Established: 1983
Products: paper wall work
Marketing Materials: brochure, photos, resume, slides. video
Size Range: 8" x 11" to 7' x 4'
Price Range: $50 - $4,000

Judith Poxson Fawkes, *Theater & Boat Landing,* 1992, linen tapestry, 6'7"W x 3'8"H

Sheet formation is the basis for all of Joseph Gallo's work. Figurative images are created by templates, multiple pulls and drawing with water. Other works involve wet collage and air brushing. Mono casts and low-relief floral prints are also available. All works consist of pigmented cotton rag, linen and abaca. See page 13 for photographs and additional information.

LORE EDZARD

815 Running Deer
Nashville, TN 37221
(615) 662-2583
Established: 1967
Products: tapestries
Techniques: weaving, dyeing, embroidery
Marketing Materials: photos, slides, resume
Size Range: 4' x 4' to 10' x 8'
Price Range: $75 sq. ft. - $100 sq. ft.

SYLVIA H. EINSTEIN

11 Oak Ave.
Belmont, MA 02178
(617) 484-9541
Established: 1980
Products: art quilts
Techniques: quilting
Marketing Materials: slides, resume
Size Range: 8" x 8" to 90" x 60"
Price Range: $150 - $3,000

SUSANA ENGLAND

PO Box 20601
Oakland, CA 94620
(510) 261-5646
Established: 1970
Products: paper wall work
Techniques: dyeing, painting
Marketing Materials: brochure, photos, resume, slides
Size Range: 8" x 10" to 5' x 7'
Price Range: $30 - $2,000

Susana England, whose work is included in private and corporate collections, uses a wide range of techniques to enhance the textural qualities in the abstract images of her dimensional wall pieces and free-standing sculpture. These fiber collage 'paintings' of cloth and handmade paper are embellished with stitching and painted forms. See page 12 for photographs and additional information.

JOHANNA ERICKSON

48 Chester St.
Watertown, MA 02172
(617) 926-1737
Established: 1972
Products: fiber installations
Techniques: weaving
Marketing Materials: photos, slides, resume, brochure
Size Range: 2' x 3' to 6' x 10'
Price Range: $120 - $1,200

NANCY N. ERICKSON

Dancing Rabbit Studios
3250 Pattee Canyon Rd.
Missoula, MT 59803
(406) 549-4671

Established: 1963
Products: art quilts
Techniques: quilting, appliqué, painting
Marketing Materials: photos, slides, resume
Size Range: 22" x 30" to 8' x 9'
Price Range: $750 - $8,000

EURO-ARTS

Beata Pies
543 Pacific St.
Brooklyn, New York, NY 11217
(212) 229-2854
FAX (212) 229-2854
Established: 1983
Products: tapestries
Techniques: painting, weaving
Marketing Materials: photos, slides, resume
Size Range: 1' x 1' to 7' x 10'
Price Range: $500 - $15,000

PHYLLIS CERATTO EVANS

PO Box 10761
Bainbridge Island, WA 98110
(206) 842-5042
Established: 1987
Products: fiber installations
Techniques: laminating
Marketing Materials: slides, resume
Size Range: 15" x 12" to 36" x 48"
Price Range: $250 - $2,500

JUDITH POXSON FAWKES

c/o Lauro Russo Gallery
805 NW 21st Ave.
Portland, OR 97209
(503) 226-2754
Established: 1970
Products: tapestries
Techniques: weaving
Marketing Materials: photos, slides, resume
Size Range: 3' x 3' to 8' x 20'
Price Range: $150 sq. ft.

See photograph on page 60.

LINDA FELIZ

Blue Heron Concepts
PO Box 1103
Westminster, CA 92683
(714) 894-8880
Established: 1972
Products: fiber installations
Techniques: weaving, dyeing, painting
Marketing Materials: photos, slides, resume
Size Range: 30" x 14" to 72" x 45"
Price Range: $100 - $3,000

LUCY FELLER

Photo Linens
941 Park Ave.
New York, NY 10028
(212) 628-1361
Established: 1957
Products: art quilts
Techniques: appliqué, embroidery
Marketing Materials: photos, slides, resume
Size Range: 10" x 15" to 5' x 5'
Price Range: $500 - $10,000

CATHERINE FERRO

KAIDA
3405 Honeywood Dr.
Johnson City, TN 37604
(615) 282-5847
Established: 1971
Products: paper wall work
Techniques: painting
Marketing Materials: photos, resume, brochure
Size Range: 8" x 10" to 4' x 5'
Price Range: $150 - $4,000

Catherine Ferros's palettes vary from combinations of intense hot colors to works involving the softest pastel hues. Acrylics, inks, dyes and assorted media are applied to papers that, once dry, are pulled, manipulated, folded, cut and reconstructed. These works contrast freeform with hard-edge dimension with surface plane and color with pattern. See photograph on this page.

PAMELA FLANDERS

Flanders Fine Arts
5864 Bridgeport Lake Way
San Jose, CA 95123
(408) 997-8438
Established: 1978
Products: paper wall work
Techniques: painting, laminating
Marketing Materials: slides, resume
Size Range: 8" x 10" to 40" x 60"
Price Range: $50 - $1,000

BARBARA FLETCHER

88 Beals St.
Brookline, MA 02146
(617) 277-3019
Established: 1986
Products: paper wall work
Techniques: casting, dyeing, airbrush
Marketing Materials: photos, slides, resume
Size Range: 3" x 3" to 45" x 45"
Price Range: $20 - $1,500

Catherine Ferro, *Latin Rhythms*, mixed media dimensional collage

FIBER ART

ROBERT FORMAN
412 Grand St.
Hoboken, NJ
(201) 659-7069
Established: 1975
Products: fiber installations
Marketing Materials: photos, slides, resume
Size Range: 10" x 15" to 60" x 72"
Price Range: $1,000 - $15,000

ROBERTA A. FOUNTAIN
PO Box 82
Ludlow, MA 01056
FAX (413) 789-4630
Established: 1975
Products: paper wall work
Techniques: laminating, dyeing, quilting
Marketing Materials: slides, resume
Size Range: 1' x 1' to 5' x 5'
Price Range: $50 - $1,250

FOWLER AND THELEN STUDIO
Laurie Fowler
Bill Thelen
201 Fairbrook
Northville, MI 48167
(313) 348-6654
Established: 1979
Products: fiber installations
Techniques: weaving
Marketing Materials: brochure, photos, slides, resume
Size Range: 1.5' x 2' to 3.5' x 8'
Price Range: $380 - $4,000

ALEXANDRA FRIEDMAN
56 Arbor St.
Hartford, CT 06106
(203) 236-3311
Established: 1987
Products: tapestries
Techniques: weaving
Marketing Materials: resume, slides
Price Range: $125 sq. ft.-$200 sq. ft.

Alexandra Friedman approaches the traditional art form of tapestry weaving with refreshing contemporary imagery. Her award-winning tapestries have been exhibited and collected by corporate and residential clients both nationally and internationally. She enjoys working on commissions and will collaborate with the client to design a tapestry that best suits a specific site. See page 23 for photographs and additional information.

JAN FRIEDMAN
1409 E. Davenport St.
Iowa City, IA 52245
(319) 338-1934
Established: 1979
Products: tapestries
Techniques: weaving, dyeing, appliqué
Marketing Materials: photos, slides, resume
Size Range: 24" x 20" to 15' x 10'
Price Range: $95 sq. ft.

WAYNE A.O. FUERST
Orchid Handmade Paper Studio
40 Woodland Rd.
Ashland, MA 01721
(508) 881-2525
Established: 1985
Products: paper wall work
Techniques: laminating
Marketing Materials: photos, slides, resume, brochure, video
Size Range: 20" x 45" to 45" x 92"
Price Range: $900 - $4,140

SUSAN GARDELS
1316 Arthur Ave.
Des Moines, IA 50316
(515) 265-2361
Established: 1978
Products: paper wall work
Techniques: painting, quilting
Marketing Materials: brochure, photos, resume, slides
Size Range: 5" x 5" to 40" x 40"
Price Range: $150 - $1,650

For the past 15 years, Susan Gardels has created archival-quality paper pieces for corporate and private clients. Pieces are constructed of acid-free rag, mulberry, and esparto grass papers, painted with acrylic glazes, and machine sewn for durability. After framing, the works require no further care. Large pieces are backed with canvas. See page 14 for photographs and additional information.

ARLENE GAWNE
Nature in Tapestry
73470 Dalea Ln.
Palm Desert, CA 92260
(619) 340-3628
Established: 1981
Products: tapestries
Techniques: weaving
Marketing Materials: photos, slides, resume
Size Range: 2' x 2' to 6' x 6'
Price Range: $250 - $12,000

CAROL H. GERSEN
Studio Art Quilts
18839 Manor Church Rd.
Boonsboro, MD 21713
(301) 432-6484
Established: 1981
Products: art quilts
Techniques: dyeing, quilting
Marketing Materials: photos, slides, resume
Size Range: 3' x 3' to 5' x 8'
Price Range: $900 - $5,000

JAMES R. GILBERT
Woven Structures
PO Box 474
Bloomfield Hills, MI 48303-0474
(313) 772-7087
FAX (313) 881-7787
Established: 1970
Products: fiber installations
Techniques: weaving, silkscreen, dyeing
Marketing Materials: photos, slides, resume, brochure, video
Size Range: 3' x 3' to 90' x 6'
Price Range: $350 - $7,000

SUSAN GILLER
291 Central Ave.
Englewood, NJ 07631
(201) 569-4570
FAX (201) 569-1903
Established: 1987
Products: tapestries
Techniques: weaving
Marketing Materials: photos, slides
Size Range: 20" x 15" to 10' x 8'
Price Range: $600 - $25,000

SUELLEN GLASHAUSSER
202 South Second Ave.
Highland Park, NJ 08904
(908) 545-6928
Established: 1971
Products: mixed media wall installations
Techniques: embroidery, painting, laminating
Marketing Materials: slides, resume
Size Range: 3" x 6" to 85" x 120"
Price Range: $400 - $1,500

MARY GOLDEN
Golden Quilts
PO Box 333
New Hampton, NH 03256
(603) 744-5650
Established: 1972
Products: art quilts
Techniques: quilting, appliqué
Marketing Materials: photos, slides, resume, brochure
Size Range: 20" x 20" to 96" x 96"
Price Range: $100 - $2,000

LAYNE GOLDSMITH
PO Box 563
Snohomish, WA 98291-0563
(206) 334-5569
Established: 1972
Products: mixed media wall installations
Techniques: felting, dyeing, laminating
Marketing Materials: brochure, photos, resume, slides
Size Range: 6' x 4' to 20' x 60'

Layne Goldsmith—recipient of a National Endowment for the Arts Individual Artist's grant—specializes in contemporary textiles with a focus on color and content. Her dimensional, wall-mounted textiles maintain their form beautifully and use the relief possibilities of the non-woven medium to create a sense of depth and texture. See page 38 for photographs and additional information.

INA GOLUB
366 Rolling Rock Rd.
Mountainside, NJ 07092
(908) 232-5376
Established: 1963
Products: tapestries
Techniques: appliqué, weaving, beading
Marketing Materials: resume, brochure
Size Range: 2' x 2' to 10' x 12'
Price Range: $1,000 - $25,000

RUTH GOWELL
7010 Aronow Dr.
Falls Church, VA 22042
(703) 532-8645
Established: 1980
Products: fiber installations

Techniques: weaving, dyeing
Marketing Materials: brochure, photos, slides, resume
Size Range: 16" x 18" to 4' x 8'
Price Range: $250 - $3,500

Ruth Gowell—a three-time winner of the Niche Award for Decorative Fibers—creates shimmering weavings of rayon, hand-dyed in color progressions and woven warp-face with up to four layers of warp. Since 1980 she has developed techniques that involve exploration of light and shadow, color interaction, texture and pattern. See page 39 for photographs and additional information.

LAURA ELIZABETH GREEN
5523 Highland St. South
St. Petersburg, FL 33705
(813) 867-1204
Established: 1973
Products: art quilts
Techniques: appliqué, dyeing, quilting
Marketing Materials: photos, slides, resume
Size Range: 1' x 1' to 8' x 8'
Price Range: $250 - $2,500

BARBARA GRENELL
1132 Halls Chapel Rd.
Burnsville, NC 28714
(704) 675-4073
Established: 1972
Products: tapestries
Techniques: weaving, dyeing, painting
Marketing Materials: photos, slides, resume, brochure
Price Range: $900 - $25,000

In Barbara Grenell's dimensional constructions, two separate tapestries are broken up and presented as sculptural relief that enhances the dimensional aspects of their content. The unified coherence that results from these juxtaposed landscapes engages the viewer, whose movement about the piece becomes an integral part of the work. See pages 40 and 41 for photographs and additional information.

MARILYN GRISHAM
315 Post Rd.
Eldorado, KS 67042
(316) 321-1996
Established: 1970
Products: tapestries
Techniques: weaving, embroidery, dyeing
Marketing Materials: photos, slides, resume
Size Range: 3' x 5' to 12' x 24'
Price Range: $2,500 - $55,000

KATRYNA HADLEY
53 Wendell St.
Cambridge, MA 02138
(617) 492-6857
Established: 1978
Products: paper wall work
Techniques: stamping/printing, painting, quilting
Marketing Materials: slides, resume
Size Range: 10" x 10" to 4' x 5'
Price Range: $200 - $1,000

MARCIA HAMMOND
Rt. 1 Box 898
Putney, VT 05346
(802) 387-2202
Established: 1977
Products: fiber installations
Techniques: weaving, dyeing
Marketing Materials: slides,
resume, brochure
Price Range: $40 sq. ft. - $150 sq. ft.

TIM HARDING
Harding Design Studio
2402 University Ave.
St. Paul, MN 55114
(612) 645-0544
Established: 1974
Products: fiber installations
Techniques: quilting, dyeing
Marketing Materials: photos,
slides, resume, brochure
Size Range: 54" x 72"
Price Range: $4,000

PETER HARRIS
Tapestry and Design Peter Harris
RR 2
Ayton, Ontario
Canada N0G 1C0
(519) 665-2245
Established: 1973
Products: tapestries
Techniques: weaving
Marketing Materials: slides, resume
Size Range: 36" x 48" to 60" x 96"
Price Range: $2,500 - $10,000

ANN L. HARTLEY
Tree House Studio
13515 Sea Island Dr.
Houston, TX 77069
(713) 444-1118
Established: 1975
Products: mixed media wall
installations
Techniques: painting, stamp-
ing/printing
Marketing Materials: photos,
slides, resume, brochure
Size Range: 12" x 12" to 4' x 6'
Price Range: $300 - $1,500

SARAH D. HASKELL
30 N. Main St.
Newmarket, NH 03857
(603) 659-5250
Established: 1976
Products: tapestries
Techniques: weaving
Marketing Materials: photos,
slides, resume, brochure
Size Range: 3' x 4' to 20' x 16'
Price Range: $1,560 - $44,600

SHARON HEIDINGSFELDER
8010 Dan Thomas Rd.
Little Rock, AR 72206-4148
(501) 671-2251
FAX (501) 671-2251
Established: 1973
Products: art quilts
Techniques: quilting, silkscreen,
dyeing
Marketing Materials: slides, resume
Size Range: 72" x 72" to 78" x 84"
Price Range: $4,000 - $6,500

MARTHA HEINE
7 Haggis Court
Durham, NC 27705
(919) 479-3270
Established: 1980
Products: tapestries
Techniques: weaving
Marketing Materials: photos,
slides, resume
Size Range: 36" x 48" to 48" x 60"
Price Range: $1,860 - $3,100

SHEILA A. HELD
2363 North 47th St.
Milwaukee, WI 53210
(414) 873-3419
Established: 1975
Products: tapestries
Techniques: weaving
Marketing Materials: slides, resume
Size Range: 30" x 20" to 80" x 54"
Price Range: $500 - $5,000

HELIO GRAPHICS
Dawn Wilkins
PO Box 6213
Key West, FL 33041
(305) 294-7901
Established: 1980
**Products: mixed media wall
installations**
Techniques: painting, silkscreen
**Marketing Materials: brochure,
photos, resume, slides**
Size Range: 20" x 20" to 50" x 60"
Price Range: $200 - $1,000

**Dawn Wilkins captures the
vibrant colors and ambiance of
the tropics in her design work.
Stretched canvas wall pieces
include prints of actual leaves in
custom colors and a variety of
tropical- and wildlife-inspired
designs. Using textile inks and
acrylics handpainted with bristle
brushes, vivid shading is emphasized with attention to detail.
Works also incorporate variations
of ancient printing techniques.
See page 167 for photographs
and additional information.**

BARBARA HELLER
Fibre Arts Studio
1610 Johnston St.
Vancouver, B.C., Canada
V6H 3S2
(604) 224-2060
Established: 1975
Products: tapestries
Techniques: dyeing, weaving
Marketing Materials: photos,
slides, resume
Size Range: 12" x 12" to 4' x 6'
Price Range: $400 - $8,000

SUSAN HART HENEGAR
5449 Bellevue Ave.
La Jolla, CA 92037
(619) 459-5681
FAX (619) 459-5693
Established: 1973
Products: tapestries
Techniques: weaving, quilting
Marketing Materials: photos,
slides, resume, brochure
Size Range: 3' x 3' to 7'6" x 25'
Price Range: $300 - $45,000

NANCY CLEARWATER HERMAN
275 North Latches Ln.
Merion, PA 19066
(215) 667-4705
Established: 1978
Products: art quilts
Techniques: appliqué
Marketing Materials: photos,
slides, resume
Size Range: 36" x 36" to 72" x 72"
Price Range: $150 sq. ft.

HICKORY MOUNTAIN WEAVERY
Jean Vollrath
10435 U.S. Highway 64E
Staley, NC 27355-8154
(919) 742-3325
Established: 1984
Products: fiber installations
Techniques: weaving
Marketing Materials: slides
Size Range: 36" x 24" to 80" x 60"
Price Range: $35 - $1,200

PAMELA HILL
PO Box 800
8500 Lafayette
Mokelumne Hill, CA 95245
(209) 286-1217
Established: 1975
Products: art quilts
Techniques: quilting
Marketing Materials: photos,
slides, resume
Size Range: 36" x 50" to 120" x 144"
Price Range: $600 - $3,500

DEBORAH HOBBINS
2925 Branch St.
Duluth, MN 55812
(218) 728-2651
FAX (218) 728-2651
Established: 1985
Products: fiber installations
Techniques: painting, weaving
Marketing Materials: photos,
slides, resume
Price Range: $450 - $2,500

JEAN HOBLITZELL
20 East Randall St.
Baltimore, MD 21230
(410) 332-8032
Established: 1985
Products: art quilts
Techniques: appliqué, quilting
Marketing Materials: photos,
slides, resume
Size Range: 12" x 10" to 104" x 104"
Price Range: $200 - $3,000

DOROTHY HOLDEN
1934 Lewis Mountain Rd.
Charlottesville, VA 22903
(804) 971-5803
Established: 1979
Products: art quilts
Techniques: quilting, appliqué,
embroidery
Marketing Materials: photos,
slides, resume
Size Range: 18" x 14" to 118" x 129"
Price Range: $500 - $5,000

BONNIE LEE HOLLAND
6407 Landon Ln.
Bethesda, MD 20817
(301) 229-4388
Established: 1982
Products: fiber installations
Techniques: dyeing, painting,
silkscreen
Marketing Materials: photos,
slides, resume, brochure
Size Range: 8" x 5" to 35' x 30'
Price Range: $200 - $30,000

ELIZABETH HOLSTER
Paper By Holster
727 East A St.
Iron Mountain, MI 49801
(906) 779-2592
Established: 1976
Products: paper wall work
Techniques: painting
Marketing Materials: slides, resume
Size Range: 20" x 20" to 60" x 60"
Price Range: $300 - $3,000

KATHERINE HOLZKNECHT
22828 57th Ave. S.E.
Woodinville, WA 98072
(206) 481-7788
Established: 1976
**Products: mixed media wall
installations**
**Techniques: dyeing, laminating,
embroidery**
**Marketing Materials: brochure,
photos, resume, slides**
Size Range: 2' x 2' to 20' x 60'
Price Range: $200 sq. ft.

**Katherine Holzknecht creates
unique mixed-media artworks for
architectural spaces. She specializes in full-spectrum colors
and visual textures to enhance
existing design features.
Constructed with dyed and
painted wood, metal, wire, fabric
and paper, her artworks are
ideal for interiors because of their
durability and lightfastness. See
page 100 for photographs and
additional information.**

DORA HSIUNG
Hsiung Design
95 Warren St.
Newton Centre, MA 02159
(617) 969-4630
Established: 1978
Products: tapestries
Techniques: weaving
Marketing Materials: photos,
slides, resume
Size Range: 12" x 12" to 21' x 16'
Price Range: $200 - $30,000

JOHN D. HUBBARD
53 Stonegate
Marquette, MI 49855
(906) 249-1188
Established: 1969
Products: paper wall work
Techniques: painting, laminating
Marketing Materials: photos,
slides, resume
Size Range: 20" x 24" to 48" x 60"
Price Range: $500 - $5,000

FIBER ART

JUDY HUBBARD
2719 Preston St.
Columbia, SC 29205
(803) 799-8138
Established: 1983
Products: fiber installations
Techniques: dyeing, painting
Marketing Materials: photos, slides, resume, brochure
Size Range: 16" x 84" to 12' x 24'
Price Range: $100 sq. ft.-$150 sq. ft.

HUGHES-HUNTER
Jeanne Hughes
3542 Veteran Ave.
Los Angeles, CA 90034
(310) 839-8601
FAX (310) 839-6116
Established: 1981
Products: mixed media wall installations
Techniques: painting
Marketing Materials: photos
Size Range: 16" x 20" to 4' x 8'
Price Range: $80 - $2,800

LENORE HUGHES
PO Box 1862
La Jolla, CA 92038
(619) 456-1144
FAX (619) 291-8362
Established: 1987
Products: paper wall work
Techniques: painting, stamping/printing
Marketing Materials: brochure, photos, resume, slides
Size Range: 3" x 2" to 108" x 156"
Price Range: $150 - $6,000

Lenore Hughes hand cuts and weaves her original watercolor paintings into unique abstracts that hint of landscape or still life. Hughes' palate includes pure, bright, summer colors, soft spring tones, decorator colors, or sophisticated grays and tans. She produces top-quality pieces as large as a full-scale mural or as small as a wine label. See page 15 for photographs and additional information.

WENDY C. HUHN
81763 Lost Creek Rd.
Dexter, OR 97431
(503) 937-3147

Elaine Ireland, *Risk Factor*, ceramic tile panel above, woven tapestry below, cotton warp; wool, cotton, silk weft, 56" x 36"

Established: 1983
Products: art quilts
Techniques: stamping/printing, quilting
Marketing Materials: photos, slides, resume
Size Range: 36" x 36" to 70" x 70"
Price Range: $850 - $2,200

JOYCE HULBERT
Joyce Hulbert, Tapestry and Textile Restoration
572 Church St.
San Francisco, CA 94114
(415) 552-8580
Established: 1982
Products: tapestries
Techniques: weaving, dyeing
Marketing Materials: photos, slides, resume
Size Range: 8" x 8" to 4' x 6'
Price Range: $300 - $7,200

CONSTANCE HUNT
1270 Sanchez St.
San Francisco, CA 94114
(415) 282-5170
Established: 1980
Products: tapestries
Techniques: weaving
Marketing Materials: photos, slides, resume
Size Range: 9" x 6" to 80" x 72"
Price Range: $400 - $19,500

LINDA HUTCHINS
2951 NW Quimby St.
Portland, OR 97210
(503) 274-9498
FAX (503) 248-9252
Established: 1988
Products: tapestries
Techniques: weaving
Marketing Materials: slides, resume
Size Range: 1' x 1' to 8' x 8'
Price Range: $250 - $16,000

MARIE-LAURE ILIE
M-Laure Studio/Cocoon
1241 Kolle Ave.
South Pasadena, CA 91030
(213) 254-8073
Established: 1975
Products: fiber installations
Techniques: painting, appliqué
Marketing Materials: photos, slides, resume, brochure
Size Range: 3' x 3' to 7' x 11'
Price Range: $900 - $10,000

Laure Ilie creates two styles of silk wall hangings. One style transposes the European Medieval tapestries and other scenes from ancient art with an antique appearance. Her other silk tapestry paintings are abstract, painterly and contemporary. They explore the richness of an appliqué technique that involves layers of transparent organza on a hand-painted silk background. See pages 42 and 43 for photographs and additional information.

INSPIRED PATCHES
Bernidett Gayles
8948 E. Town & Country Blvd.
Ellicott City, MD 21043
(410) 461-1614

Established: 1982
Products: art quilts
Techniques: quilting, beading, appliqué
Marketing Materials: photos, slides
Size Range: 36" x 36" to 100" x 100"
Price Range: $500 - $1,000

ELAINE IRELAND
450 Alabama St.
San Francisco, CA 94110
(415) 863-2765
Established: 1972
Products: tapestries
Techniques: weaving
Marketing Materials: photos, slides, resume
Size Range: 3' x 3' to 4' x 17'
Price Range: $4,500 - $50,000

See photograph on this page.

PEG IRISH
114 Metoxit Rd.
Waquoit, MA 02536
(508) 548-3230
Established: 1988
Products: fiber installations
Techniques: dyeing, embroidery
Marketing Materials: photos, slides, resume, brochure
Size Range: 8" x 10" to 3' x 5'
Price Range: $250 - $5,000

CAROL IRVING
The Weavers Web
1204 8th Ave. South
Escanaba, MI 49829
(906) 786-0331
Established: 1977
Products: fiber installations
Techniques: weaving
Marketing Materials: slides, resume
Size Range: 5' x 3'
Price Range: $250

SUSAN IVERSON
Susan Iverson—Tapestries
904 Buford Oaks Circle
Richmond, VA 23235
(804) 272-0225
Established: 1975
Products: tapestries
Techniques: weaving, dyeing
Marketing Materials: slides, resume
Size Range: 3' x 7' to 8' x 10'
Price Range: $2,500 - $10,000

DALE JACKSON
101 Hammersmith Ave. Unit 212
Toronto, Ontario, Canada
M4E 2W3
(416) 699-0950
Established: 1980
Products: tapestries
Techniques: weaving, painting, embroidery
Marketing Materials: photos, slides, resume
Size Range: 2' x 1' to 8' x 5'
Price Range: $400 - $8,000

DAMARIS JACKSON
3317 Elliot Ave. S.
Minneapolis, MN 55407
(612) 825-3524
Established: 1982
Products: art quilts
Techniques: quilting

Fiber Art

Marketing Materials: slides, resume
Size Range: 3' x 3' to 8' x 8'
Price Range: $400 - $3,500

VICTOR JACOBY
1086 17th St.
Eureka, CA 95501
(707) 442-3809
Established: 1975
Products: tapestries
Techniques: weaving
Marketing Materials: slides,
resume, brochure
Size Range: 2' x 2' to 8' x 24'
Price Range: $1,000 - $48,000

Victor Jacoby has been creating
woven tapestries and exhibiting
them nationally for more than 20
years. Since 1975 he has also
woven numerous commissions
for both corporate and residential spaces. He has explored
landscape, floral and figurative
themes as well as other themes
appropriate to individual client's
needs. See page 25 for photographs and additional information.

LUCY A. JAHNS
12 Auburn Court
Vernon Hills, IL 60061
(708) 362-2144
Established: 1982
Products: fiber installations
Techniques: painting, embroi-
dery, appliqué
Marketing Materials: photos,
slides, resume
Size Range: 24" x 36" to 48" x 120"
Price Range: $350 - $2,340

MICHAEL JAMES
Studio Quilts
258 Old Colony Ave.
Somerset Village, MA 02726
(508) 672-1370
Established: 1973
Products: art quilts
Techniques: quilting
Marketing Materials: photos,
slides, resume
Size Range: 39" x 39" to 108" x 108"
Price Range: $3,500 - $16,000

CATHERINE JANSEN
152 Heacock Ln.
Wyncote, PA 19095
(215) 884-3174
Established: 1976
Products: art quilts
Marketing Materials: photos,
slides, resume
Size Range: 8" x 10" to room sized
Price Range: $225 - $20,000

LIISA SALOSAARI JASINSKI
6828 Shiloh Ridge Ln.
Charlotte, NC 28212
(704) 563-5395
Established: 1991
Products: fiber installations
Techniques: painting, laminating
Marketing Materials: photos,
slides, resume, brochure
Size Range: 24" x 18" to 57" x 35"
Price Range: $200 - $700

DAVID C. JOHNSON
4727 W. Moorhead Circle
Boulder, CO 80303
(303) 499-0986
Established: 1981
Products: tapestries
Techniques: weaving, dyeing,
stamping/printing
Marketing Materials: photos,
slides, resume
Size Range: 2' x 3' to 5' x 15'
Price Range: $300 - $3,750

VICKI L. JOHNSON
225 Muir Dr.
Soquel, CA 95073
(408) 476-7567
FAX (408) 476-7567
Established: 1981
Products: art quilts
Techniques: painting, applique,
quilting
Marketing Materials: photos,
slides, resume, brochure
Size Range: 24" x 30" to 6' x 8'
Price Range: $400 - $6,500

ANN JOHNSTON
Ann Johnston, Quiltmaker
910 York Rd.
Lake Oswego, OR 97034
(503) 635-1173
Established: 1980
Products: art quilts
Techniques: dyeing, quilting,
painting
Marketing Materials: photos,
slides, resume
Size Range: 8" x 8" to 9' x 9'
Price Range: $250 - $8,000

OLGALYN JOLLY
O. Jolly
63 Greene St.
New York, NY 10012
(212) 966-0185
Established: 1984
Products: tapestries
Techniques: dyeing, painting
Marketing Materials: photos,
slides, resume
Size Range: 8" x 10" to 7' x 8'
Price Range: $125 sq. ft.-$200 sq. ft.

HENDRIKA KAMSTRA
Ginkgo Studio
1825 West Cottage St.
Stevens Point, WI 54481
(715) 341-8277
Established: 1984
Products: mixed media wall
installations
Techniques: casting, dyeing
Marketing Materials: photos,
slides, resume, brochure
Size Range: 15" x 10" to 30" x 40"
Price Range: $195 - $1,350

JANIS KANTER
1923 W. Dickens
Chicago, IL 60614
(312) 252-2119
Established: 1986
Products: mixed media wall
installations
Techniques: weaving, silkscreen
Marketing Materials: brochure,
photos, resume, slides
Size Range: 3' x 3' to 8' x 5'
Price Range: $1,000 - $5,000

Tapestry artist Janis Kanter thinks
of her work as painting with yarn.

Her woven images are filled with
an intriguing variety of rich texture
and color, much like the impasto
of a painter's palette. Kanter also
uses colorful neon tubing, interlaced and floating over the textural imagery to create two-
dimensional, sculptural work. See
page 44 for photographs and
additional information.

ANNA KARESH
Art Studio West
PO Box 900528
San Diego, CA 92190
(619) 258-0766
Established: 1970
Products: mixed media wall
installations
Techniques: painting, casting
Marketing Materials: photos,
slides, resume, brochure
Size Range: 16" x 22" to 60" x 8'4"
Price Range: $500 - $4,000

MARY LUCE KASPER
MK Handweaving
106 High St.
Florence, MA 01060
(413) 584-6667
Established: 1980
Products: fiber installations
Techniques: dyeing, weaving
Marketing Materials: slides,
resume, brochure
Size Range: 5' x 3' to 7' x 5'
Price Range: $1,050 - $2,250

DONNA J. KATZ
540 W. Briar Pl., #4K
Chicago, IL 60657
(312) 525-3390
Established: 1975
Products: art quilts
Techniques: painting, quilting
Marketing Materials: photos,
slides, resume
Size Range: 18" x 24" to 8' x 8'
Price Range: $200 - $6,400

JUDI KEEN
923 20th St.
Sacramento, CA 95814
(916) 446-4777
Established: 1976
Products: tapestries
Techniques: embroidery, weaving
Marketing Materials: photos,
slides, resume
Size Range: 3' x 3' to 9' x 12'
Price Range: $400 - $4,800

ANN KEISTER
410 S. Serena Ln.
Bloomington, IN 47401
(812) 333-8022
Established: 1978
Products: tapestries
Techniques: weaving
Marketing Materials: slides, resume
Size Range: 30" x 40" to 5' x 8'
Price Range: $3,200 - $16,000

KATHY KENLEY
RR2 Box 103 RT 542
Green Bank, NJ 08215
(609) 965-7167
Established: 1972
Products: mixed media wall
installations

Techniques: casting, laminating,
airbrush
Marketing Materials: photos,
slides, resume
Size Range: 6" x 8" to 6' x 6'
Price Range: $30 - $3,500

ANNE MARIE KENNY
Fiber Work
1465 Hooksett Rd. #109
Hooksett, NH 03106
(603) 268-0336
Established: 1983
Products: art quilts
Techniques: painting, applique
Marketing Materials: photos,
slides, resume, brochure
Size Range: 22" x 24" to 5' x 6'
Price Range: $300 - $15,000

GLENDA KING
858 Malabu Dr. #26
Lexington, KY 40502
(606) 257-4669
Established: 1989
Products: art quilts
Techniques: quilting, dyeing,
embroidery
Marketing Materials: photos,
slides, resume, brochure
Size Range: 2' x 2' to 7' x 7'
Price Range: $600 - $9,000

KIMBERLY HALDEMAN KLEIN
925 Grandview Blvd.
Lancaster, PA 17601
(717) 293-9453
Established: 1976
Products: art quilts
Techniques: quilting
Marketing Materials: slides,
brochure
Size Range: 40" x 40" to 60" x 60"
Price Range: $500 - $2,000

LYNN KLEIN
3373 Dwight Way
Berkeley, CA 94702
(510) 704-9265
Established: 1976
Products: mixed media wall
installations
Techniques: dyeing, painting,
laminating
Marketing Materials: photos,
slides, resume, brochure
Size Range: 16" x 12" to 48" x 120"
Price Range: $750 - $20,000

M.A. KLEIN
3840 Thorson Dr.
Placerville, CA 95667
(916) 644-6396
FAX (916) 644-5411
Established: 1960
Products: mixed media wall
installations
Techniques: dyeing, appliqué,
embroidery
Marketing Materials: brochure,
photos, resume, slides
Size Range: 17" x 14" to 7' x 25'
Price Range: $200 sq. ft.-$300 sq. ft.

M.A. Klein creates one-of-a-kind,
mixed-media fiber collages. Her
techniques include collage and
other appliqué, fabric manipulation, hand and machine stitchery,
patchwork, quilting and hand
painting fabrics. These combined

FIBER ART

techniques result in unique, three-dimensional, heavily textured pieces whose sizes vary from large-scale installations to smaller intimate focal points. See page 45 for photographs and additional information.

MARY KLOTZ
Forestheart Studio
136 Stonegade Dr.
Frederick, MD 21702
(301) 695-4815
Established: 1980
Products: fiber installations
Techniques: weaving, dyeing, felting
Marketing Materials: photos, slides, resume
Size Range: 9" x 12" to 6' x 9'
Price Range: $400 - $6,000

ROBIN REIDER KNIGHT
Weavings by Robin
PO Box 687
Chimayo, NM 87522
(505) 351-4474
Established: 1980
Products: tapestries
Techniques: weaving
Marketing Materials: photos, slides, resume
Size Range: 45" x 16" to 80" x 50"
Price Range: $140 - $2,800

JOAN KOPCHIK
1335 Stephen Way
Southhampton, PA 18966-4349
(215) 322-1862
Established: 1974
Products: paper wall work
Techniques: painting, stamping/printing
Marketing Materials: photos, resume, slides
Size Range: 18" x 18" to 4' x 6'
Price Range: $600 - $2,500

Joan Kopchik folds and layers sheets of archival quality handmade papers and she incorporates textural elements and objects to create works of distinction. Her elegant designs are nature inspired and are suitable for many environments. She has worked with design professionals to develop site-specific works for private and corporate spaces. See page 16 for photographs and additional information.

LAURENCE KORWIN
Korwin Design
333 N. Michigan Ave.
Chicago, IL 60601
(312) 372-8687
Established: 1980
Products: tapestries
Techniques: applique
Marketing Materials: photos, slides, resume
Size Range: 3' x 5' to 20' x 50'
Price Range: $5,000 - $25,000

LIBBY KOWALSKI
41 Union Square West, Suite 502
New York, NY 10003
(212) 627-5770
FAX (212) 989-9702
Products: fiber installations
Techniques: weaving, painting

Libby Kowalski's black-and-white woven and painted pieces are delicate, yet bold, highly-patterned and hard-edged images. Although her earlier work was more constructivist in style, recent compositions reveal an exploration into symbolism. She now frequently uses computers and computer imagery to design her compositions. See page 26 for photographs and additional information.

GRACE A. KRAFT
Stone School House
Madrid, NM 87010
(505) 471-8062
Established: 1971
Products: fiber installations
Techniques: silkscreen, painting, airbrush
Marketing Materials: photos, slides, resume, brochure, video
Size Range: 32" x 32" to 45' x 45'
Price Range: $1,200 - $33,000

CANDACE KREITLOW
PO Box 113
Mazomanie, WI 53560
(608) 795-4680
Established: 1985
Products: fiber installations
Techniques: weaving, dyeing
Marketing Materials: photos, slides, resume
Size Range: 24" x 32" to 8' x 7'
Price Range: $900 - $24,000

SUSAN KRISTOFERSON
Kristoferson Studio
1150 N.W. Alder Creek Dr.
Corvallis, OR 97330
(503) 745-5554
FAX (503) 753-9010
Established: 1970
Products: fiber installations
Techniques: painting, dyeing
Marketing Materials: photos, slides, resume, brochure
Size Range: 12" x 12" to 48" x 180"
Price Range: $200 - $9,000

KT-STUDIO LTD
Kaija Tyni-Rautiainen
5390 Gordon Ave.
Burnaby, B.C. Canada
V5E 3L8
(604) 524-2455
Established: 1979
Products: tapestries
Techniques: weaving
Marketing Materials: photos, slides, resume
Size Range: 12" x 12" to 100" x 60"

LIALIA KUCHMA
2423 W. Superior
Chicago, IL 60612
(312) 227-5445
Established: 1979
Products: tapestries
Techniques: weaving
Marketing Materials: photos, slides, resume
Size Range: 36" x 36" to 8' x 8'
Price Range: $1,500 - $15,000

CHRISTINE LAFFER
Tapus
1933 O'Toole Ave. #A-102
San Jose, CA 95131-2220
(408) 922-7240
FAX (408) 922-7241
Established: 1983
Products: tapestries
Techniques: weaving
Marketing Materials: photos, slides, resume, brochure
Size Range: 3" x 3" to 5' x 8'
Price Range: $150 - $16,000

ANNE LAMBORN
Anne Lamborn, Architectural Textiles
7 Monroe Court
Los Gatos, CA 95030
(408) 354-8493
FAX (408) 354-9958
Established: 1970
Products: fiber installations
Techniques: dyeing, weaving
Marketing Materials: photos, slides, resume, brochure
Size Range: 2' x 5' to 5' x 30'
Price Range: $1,000 - $20,000

MARY LANE
PO Box 7280
Olympia, WA 98507-7280
(206) 956-9173
Established: 1982
Products: tapestries
Techniques: weaving
Marketing Materials: photos, slides, resume
Size Range: 3" x 5" to 8' x 16'
Price Range: $300 - $10,000

KAREN LARSEN
Cacophony
7 Austin Park
Cambridge, MA 02139
(617) 491-4025
Established: 1979
Products: art quilts
Techniques: quilting, weaving
Marketing Materials: slides, resume
Size Range: 22" x 22" to 96" x 120"
Price Range: $150 - $10,000

JUDITH LARZELERE
Corporate Fiber Art
226 Beech St.
Belmont, MA 02178
(617) 484-6091
Established: 1978
Products: art quilts
Techniques: quilting
Marketing Materials: photos, slides, resume
Size Range: 18" x 18" to 9' x 15'
Price Range: $600 - $25,000

ULRIKA LEANDER
Contemporary Tapestry Weaving
107 Westoverlook Dr.
Oak Ridge, TN 37830
(615) 482-6849
Established: 1971
Products: tapestries
Techniques: weaving
Marketing Materials: photos, slides, resume, brochure, video
Size Range: 4' x 4' to 30' x 12'
Price Range: $120 sq. ft. - $240 sq. ft.

Ulrika Leander has installed more than 150 tapestries—all using 100

percent natural fibers and some measuring up to 12' by 30'—commissioned for public, private and commercial settings in Scandinavia and the U.S. Inspired by her native country's traditions, Leander has established a reputation for superb craftsmanship and a remarkable range of creative and imaginative designs. See page 27 for photographs and additional information.

DAVID LECLERC
Paper People
PO Box 766
Dennisport, MA 02639
(508) 362-2414
Established: 1975
Products: paper wall work
Marketing Materials: photos, slides, resume, brochure, video
Size Range: 12" x 18" to 5' x 8'
Price Range: $20 - $2,000

SUSAN WEBB LEE
963 Woods Loop
Weddington, NC 28173
(704) 843-1323
Established: 1973
Products: art quilts
Techniques: quilting, applique, dyeing
Marketing Materials: photos, slides, resume
Size Range: 25" x 25" to 80" x 80"
Price Range: $300 - $8,000

CONNIE LEHMAN
PO Box 281
Elizabeth, CO 80107
(303) 646-4638
FAX (303) 646-4638
Established: 1975
Products: tapestries
Techniques: embroidery, beading, applique
Marketing Materials: photos, slides, resume, brochure
Size Range: 1.5" x 2" to 5" x 8"
Price Range: $250 - $1,500

BONNY LHOTKA
5658 Cascade Pl.
Boulder, CO 80303
(303) 494-5631
FAX (303) 494-3472
Established: 1972
Products: tapestries
Techniques: painting, laminating, stamping/printing
Marketing Materials: brochure, photos, resume, slides, video
Size Range: 24" x 36" to 10' x 30'
Price Range: $660 - $110 sq. ft.

Bonny Lhotka creates unique monographic transfer tapestries on tear-proof spun-bonded fiber using sheets of acrylic paint. These tapestries can be installed on curved walls, free hung with images on both sides or hung as traditional paintings. The work can be rolled for ease of presentation and shipping. See page 48 for photographs and additional information.

WENDY LILIENTHAL
740 Butterfield Rd.
San Anselmo, CA 94960
(415) 453-1019
Established: 1975
Products: paper wall work
Techniques: casting, dyeing
Marketing Materials: slides,
resume, brochure
Size Range: 18" x 24" to 30" x 40"
Price Range: $450 - $1,200

CAL LING
Cal Ling Paperworks
441 Cherry St.
Chico, CA 95928
(916) 893-0882
Established: 1978
Products: mixed media wall
installations
Marketing Materials: photos,
slides, resume
Size Range: 1' x 2' to 10' x 15'
Price Range: $300 - $20,000

Cal Ling mixes the idea of paper
and clay by producing paper
tiles that are durable as well as
aesthetically pleasing. Treated
with a waterproofing agent, the
combination of smooth and textured papers adds depth and
dimension to the surface. These
paper tiles may register as
murals, wall papers, architectural
accents or formal artworks. See
page 17 for photographs and
additional information.

M. JOAN LINTAULT
306 N. Springer
Carbondale, IL 62901
(618) 549-6540
Established: 1965
Products: art quilts
Techniques: dyeing, silkscreen,
quilting
Marketing Materials: photos,
slides, resume, brochure
Size Range: 14" x 15" to 24' x 12'
Price Range: $1,000 - $20,000

LLAMA STUDIOS
Leora Klaymer Stewart
203 Park Pl., 2F
Brooklyn, NY 11238
(718) 783-0379
Established: 1970
Products: fiber installations
Techniques: weaving
Marketing Materials: photos,
slides, resume
Size Range: 6" x 8" to 10' x 20'
Price Range: $500 - $20,000

CHRISTINE LOFASO
120 Moore St.
Providence, RI 02907-1505
(401) 273-9183
Established: 1978
Products: fiber installations
Techniques: laminating, painting,
beading
Marketing Materials: photos,
slides, resume
Size Range: 24" x 36" to 48" x 84"
Price Range: $2,000 - $6,000

SARA LONG
30060 Sherwood Rd.
Fort Bragg, NC 28307
(707) 964-5964

Established: 1969
Products: art quilts
Techniques: quilting,
stamping/printing
Marketing Materials: resume
Size Range: 22" x 15" to 8' x 8'
Price Range: $175 - $5,000

ANJA LONGENECKER
Anja's Art
2 Batesview Dr.
Greenville, SC 29607
(803) 370-9472
Established: 1990
Products: tapestries
Techniques: painting, dyeing,
airbrush
Marketing Materials: photos,
slides, resume
Size Range: 6' x 4' to 7' x 8'
Price Range: $1,500 - $2,500

JOYCE P. LOPEZ
1147 W. Ohio #304
Chicago, IL 60622
(312) 243-5033
FAX (312) 243-5033
Established: 1970
Products: fiber installations
Marketing Materials: brochure,
photos, resume, slides
Size Range: 30" x 30" to 20' x 30'

Joyce Lopez is an internationally
known sculptor who has successfully operated her studio for more
than 18 years. Known for her
innovative design solutions to
site-specific requirements, she
strictly adheres to the client's
budget and deadline. Commissioned work for easily maintained, mid-sized sculptures usually takes two to four months. See
pages 46 and 47 for photographs
and additional information.

PEGGY CLARK LUMPKINS
RR1 Box 4650
Brownville, ME 04414
(207) 965-8526
Established: 1979
Products: tapestries
Techniques: weaving
Marketing Materials: photos,
slides, resume, brochure
Size Range: 2' x 1' to 8' x 20'
Price Range: $350 - $28,000

LURIE-LAROCHETTE TAPESTRIES
Yael Lurie
Jean Pierre Larochette
2216 Grant St.
Berkeley, CA 94703
(510) 548-5744
Established: 1966
Products: tapestries
Techniques: weaving
Marketing Materials: photos,
slides, resume, brochure
Size Range: 12" x 8" to 8' x 16'
Price Range: $600 - $35,000

NANCY LYON
102 Shaker Steet
New London, NH 03257
(603) 526-6754
Established: 1971
Products: tapestries
Techniques: weaving

Marketing Materials: slides,
resume, brochure
Size Range: 25" x 25" to 10' x 50'
Price Range: $60 sq. ft.

MHS DESIGNS
Margaret Story
27 Paddock Ln.
Hampton, VA 23669
(804) 851-7930
Established: 1986
Products: fiber installations
Techniques: weaving
Marketing Materials: slides, resume
Size Range: 32" x 16" to 72" x 34"
Price Range: $90 - $320

ANN MACEACHERN
Box 80, Old Rt. 109
Acton, ME 04001
(207) 636-2539
Established: 1970
Products: mixed media wall
installations
Techniques: weaving, embroidery
Marketing Materials: slides
Size Range: 8" x 12" to 2' x 6'
Price Range: $20 - $200

MARGO MACDONALD
5814 Crescent Beach Rd.
Vaughn, WA 98394
(206) 884-2955
Established: 1980
Products: tapestries
Techniques: weaving
Marketing Materials: photos,
slides, resume
Size Range: 30" x 18" to 4'6" x 4'6"
Price Range: $500 - $2,000

IRENE MAGINNISS
770 Andover Rd.
Mansfield, OH 44907
(419) 756-2841
Established: 1970
Products: paper wall work
Techniques: laminating
Marketing Materials: photos,
slides, resume
Size Range: 6" x 6" to 50" x 50"
Price Range: $30 - $1,500

JAN MAHER
817 Greenwood Dr.
Greensboro, NC 27410
(919) 855-5746
Established: 1982
Products: art quilts
Techniques: quilting, beading,
dyeing
Marketing Materials: photos,
slides, resume
Size Range: 38" x 38" to 120" x 192"
Price Range: $1,250 - $20,000

JULIANNA S. MAHLEY
404 Council Dr. NE
Vienna, VA 22180
(703) 281-9106
Established: 1989
Products: fiber installations
Techniques: embroidery, paint-
ing, airbrush
Marketing Materials: slides,
resume
Size Range: 5" x 5" to 10" x 10"
Price Range: $400 - $1,000

PATRICIA MALARCHER
93 Ivy Ln.
Englewood, NJ 07631
(201) 568-1084
Established: 1965
Products: art quilts
Techniques: applique, painting,
embroidery
Marketing Materials: photos,
slides, resume, brochure
Size Range: 9" x 5" to 120" x 84"
Price Range: $125 sq. ft.-$200 sq. ft.

LEE A. MALERICH
1316 Dogwood Dr.
Orangeburg, SC 29115
(803) 534-0457
FAX (803) 534-0457
Established: 1980
Products: mixed media wall
installations
Techniques: embroidery, quilting,
applique
Marketing Materials: photos,
slides, resume
Size Range: 25" x 25" to 40" x 40"
Price Range: $1,500 - $2,500

BARBARA MANGER
3240 N. Summit
Milwaukee, WI 53211
(414) 964-6756
Established: 1975
Products: paper wall work
Techniques: stamping/printing,
silkscreen, quilting
Marketing Materials: photos,
slides, resume, brochure
Size Range: 36" x 36" to 80" x 80"
Price Range: $600 - $3,000

RUTH MANNING
177 Rogers Parkway
Rochester, NY 14617
(716) 467-6250
Established: 1980
Products: tapestries
Techniques: weaving, dyeing
Marketing Materials: photos,
slides, resume
Size Range: 1' x 1' to 4' x 6'
Price Range: $200 - $5,000

SHARON MARCUS
4145 S.W. Corbett
Portland, OR 97201
(503) 796-1234
FAX (503) 796-1234
Established: 1975
Products: tapestries
Techniques: weaving
Marketing Materials: slides,
resume, photos
Size Range: 3' x 3' to 7' x 13'
Price Range: $250 sq. ft.-$400 sq. ft.

Sharon Marcus—an internationally recognized artist whose work
has appeared in publications
around the world—creates
woven tapestries that combine
classical technique with expressive, innovative style. Premium
quality wool, linen and cotton
are utilized to create designs that
are dramatic and "readable" at
a distance, yet increasingly
complex in detail when viewed
more closely. See page 28 for
photographs and additional
information.

FIBER ART

JANE GOLDING-DADEY MARIE
515 M St.
Aurora, NE 68818-1946
(402) 694-2871
Established: 1975
Products: mixed media wall installations
Techniques: painting, laminating
Marketing Materials: slides, resume
Size Range: 6" x 6" to 10" x 10"
Price Range: $50 - $10,000

MARCEL MAROIS
193 Lockwell
Quebec City, P. Quebec
Canada, G1R 1V6
(418) 525-6780
Established: 1973
Products: tapestries
Techniques: weaving
Marketing Materials: photos, slides, resume, brochure
Size Range: 8" x 8" to 126" x 240"
Price Range: $15,000 - $85,000

DONNA MARTIN
Box 82 H Callenopal
Santa Fe, NM 87501
(505) 982-4748
Established: 1980
Products: tapestries
Techniques: dyeing, weaving
Marketing Materials: photos, slides, resume
Size Range: 3' x 5' to 5' x 7'
Price Range: $2,000 - $7,000

PAMELA MATIOSIAN
2607 Park Pl.
Evanston, IL 60201
(708) 475-5132
Established: 1980
Products: mixed media wall installations
Techniques: dyeing, quilting, painting
Marketing Materials: photos, slides, resume, brochure
Size Range: 30" x 40" to 12' x 40'
Price Range: $3,000 - $53,000

MARTHA MATTHEWS
Martha Matthews—Tapestry
7200 Terrace Dr.
Charlotte, NC 28211
(704) 364-3435
Established: 1973
Products: tapestries
Techniques: weaving
Marketing Materials: slides, resume
Size Range: 24" x 36" to 8' x 20'
Price Range: $1200 - $32,000

THERESE MAY
651 N. 4th St.
San Jose, CA 95112
(408) 292-3247
Established: 1965
Products: art quilts
Techniques: applique, painting, embroidery
Marketing Materials: photos, slides, resume
Size Range: 1' x 1' to 14' x 14'
Price Range: $500 - $41,000

See photograph on this page.

LYNN MAYNE
58 E. Corral Dr.
Saginaw, MI 48603
(517) 799-6249
FAX (517) 793-9771
Established: 1983
Products: tapestries
Techniques: weaving
Marketing Materials: slides, resume, video
Size Range: 12" x 10" to 3' x 4'
Price Range: $250 - $1,200

PHOEBE MCAFEE
97 Winfield Ave.
San Francisco, CA 94110
(415) 282-3448
Established: 1967
Products: tapestries

Techniques: weaving, applique, embroidery
Marketing Materials: photos, slides, resume, brochure
Size Range: 1' x 2' to 8' x 24'
Price Range: $200 - $50,000

DIANNE MCKENZIE
Comet Studios
PO Box 337
The Sea Ranch, CA 95497
(707) 785-2567
Established: 1975
Products: tapestries
Techniques: weaving, dyeing, painting
Marketing Materials: slides, resume
Size Range: 6' x 8' to 12' x 20'
Price Range: $250 sq. ft.-$500 sq. ft.

IRENE M. MCNAMARA-BOS
11744 Moorpark Unit F
Studio City, CA 91604
(818) 985-2448
Established: 1982
Products: art quilts
Techniques: quilting, painting
Marketing Materials: photos, slides, resume, brochure
Size Range: 60" x 60" to 5' x 7'
Price Range: $85 sq. ft. - $125 sq. ft.

Theresa May, *Playful Contemplations*, 1992, embellished quilt, 56" x 86"

ELIAZBETH MEARS
10160 Hampton Rd.
Fairfax Station, VA 22039
(703) 690-2545
Established: 1978
Products: fiber installations
Techniques: applique, quilting,
laminating
Marketing Materials: photos,
slides, resume
Size Range: 4' x 6' to 17' x 24'
Price Range: $500 - $20,000

GERALDINE MILLHAM
Geraldine Millham Tapestries
672 Drift Rd.
Westport, MA 02790
(508) 636-5437
Established: 1970
Products: tapestries
Techniques: weaving
Marketing Materials: photos,
slides, resume, brochure
Size Range: 2' x 2' to 15' x 3'6"
Price Range: $100 sq. ft.-$150 sq. ft.

MYRON MELNICK
Myron Melnick Studio
1366 Garfield St. #601
Denver, CO 80206
(303) 458-6486
Established: 1979
Products: paper wall work
Techniques: casting, painting,
stamping/printing
Marketing Materials: photos,
slides, resume, brochure
Size Range: 30" x 22" to 8' x 15'
Price Range: $350 - $25,000

BETH MINEAR
1115 E. Capitol St., S.E.
Washington, DC 20003
(202) 544-1714
Established: 1978
Products: fiber installations
Techniques: weaving
Marketing Materials: slides, resume
Size Range: 50" x 30" to 96" x 60"
Price Range: $500 - $2,200

NORMA MINKOWITZ
25 Broadview Rd.
Westport, CT 06880
(203) 227-4497
Established: 1960
Products: fiber installations
Techniques: painting
Marketing Materials: photos,
slides, resume
Size Range: 12" x 23" to 50" x 63"
Price Range: $1,200 - $8,000

JULIA MITCHELL
Julia Mitchell Tapestry Designer
and Weaver
PO Box 1512
Vineyard Haven, MA 02568
(508) 693-6837
Established: 1978
Products: tapestries
Techniques: weaving
Marketing Materials: photos,
slides, resume
Size Range: 16" x 16" to 8' x 14'
Price Range: $850 sq. ft.

PATTI MITCHEM
28 Witchtrot Rd.
South Berwick, ME 03908
(207) 384-2195
FAX (207) 384-1938
Established: 1976
Products: fiber installations
Marketing Materials: photos,
slides, resume
Price Range: $90 sq. ft. - $160 sq. ft.

KATHLEEN MOLLOHAN
524 South Roberts
Helena, MT 59601
(406) 442-9028
Established: 1983
Products: tapestries
Techniques: weaving, beading,
painting
Marketing Materials: slides, resume
Size Range: 5' x 4' to 8' x 6'
Price Range: $2,500 - $5,000

DOTTIE MOORE
1134 Charlotte Ave.
Rockhill, SC 29732
(803) 327-5088
Established: 1976
Products: art quilts
Techniques: appliqué, quilting,
embroidery
Marketing Materials: brochure,
photos, resume, slides, video

Dottie Moore's art quilts are conversations with the earth and sky,
visually conveying quiet moments in nature. Each piece is
one-of-a-kind, appliquéed, quilted and embellished with hand
embroidery. Carefully selected
cloth is sometimes hand-dyed or
hand-painted, and then stitched
intricately to produce a striking
sculptural dimension. See page
49 for photographs and additional
information.

JENNIFER MOORE
520 S. 19th St.
Philomath, OR 97370
(503) 929-4329
FAX (503) 929-5244
Established: 1984
Products: tapestries
Techniques: weaving, dyeing,
embroidery
Marketing Materials: photos,
slides, resume
Size Range: 12" x 12" to 8' x 8'
Price Range: $250 - $16,000

LORETTA MOSSMAN
2416 Aspen St.
Philadelphia, PA 19130
(215) 765-3248
(215) 483-4864
Established: 1978
Products: tapestries
Techniques: appliqué, embroidery
Marketing Materials: brochure,
photos, resume, slides
Size Range: 4' x 3' to 8' x 9'
Price Range: $1,500 - $6,000

Loretta Mossman develops
tapestries for individual spaces
and design concepts. A colorist,
she creates moods with her rich
palette. Using traditional techniques, pure wools are colored
with luxurious natural pigments

and woven to form single panels
or multi-dimensional constructions. Designs and textures are
created and enhanced with
eclectic accents such as
appliquéed fabrics, buttons and
found objects. See page 29 for
photographs and additional
information.

JAN MYERS-NEWBURY
7422 Ben Hur St.
Pittsburgh, PA 15208
(412) 731-9569
Established: 1980
Products: art quilts
Techniques: dyeing, quilting
Marketing Materials: slides, resume
Size Range: 24" x 24" to 90" x 80"
Price Range: $600 - $7,500

DOMINIE NASH
8612 Rayburn Rd.
Bethesda, MD 20817
(202) 722-1407
Established: 1972
Products: art quilts
Techniques: quilting, dyeing,
silkscreen
Marketing Materials: photos,
slides, resume
Size Range: 20" x 16" to 84" x 72"
Price Range: $300 - $5,000

MIRIAM NATHAN-ROBERTS
1351 Acton St.
Berkeley, CA 94706
(510) 525-5432
Established: 1982
Products: art quilts
Techniques: quilting, painting,
applique
Marketing Materials: slides, resume
Size Range: 20" x 20" to 96" x 96"
Price Range: $500 - $10,000

JEAN NEBLETT
628 Rhode Island St.
San Francisco, CA 94107-2628
(415) 550-2613
FAX (415) 821-2772
Established: 1977
Products: art quilts
Techniques: applique, painting,
quilting
Marketing Materials: slides,
resume
Size Range: 4" x 5" to 75" x 58"
Price Range: $300 - $11,600

ROCHELLE NEWMAN
Pythagorean Press
PO Box 5162
Bradford, MA 01835-0162
(508) 372-3129
Established: 1962
Products: tapestries
Techniques: weaving, painting
Marketing Materials: photos,
slides, resume
Size Range: 1' x 1' to 8' x 8'
Price Range: $100 sq. ft.-$500 sq. ft.

ANNE MCKENZIE
NICKOLSON
5020 N. Illinois St.
Indianapolis, IN 46208
(317) 257-8929
Established: 1978

Products: art quilts
Techniques: embroidery, airbrush
Marketing Materials: photos,
slides, resume, brochure
Size Range: 15" x 15" to 12' x 18'
Price Range: $450 - $26,000

ELIZABETH NORDGREN
6 Ryan Way
Durham, NH 03824
(603) 868-2873
Established: 1954
Products: fiber installations
Techniques: painting, weaving
Marketing Materials: slides
Size Range: 5" x 3" to 6" x 55"
Price Range: $80 sq. ft. - $90 sq. ft.

INGE NØRGAARD
907 Pierce St.
Port Townsend, WA 98368-8046
(206) 385-0637
Established: 1972
Products: tapestries
Techniques: weaving
Marketing Materials: photos,
slides, resume
Size Range: 3" x 3" to 10' x 15'
Price Range: $100 - $20,000

SHEILA O'HARA
7101 Thorndale Dr.
Oakland, CA 94611
(510) 339-3014
Established: 1977
Products: tapestries
Techniques: weaving
Marketing Materials: slides, resume
Size Range: 12" x 20" to 20' x 20'
Price Range: $250 sq. ft. -
$1,000 sq. ft.

IRA ONO
Ira Ono Designs
PO Box 112
Volcano, HI 96785
(808) 967-7261
Established: 1968
Products: mixed media wall
installations
Techniques: casting, painting
Marketing Materials: photos,
slides, resume, brochure
Size Range: 8" x 10" to 4' x 6'
Price Range: $225 - $3,000

ELLEN OPPENHEIMER
448 Clifton St.
Oakland, CA 94618
(510) 658-9877
Established: 1982
Products: art quilts
Techniques: applique, dyeing,
quilting
Marketing Materials: photos,
slides, resume
Size Range: 36" x 36" to 84" x 84"
Price Range: $1,350 - $7,000

CAROL OWEN
54 Fearrington Post
Pittsboro, NC 27312
(919) 542-0616
Established: 1972
Products: paper wall work
Techniques: painting
Marketing Materials: photos,
slides, resume, brochure
Size Range: 22" x 22" to 3' x 5'
Price Range: $400 - $2,000

FIBER ART

SOYOO HYUNJOO PARK
Soyoo Art Studio
193 Closter Dock Rd.
Closter, NJ 07624
(201) 767-8766
FAX (201) 767-0497
Established: 1978
Products: tapestries
Techniques: weaving, painting, embroidery
Marketing Materials: photos, slides, resume
Size Range: 7" x 7" to 10' x 10'
Price Range: $250 - $50,000

ESTER PARKHURST
6677 Drexel Ave.
Los Angeles, CA 90048
(213) 651-1318
Established: 1979
Products: art quilts
Techniques: quilting
Marketing Materials: slides, resume
Size Range: 2' x 2' to 6' x 13'
Price Range: $400 - $12,000

JACQUE PARSLEY
2005 Indian Chute
Louiseville, KY 40207
(502) 893-2092
Established: 1976
Products: mixed media wall installations
Techniques: applique, embroidery, laminating
Marketing Materials: photos, slides, resume, brochure
Price Range: $500 - $3,000

PAM PATRIE
Patrie Studios
314 S.W. 9th #5
Portland, OR 97205
(503) 284-2963

Established: 1974
Products: tapestries
Techniques: weaving, painting, stamping/printing
Marketing Materials: photos, slides, resume, video
Size Range: 2' x 3' to 10' x 24'
Price Range: $400 - $25,000

EVE S. PEARCE
RR1
Box 3880, Carpenter Hill Rd.
Bennington, VT 05201
(802) 823-5580
Established: 1980
Products: tapestries
Techniques: weaving
Marketing Materials: photos, slides, resume
Size Range: 3' x 2' to 4' x 8'
Price Range: $900 - $4,000

PENELOPE'S WEB
Linda Pardue Winse
7915 W. Bridle Trial
Flagstaff, AZ 86001
(602) 779-3776
Established: 1981
Products: tapestries
Techniques: weaving, beading
Marketing Materials: photos, slides, resume, brochure
Size Range: 12" x 12" to 15' x 5'
Price Range: $350 - $15,000

KAREN PERRINE
512 N. K St.
Tacoma, WA 98403
(206) 627-0449
Established: 1977
Products: fiber installations
Techniques: dyeing, quilting, stamping/printing
Marketing Materials: brochure, photos, resume, slides

Size Range: 8" x 12" to 8' x 16'
Price Range: $150 sq. ft.

Nature inspires Karen Perrine's distinctive fiber designs. A surface designer for 20 years who exhibits nationally and internationally, Perrine dyes and paints cotton, linen, rayon and silk fabrics with layers of color, creating unique yardage to cut and assemble into evocative landscapes. Finished work is presented as framed collage or quilted textile. See page 50 for photographs and additional information.

LINDA S. PERRY
Art Quilts
96 Burlington St.
Lexington, MA 02173
(617) 863-1107
Established: 1972
Products: art quilts
Techniques: dyeing, applique
Marketing Materials: slides, resume, brochure
Size Range: 3' x 2' to 8' x 5'
Price Range: $750 - $5,000

PAMELA VEA PERRY
7 Hill Top Rd.
Weston, MA 02193
(617) 894-4508
Established: 1970
Products: tapestries
Techniques: weaving, embroidery, dyeing
Marketing Materials: photos, slides, resume
Size Range: 6" x 6" to 16' x 10'
Price Range: $400 - $10,000

PHILADELPHIA FIBER STUDIO
Christine Roll
114 N. Wayne Ave.
Wayne, PA 19087
(215) 254-8476
Established: 1983
Products: tapestries
Techniques: weaving
Marketing Materials: photos, slides, resume, brochure
Size Range: 2' x 2' to 6' x 8'
Price Range: $250 sq. ft.-$300 sq. ft.

SUE PIERCE
Pierceworks
14414 Wodcrest Dr.
Rockville, MD 20853
(301) 460-8111
Established: 1978
Products: art quilts
Techniques: quilting, applique, painting
Marketing Materials: photos, slides, resume
Size Range: 12" x 12" to 6' x 12'
Price Range: $125 - $9,000

BEVERLY PLUMMER
2720 White Oak, Left
Burnsville, NC 28714
(704) 675-5208
Established: 1978
Products: paper wall work
Techniques: casting, laminating
Marketing Materials: photos, slides, resume
Size Range: 24" x 24" to 5' x 40'
Price Range: $300 - $3,000

See photograph on this page.

JUNCO SATO POLLACK
11 Polo Dr. NE
Atlanta, GA 30309
(404) 892-2155
FAX (404) 892-2155
Established: 1980
Products: fiber installations
Techniques: weaving, dyeing
Marketing Materials: photos, slides, resume, brochure
Size Range: 30" x 30" to 5' x 25'
Price Range: $2,000 - $30,000

JASON POLLEN
4348 Locust St.
Kansas City, MO 64110
(816) 561-4882
Established: 1970
Products: fiber installations
Techniques: airbrush, applique, dyeing
Marketing Materials: photos, slides, resume
Size Range: 20" x 15" to 5' x 7'
Price Range: $1,500 - $7,000

DEE FORD POTTER
45 NW Greeley Ave.
Bend, OR 97701
(503) 382-4797
Established: 1969
Products: fiber installations
Techniques: weaving, painting
Marketing Materials: photos, slides, resume
Size Range: 1' x 1' to 6' x 20'
Price Range: $300 - $12,000

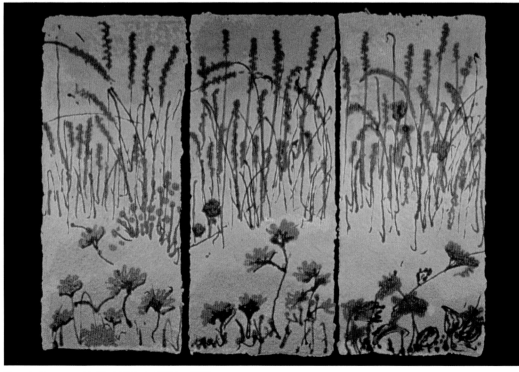

Beverly Plummer, Untitled triptych, 31"H x 41"W

SUZANNE PRETTY

Suzanne Pretty Tapestry Studio
4 Elm St.
Farmington, NH 03835
(603) 755-3964
Established: 1969
Products: tapestries
Techniques: weaving, dyeing, painting
Marketing Materials: photos, slides, resume, brochure
Size Range: 35" x 45" to 4' x 6'
Price Range: $4,000 - $8,000

NANCY PRICHARD

2604 Chubb Lake Ave.
Virginia Beach, VA 23455
(804) 363-9272
Established: 1974
Products: paper wall work
Techniques: dyeing, stamping/printing
Marketing Materials: slides, resume
Size Range: 18" x 16" to 36" x 36"
Price Range: $295 - $475

QUINT-ROSE STUDIO

Quint-Rose
Box 54
Tenants Harbor, ME 04860
(207) 372-8128
Established: 1956
Products: mixed media wall installations
Techniques: painting
Marketing Materials: photos, slides, resume
Size Range: 18" x 24" to 9' x 3'
Price Range: $450 - $10,000

JANE REEVES

3100 Logan Ave. N.W.
Canton, OH 44709
(216) 492-3833
Established: 1982
Products: art quilts
Techniques: quilting, dyeing, applique
Marketing Materials: slides, resume
Size Range: 3' x 3' to 8' x 10'
Price Range: $900 - $10,000

MYRA REICHEL

121 East Sixth St.
Media, PA 19063
(215) 565-5028
Established: 1973
Products: tapestries
Techniques: weaving
Marketing Materials: photos, slides, resume, brochure
Size Range: 6" x 6" to 9' x 12'
Price Range: $500 - $30,000

SISTER REMY REVOR

Mount Mary College
2900 Menomonee River Park
Milwaukee, WI 53222
(414) 258-4810
Products: tapestries
Techniques: silkscreen
Marketing Materials: slides, resume
Size Range: 32" x 24" to 4' x 40"
Price Range: $200 - $400

SAGE REYNOLDS

Fourhands Design Studio
129 Tysen St.
Staten Island, NY 10301
(718) 816-0682

Established: 1971
Products: tapestries
Techniques: weaving
Marketing Materials: slides
Size Range: 14" x 14" to 60" x 60"
Price Range: $600 - $5,000

AMANDA RICHARDSON

Richardson Kirby
PO Box 2147
Friday Harbor, WA 98250
(206) 378-3224
Established: 1978
Products: fiber installations
Marketing Materials: brochure, photos, resume, slides
Size Range: 45" x 60" to 15'6" x 10'
Price Range: $500 sq. ft.

The rich, light-reflective tapestries of Amanda Richardson respond to their environments, the image varying with the angle and intensity of light. Fabrics are hand-dyed, cut into intricate forms, and bonded together, layer on layer, to build up a rich and complex final image, giving the impression of great spatial depth. See pages 52 and 53 for photographs and additional information.

EVA R. ROBBINS

Eva R Works & Yarn, Inc.
109 Towne Rd.
Oak Ridge, TN 37830
(615) 483-7492
Established: 1973
Products: fiber installations
Techniques: embroidery
Marketing Materials: slides, resume
Size Range: 40" x 14" to 60" x 40"
Price Range: $250 - $1,000

See photograph on this page.

MARTHA VICK ROBBINS

674 West Dr.
Memphis, TN 38112
(901) 327-7456
Established: 1989
Products: fiber installations
Techniques: stamping/printing, silkscreen, dyeing
Marketing Materials: photos, slides, resume
Size Range: 9' x 12' to 9' x 60'
Price Range: $50 yd. - $100 yd.

GRETCHEN ROMEY-TANZER

Tanzer's Fiberworks
33 Monument Rd.
Orleans, MA 02653
(508) 255-9022
Established: 1986
Products: tapestries
Techniques: weaving, silkscreen, painting
Marketing Materials: photos, slides, resume, brochure
Size Range: 19" x 19" to 46" x 36"
Price Range: $300 - $900

Eva R. Robbins, *Harvest Colors*, 15" x 39"

FIBER ART

GLORIA F. ROSS
Gloria F. Ross tapestries
21 East 87th St.
New York, NY 10128
(212) 369-3337
Established: 1965
Products: tapestries
Techniques: weaving
Marketing Materials: photos, slides, resume, brochure
Size Range: 9' x 3' to 12' x 45'
Price Range: $3,000 - $200,000

BERNIE ROWELL
1525 Branson Ave.
Knoxville, TN 37917
(615) 523-5244
Established: 1975
Products: fiber installations
Techniques: applique, embroidery, painting
Marketing Materials: photos, slides, resume, brochure
Size Range: 24" x 30" to 72" x 108"
Price Range: $450 - $5,000

KRISTIN CARLSEN ROWLEY
817 N. Gilbert St.
Iowa City, IA 52245
(319) 339-1926
Established: 1979
Products: tapestries
Techniques: weaving, dyeing
Marketing Materials: slides, resume
Size Range: 4" x 6" to 4' x 18'
Price Range: $150 - $3,000

DEANN RUBIN
Deann Joy
990-A La Mesa Terrace
Sunnyvale, CA 94086
(408) 739-9609
Established: 1968
Products: tapestries
Techniques: weaving, painting
Marketing Materials: slides, resume, brochure, photos
Size Range: 2" x 8" to 48" x 96"
Price Range: $50 - $350 sq. ft.

Incorporating the finest yarns available, Deann Rubin weaves her powerful graphic designs into contemporary gobelin-style tapestries. Her work ranges from pieces based on photorealism to more graphic abstractions. Many of her works reflect urban themes that use human imagery. Her tapestries require little care and are made to last. See page 30 for photographs and additional information.

KAREN JENSON RUTHERFORD
Karen Jenson Rutherford Studio
513 South 21 St.
Terre Haute, IN 47803
(812) 234-2928
Established: 1976
Products: fiber installations
Techniques: weaving, dyeing
Marketing Materials: photos, slides, resume
Size Range: 5" x 10" to 5' x 10'
Price Range: $250 - $4,000

TERESA GRAHAM SALT
1603 East Fourth St.
Greenville, NC 27858
(919) 830-0898
Established: 1980
Products: tapestries
Techniques: weaving, beading
Marketing Materials: photos, slides, resume
Size Range: 6" x 6" to 16" x 16"
Price Range: $600 - $1,000

FRANCIS SANDERS
17 Hanging Moss Rd.
Savannah, GA 31410
(912) 897-6579
Established: 1980
Products: fiber installations
Techniques: weaving
Marketing Materials: photos, slides, resume
Size Range: 1' x 2" to 8' x 40"
Price Range: $60 sq. ft.

ARTURO ALONZO SANDOVAL
PO Box 237
Lexington, KY 40584-0237
(606) 273-8898
Products: art quilts
Techniques: applique, dyeing, embroidery
Marketing Materials: photos, slides, resume, brochure
Size Range: 32" x 40" to 7' x 22'
Price Range: $3,400 - $25,000

STEPHANIE SANTMYERS
ArtQuilts
7 Pipers Glen Court
Greensboro, NC 27406
(919) 852-6439
Established: 1985
Products: art quilts
Techniques: quilting
Marketing Materials: photos, slides, resume
Size Range: 4'2" x 4'2" to 72" x 72"
Price Range: $1,500 - $2,200

JOY SAVILLE
244 Dodds Ln.
Princeton, NJ 08540
(609) 924-6824
Established: 1976
Products: fiber installations
Marketing Materials: photos, slides, resume, brochure
Size Range: 2' x 2' to 10' x 25'
Price Range: $1,000 - $62,500

SUSAN SAWYER
RD 1 Box 107
East Calais, VT 05650
(802) 456-8836
Established: 1971
Products: art quilts
Techniques: quilting, applique
Marketing Materials: slides, resume, brochure
Size Range: 8" x 8" to 84" x 84"
Price Range: $100 - $7,000

DEIDRE SCHERER
PO Box 156
Williamsville, VT 05362
(802) 348-7807
Established: 1973
Products: fiber installations

Marketing Materials: slides, resume
Size Range: 18" x 15" to 62" x 72"
Price Range: $500 - $8,000

JULIA SCHLOSS
Eagle Lake Rd. RR1 Box 5053
Bar Harbor, ME 04609
(207) 288-9882
Established: 1976
Products: tapestries
Techniques: weaving
Marketing Materials: photos, slides, resume
Size Range: 24" x 24" to 150" x 56"
Price Range: $500 - $10,000

JOAN SCHULZE
808 Piper Ave.
Sunneyvale, CA 94087
(408) 736-7833
Established: 1970
Products: art quilts
Techniques: painting, quilting
Marketing Materials: brochure, photos, resume, slides
Size Range: 20" x 16" to 9' x 9'
Price Range: $400 - $12,000

Jazz-like improvisation, exploring the unexpected possibilities of invention, pushing traditional aspects of the quilt into new territory, all describe Joan Schulze's approach to the art quilt. Her work—including two-sided quilts—is the continuous dialogue between subject and materials leading to her unique, complex and rich expression. See page 51 for photographs and additional information.

JUDY SCHUSTER
Judy Schuster Tapestries
212 18th St.
Manhattan Beach, CA 90266
(310) 545-3995
FAX (310) 545-3995
Established: 1974
Products: tapestries
Techniques: weaving, dyeing, painting
Marketing Materials: photos, slides, resume, brochure
Size Range: 18" x 26" to 55" x 75"
Price Range: $2,000 - $10,000

WARREN SEELIG
7723 Union Ave.
Elkins Park, PA 19117
(215) 635-0398
FAX (215) 635-0398
Established: 1974
Products: fiber installations
Marketing Materials: photos, slides, resume, brochure
Price Range: $2,500 - $45,000

H. JEANETTE SHANKS
Box 25, Jackson's Point
Ontario, Canada
LOE 1L0
(416) 722-8584
FAX (416) 722-3351
Established: 1983
Products: art quilts
Techniques: applique, beading, dyeing
Marketing Materials: photos, slides, resume
Size Range: 36" x 36" to 65" x 52"
Price Range: $600 - $1,200

IRA SHAREFF
Shareff Designs
81 Irving Pl.
New York, NY 10003
(212) 475-3963
Established: 1968
Products: fiber installations
Techniques: weaving, dyeing, beading
Marketing Materials: photos, slides, resume, brochure
Size Range: 24" x 12" to 108" x 96"
Price Range: $500 - $12,000

KATHLEEN SHARP
17360 Valley Oak Dr.
Monte Sereno, CA 95030
(408) 395-3014
Established: 1978
Products: art quilts
Techniques: applique, painting
Marketing Materials: photos, slides, resume, brochure
Size Range: 30" x 30" to 90" x 90"
Price Range: $1,500 - $10,000

BARBARA SHAWCROFT
4 Anchor Dr. #243
Emeryville, CA 94608
(510) 698-6694
Established: 1967
Products: fiber installations
Marketing Materials: photos, slides, resume, brochure
Size Range: 3" x 3" to 50' x 25'
Price Range: $2,500 - $250,000

SUSAN SHIE
JAMES ACORD
Turtle Moon Studios
2612 Armstrong Dr.
Wooster, OH 44691
(216) 345-5778
Established: 1977
Products: art quilts
Techniques: painting, embroidery, beading
Marketing Materials: photos, slides, resume
Size Range: 1' x 1' to 7' x 7'
Price Range: $2,000 - $30,000

REBECCA SHORE
2038 N. Oakley
Chicago, IL 60647
(312) 227-3478
Established: 1981
Products: art quilts
Techniques: quilting, applique
Marketing Materials: slides, resume
Size Range: 6" x 8" to 100" x 100"
Price Range: $200 - $4,000

SALLY SHORE
Sally Shore/Weaver
Ludlam Ln.
Locust Valley, NY 11560
(516) 671-7276
Established: 1970
Products: fiber installations
Techniques: weaving
Marketing Materials: photos, slides, resume
Size Range: 3" x 5" to 5' x 17'
Price Range: $125 - $6,500

Fiber Art

ANE SHUSTA
PO Box 18
Snoqualmie Pass, WA 98068
(206) 434-6115
Established: 1983
Products: tapestries
Techniques: weaving
Marketing Materials: photos,
slides, resume
Size Range: 3' x 5' to 5' x 7'
Price Range: $1,000 - $2,000

ELIZABETH SIBLEY
9 Union St.
Nantucket, MA 02554
(508) 228-6262
FAX (508) 325-5991
Established: 1972
Products: mixed media wall
installations
Techniques: painting, dyeing,
embroidery
Marketing Materials: photos,
slides, resume
Size Range: 2" x 2" to 2.5' x 2.5'

LAURA LAZAR SIEGEL
10 Crossway
Scarsdale, NY 10583
(914) 723-9392
FAX (212) 808-0406
Established: 1965
Products: fiber installations
Techniques: painting, dyeing
Marketing Materials: photos,
slides, resume
Size Range: 18" x 24" to 5' x 7'
Price Range: $350 - $2,500

See photograph on this page.

LOUISE SILK
City Quilt
210 Conover Rd.
Pittsburg, PA 15208
(412) 361-1158
Established: 1978
Products: art quilts
Techniques: quilting
Marketing Materials: photos,
slides, resume, brochure
Size Range: 8" x 8" to 9' x 18'
Price Range: $50 - $5,500

ELLY SIMMONS
Box 463, 36 Spring
Lagunitas, CA 94938
(415) 488-4177
FAX (415) 488-4652
Established: 1980
Products: tapestries
Techniques: weaving, painting
Marketing Materials: photos,
slides, resume
Size Range: 14" x 21" to 5' x 7'
Price Range: $800 - $5,500

MARY JO SINCLAIR
10 Milton St.
St. Augustine, FL 32084
(904) 824-1441
FAX (904) 824-1441
Established: 1978
Products: paper wall work
Techniques: weaving, laminat-
ing, painting
Marketing Materials: photos,
slides, resume, brochure
Size Range: 3' x 4' to 7' x 16'
Price Range: $3,000 - $27,000

LOUISE SLOBODAN
Textile Context Studio
1420 Old Bridge Rd.,
Granville Island
Vancouver, B.C. Canada
V6H 3S6
(604) 684-6661
Established: 1979
Products: art quilts
Techniques: silkscreen, quilting
Marketing Materials: photos,
slides, resume, brochure
Size Range: 2' x 2' to 3'6" x 13"
Price Range: $200 - $2,000

SHIGEKO SPEAR
University of North Texas
2042 Scripture
Denton, TX 76201
(817) 565-4125
FAX (817) 565-4717
Established: 1977
Products: fiber installations
Techniques: silkscreen, dyeing
Marketing Materials: slides, resume
Size Range: 30" x 37" to 53" x 106"
Price Range: $1,000 - $3,000

KATHY SPOERING
Kathy Spoering, Tapestries
2306 Dogwood Court
Grand Junction, CO 81506
(303) 242-9081
Established: 1989
Products: tapestries
Techniques: weaving, painting,
beading
Marketing Materials: photos,
slides, resume
Size Range: 18" x 18" to 42" x 42"
Price Range: $600 - $1,600

JEAN STAMSTA
9313 Center Oak Rd.
Hartland, WI 53029
(414) 966-2923
Established: 1959
Products: paper wall work
Techniques: painting, casting
Marketing Materials: slides, resume
Size Range: 15" x 20" to 8' x 16'
Price Range: $350 - $20,000

STANDLEY/VANDIANCHI
Peggy Vanbianchi
Emily Standley
7035 Crawford Dr.
Kingston, WA 98346
(206) 297-3068
Established: 1975
Products: fiber installations
Techniques: stamping/printing,
painting, dyeing
Marketing Materials: photos,
slides, resume
Size Range: 12" x 12" to 10' x 10'
Price Range: $250 - $10,000

HILLARY STEEL
Hillary Steel—Handweaver
2216 Hampton Ave.
Pittsburg, PA 15218
(412) 731-4145
Established: 1983
Products: tapestries
Techniques: weaving, dyeing,
stamping/printing
Marketing Materials: photos,
slides, resume
Size Range: 14" x 14" to 8' x 8'
Price Range: $400 - $15,000

ELINOR STEELE
61 Weybridge St.
Middlebury, VT 05753
(802) 388-6546
Established: 1974
Products: tapestries
Techniques: weaving
Marketing Materials: photos,
slides, resume, brochure
Size Range: 2' x 3' to 8' x 12'
Price Range: $1,200 - $19,200

JOY STOCKDALE
2145 Oregon St.
Berkeley, CA 94705
(510) 841-2008
Established: 1981
Products: fiber installations
Techniques: silkscreen, quilting,
painting
Marketing Materials: photos,
slides, resume
Size Range: 3' x 4' to 5' x 10'
Price Range: $250 - $1,000

GLENNE STOLL
Glenne Stoll Quilts
1723 E. 16th Ave.
Denver, CO 80218
(303) 399-2013
Established: 1972
Products: art quilts
Techniques: quilting, beading,
applique
Marketing Materials: slides,
resume, brochure
Size Range: 24" x 24" to 100" x 100"
Price Range: $400 - $8,000

Laura Lazar Siegel, *Generation to Generation*, Parker Jewish Geriatric Center, handpainted multi-layers of silk, enhanced with fabrics and textures to create a three dimensional piece.

FIBER ART

MEREDITH STRAUSS
2621 Kennington Dr.
Glendale, CA 91206
(818) 246-2600
Established: 1978
Products: mixed media wall installations
Techniques: weaving, dyeing
Marketing Materials: photos, slides, resume
Size Range: 2' x 3' to 6' x 16'
Price Range: $180 sq. ft.

JOAN STUBBINS
2616 S. Mahoning Ave.
Alliance, OH 44601
(215) 823-7328
Established: 1988
Products: tapestries
Techniques: weaving, dyeing, embroidery
Marketing Materials: slides, resume
Size Range: 30" x 20" to 55" x 40"
Price Range: $500 - $4,000

The art of Joan Stubbins is intuitive and personal, reflecting the unique structural and textural qualities of the woven textile. The one-of-a-kind pieces are crafted in natural fibers and colorfast, fiber-reactive dyes. Ms. Stubbins exhibits nationally and is represented in private and corporate collections. See page 54 for photographs and additional information.

KUMIKO SUDO
87326 Green Hill Rd.
Eugene, OR 97402
(503) 345-9026
Established: 1970
Products: art quilts
Techniques: applique, embroidery, laminating
Marketing Materials: photos, slides, resume
Size Range: 16" x 16" to 74" x 100"
Price Range: $300 - $12,000

JANICE M. SULLIVAN
Textile Design
4166 A 20th St.
San Francisco, CA 94114
(415) 431-6835
Established: 1984
Products: fiber installations
Techniques: weaving, painting, airbrush
Marketing Materials: photos, slides, resume, brochure
Size Range: 24" x 36" to 96" x 84"
Price Range: $150 sq. ft.

LYNNE SWARD
625 Bishop Dr.
Virginia Beach, VA 23455
(804) 497-7917
Established: 1970
Products: art quilts
Techniques: embroidery, applique, laminating
Marketing Materials: photos, slides, resume
Size Range: 8" x 8" to 60" x 72"
Price Range: $150 - $4,000

CAMERON TAYLOR-BROWN
418 South Mansfield Ave.
Los Angeles, CA 90036
(213) 938-0088
Established: 1982
Products: fiber installations
Techniques: weaving, embroidery, painting
Marketing Materials: photos, slides, resume, brochure
Size Range: 24" x 24" to 8' x 120'
Price Range: $100 sq. ft.-$150 sq. ft.

WENDY TEISBERG
Zephyr Studio
1460 Simpson St.
St. Paul, MN 55108
(612) 644-7028
Established: 1980
Products: tapestries
Techniques: weaving, dyeing
Marketing Materials: slides, resume
Size Range: 30" x 60" to 11'3" x 5'
Price Range: $1,000 - $8,000

GAIL TEMPLE
Gail Temple Tapestries
21402 President Point Rd. NE
Kingston, WA 98346
(206) 297-3218
Established: 1975
Products: tapestries
Techniques: weaving
Marketing Materials: photos, slides, resume
Size Range: 12" x 18" to 5' x 7'
Price Range: $375 - $3,000

NANCY THAYER
Archiforms
18815 Saratoga Blvd.
Lathrup Village, MI 48076
(313) 569-2178
Established: 1972
Products: mixed media wall installations
Techniques: casting, painting
Marketing Materials: photos, slides, resume
Size Range: 2' x 3' to 12' x 14'
Price Range: $1,000 - $6,500

LINDA THEEDE
178 Old Wurtemburg Rd.
Rhinebeck, NY 12572
(914) 876-6130
Established: 1977
Products: tapestries
Techniques: weaving
Marketing Materials: photos, slides, resume
Size Range: 12" x 15" to 4' x 3'
Price Range: $500 - $2,000

JAYN THOMAS
Giant Slide Rd.
Mount Desert, ME 04660
(207) 276-5612
FAX (207) 276-4221
Established: 1978
Products: fiber installations
Techniques: weaving
Marketing Materials: slides, resume
Size Range: 2' x 2' to 30' x 30'
Price Range: $150 sq. ft.-$300 sq. ft.

RENA THOMPSON
705 Almshouse Rd.
Chalfont, PA 18914
(215) 345-8185
Established: 1980
Products: tapestries
Techniques: weaving, dyeing, painting
Marketing Materials: slides, resume
Size Range: 54" x 88" to 8' x 6"
Price Range: $300 - $4,500

LYNN THOR
Contemporary Fiber Designs
PO Box 70
Tunnel, NY 13848
(607) 693-1572
Established: 1976
Products: fiber installations
Techniques: weaving, painting
Marketing Materials: resume, brochure
Size Range: 14" x 14" to 30" x 30"
Price Range: $90 - $500

THORNAPPLE DESIGNS
Lori Kammeraad
2822 Thornapple River Dr. SE
Grand Rapids, MI 49546
(616) 942-7042
Established: 1978
Products: tapestries
Techniques: weaving, dyeing, casting
Marketing Materials: brochure
Size Range: 40" x 10" to 60" x 96"
Price Range: $70 - $2,000

RAYMOND D. TOMASSO
Inter-Ocean Curiosity Studio
2998 South Bannock
Englewood, CO 80110
(303) 789-0282
Established: 1972
Products: paper wall work
Techniques: laminating, painting
Marketing Materials: photos, slides, resume
Size Range: 15" x 21" to 4' x 6'
Price Range: $500 - $2,500

MARJORIE TOMCHUK
44 Horton Ln.
New Canaan, CT 06840
FAX (203) 972-3182
Established: 1962
Products: paper wall work
Techniques: casting, painting, airbrush
Marketing Materials: brochure, photos, resume, slides
Size Range: 20" x 15" to 4' x 16'
Price Range: $350 - $6,000

As a professional for 30 years, Marjorie Tomchuk has art placed in more than 50 major corporations, including IBM, Xerox, Citicorp, AT&T, GE, and also in museums including the Library of Congress. She specializes in paintings and embossings on artist-made paper, the style is semi-abstract. See page 18 for photographs and additional information.

PAMELA TOPHAM
Pamela Topham, Landscape Tapestries
PO Box 1057
Wainscott, NY 11975
(516) 537-2871

Established: 1976
Products: tapestries
Techniques: weaving
Marketing Materials: photos, slides, resume
Size Range: 20" x 23" to 10' x 16'
Price Range: $1,600 - $64,000

MICHELE TUEGEL
Michele Tuegel Paperworks
433 Monte Cristo Blvd.
Tierra Verde, FL 33715
(813) 821-7391
FAX (813) 821-7391
Established: 1978
Products: paper wall work
Marketing Materials: slides, resume
Size Range: 10" x 8" to 40" x 70"
Price Range: $75 - $2,500

CONSUELO JIMENEZ UNDERWOOD
Tu'Tuli Enterprises
21850 Byrne Court
Monta Vista, CA 95014
(408) 993-8607
Established: 1981
Products: mixed media wall installations
Techniques: weaving, dyeing, painting
Marketing Materials: photos, slides, resume
Size Range: 4' x 4' to 11' x 2'
Price Range: $800 - $3,000

CONNIE UTTERBACK
3641 Midvale Ave., #204
Los Angeles, CA 90034
(310) 841-6675
Established: 1981
Products: fiber installations
Marketing Materials: photos, slides, resume
Size Range: 2' x 3' to 5' x 8'
Price Range: $700 - $5,000

LYDIA VAN GELDER
Fiber Arts
758 Sucher Ln.
Santa Rosa, CA 95401
(707) 546-4139
Established: 1950
Products: tapestries
Techniques: weaving, dyeing
Marketing Materials: photos, slides
Size Range: 72" x 30" to 6' x 9'
Price Range: $750 - $3,000

ALICE VAN LEUNEN
PO Box 408
Lake Oswego, OR 97034
(503) 636-0787
FAX (503) 636-0787
Established: 1968
Products: mixed media wall installations
Techniques: weaving, airbrush, embroidery
Marketing Materials: photos, slides, resume
Size Range: 12" x 12" to 11' x 12'
Price Range: $200 - $30,000

AASE VASLOW
100 Orchard Ln.
Oak Ridge, TN 37830
(615) 483-3650
Established: 1976
Products: tapestries
Techniques: weaving, beading, applique
Marketing Materials: photos, slides, resume
Size Range: 30" x 30" to 5' x 10'
Price Range: $120 sq. ft.-$240 sq. ft.

JUDITH VEROSTKO-PETREE
PO Box 25492
Richmond, VA 23260
(804) 358-7659
Established: 1987
Products: tapestries
Techniques: weaving
Marketing Materials: photos, slides, resume
Size Range: 1' x 2' to 6' x 10'
Price Range: $500 - $18,000

BARBARA ALLEN WAGNER
The Crow's Nest
7 Skyline Pl.
Astoria, OR 97103
(503) 325-5548
Established: 1953
Products: tapestries
Techniques: weaving, embroidery
Marketing Materials: photos, slides, resume
Size Range: 5' x 3' to 7' x 5'
Price Range: $5,000 - $15,000

DAVID WALKER
2905 Probasco Court
Cincinnati, OH 45220
(513) 961-9065
Products: art quilts
Techniques: quilting, applique, dyeing
Marketing Materials: slides, resume
Size Range: 30" x 30" to 95" x 95"
Price Range: $1,000 - $6,000

GRACEANN WARN
Granceann Warn Studio
117 West Liberty St.
Ann Arbor, MI 48104
(313) 665-2374
Established: 1985
Products: mixed media wall installations
Techniques: painting, stamping/printing
Marketing Materials: photos, slides, resume
Size Range: 18" x 12" to 48" x 36"
Price Range: $750 - $1,800

MONA WATERHOUSE
102 Delbank Point
Peachtree City, GA 30269
(404) 487-2881
Established: 1978
Products: paper wall work
Techniques: painting, dyeing
Marketing Materials: photos, slides, resume
Size Range: 20" x 16" to 37" x 37"
Price Range: $350 - $1,000

HELEN FROST WAY
20 Oenoke Ln.
New Canaan, CT 06840
(203) 966-4484
FAX (203) 966-3886
Established: 1968
Products: mixed media wall installations
Marketing Materials: slides, resume
Price Range: $100 - $10,000

HELEN WEBBER
Helen Webber Designs
555 Pacific
San Francisco, CA 94133
(415) 989-5521
FAX (415) 989-5746
Established: 1973
Products: tapestries
Techniques: painting
Marketing Materials: photos, slides, resume, brochure
Size Range: 4' x 5' to 35' x 12'
Price Range: $4,000 - $84,000

LEANNE WEISSLER
50 Webster Ave.
New Rochelle, NY 10801
(914) 235-7632
Established: 1970
Products: mixed media wall installations
Techniques: silkscreen
Marketing Materials: photos, slides, resume
Size Range: 12" x 12" to 3' x 4'
Price Range: $150 - $1,200

EFREM WEITZMAN
Efrem Weitzman, Art Work, Inc.
P.O. Drawer 1092
South Fallsburg, NY 12779
(914) 434-2408
Established: 1960
Products: tapestries
Techniques: appliqué, embroidery
Marketing Materials: brochure
Size Range: 10' x 6' to 10' x 156'
Price Range: $120 sq. ft.-$300 sq. ft.

Efrem Weitzman's hand-tufted wool tapestries are the result of a dialogue between the artist and client. Because he is interested in creating art works that are uniquely suited to their setting, Weitzman employs other media—such as metal, fiber, and mosaic—for his walls. Clients include Worthen Bank, Little Rock AR, Liberty Bank, Oklahoma City, OK, and General Battery, Reading, PA. See page 31 for photographs and additional information.

JUDI MAUREEN WHITE
Renaissance Fibres
2062 East Malibu Dr.
Tempe, AZ 85282
(602) 820-3808
Established: 1970
Products: mixed media wall installations
Techniques: painting, weaving, embroidery
Marketing Materials: photos, slides, resume
Size Range: 3' x 4' to 8' x 20'
Price Range: $1,200 - $25,000

NANCY WHITTINGTON
105 Walters Rd.
Carrboro, NC 27510
(919) 933-0624
FAX (919) 933-0631
Established: 1976
Products: art quilts
Techniques: dyeing, painting, applique
Marketing Materials: photos, slides, resume
Size Range: 36" x 48" to 100" x 100"
Price Range: $4,000 - $12,000

PATRYC WIGGINS
Mill Tapestry Project
58 North Main St.
Newport, NH 03773
(603) 863-3430
Established: 1988
Products: tapestries
Techniques: weaving
Marketing Materials: photos, slides, resume, brochure, video
Size Range: 8" x 8" to 6' x 13'
Price Range: $250 - $50,000

JAY D. WILSON
Wilson & Yamada Art Studio
3155 Nahenahe Pl.
Kihei, HI 96753-9314
(808) 874-3597
Established: 1976
Products: tapestries
Techniques: weaving, dyeing
Marketing Materials: photos, slides, resume
Size Range: 6' x 4' to 8' x 12'
Price Range: $15,000 - $75,000

NANCY E. WINES-DEWAN
Contemporary Maine Textiles
PO Box 861
Yarmouth, ME 04096
(207) 846-6058
Established: 1970
Products: tapestries
Techniques: weaving, dyeing
Marketing Materials: photos, slides, resume, brochure
Size Range: 12" x 12" to 72" x 120"
Price Range: $150 - $9,000

JOEN WOLFROM
Joen Wolfrom, Textile Artist
104 Bon Bluff
Fox Island, WA 98333
(206) 549-2395
Established: 1977
Products: art quilts
Techniques: quilting
Marketing Materials: photos, slides, resume
Size Range: 24" x 30" to 120" x 120"
Price Range: $100 sq. ft.-$250 sq. ft.

CHARLOTTE ZIEBARTH
Charlotte Ziebarth Tapestries
3070 Ash Ave.
Boulder, CO 80303
(303) 494-2601
Established: 1978
Products: tapestries
Techniques: weaving, dyeing
Marketing Materials: photos, slides, resume, brochure
Size Range: 24" x 30" to 5' x 10'
Price Range: $400 - $10,000

BHAKTI ZIEK
5225 Greene St.
Philadelphia, PA 19144
(215) 844-4402
Established: 1979
Products: tapestries
Techniques: weaving, dyeing, painting
Marketing Materials: photos, slides, resume
Size Range: 3' x 8' to 9' x 20'
Price Range: $200 - $20,000

ELLEN ZOHOREC
1418 Country Club Rd.
Brevard, NC 28712
(704) 883-2254
Established: 1980
Products: paper wall work
Techniques: painting, quilting
Marketing Materials: brochure, photos, resume, slides
Size Range: 8" x 10" to 15' x 15'
Price Range: $200 - $125 sq. ft.

Ellen Zahorec creates one-of-a-kind, contemporary, mixed-media, canvas constructions and handmade-paper collages. She fuses fine-art media and craft processes resulting in rich patterned surfaces of color and texture. Collages and canvas constructions are available for private and corporate collections and are designed for specific dimensions and color range. See page 19 for photographs and additional information.

The Care and Maintenance of Fiber Art

Hand-crafted works in fiber have enriched the lives of both royalty and peasantry since the beginning of humankind. Persian brocades, Indian chilkats, Indonesian ship cloths, Asian ikats, Turkish rugs -- the artistry and craftsmanship of textiles from centuries past are kept alive in countless museums around the world. And, it's a marvel that they exist at all for us to enjoy today. Homage is paid first to the artists who toiled over these works and second to the conservators who have preserved them for safe passage into this century.

Likewise, today's fiber art deserves our thoughtful attention to care and maintenance. Regarding contemporary textiles as the heirlooms of tomorrow is the best way to ensure their preservation for future generations to enjoy.

You don't have to be a museum curator to purchase and display contemporary textiles, but you do have to remember that they are perishable works of art. While a designer's most important function is to choose the right art or artist for a client's taste, project and budget, in this medium there is also an important role to be played in several pragmatic areas. The most exquisite art in the world will be diminished by inappropriate positioning, lighting and overall maintenance. Aesthetics and conservation should get equal consideration.

Successful presentation begins with selecting the right environment -- a space, position and illumination that shows off the ultimate quality of a piece. On an artistic level, attention must be given to spatial considerations, proportions, focal points. On a practical level, solutions must be found for safely showcasing fiber art.

If the art is commissioned as part of the overall design process and the installation plan thought through in the conception stage, this task is easier. But if a work has been commissioned or purchased for an existing space, solutions need to be found for lighting that will neither diminish the piece aesthetically nor destroy it physically. Because fiber is somewhat fragile, these questions of endurance and care are important. Fiber art that has become shabby, or soiled, with its color faded is an all too familiar and disheartening sight.

Jean West, former director of the Center for Tapestry Arts in New York City, brings home the point with a reminder of the short-lived craze of the 1960s and 70s. Jute and sisal, many clients learned the hard way, are extremely fragile -- if unprotected, they deteriorate rapidly. Because there was little history in this field, and scarce information on protection was available, a large body of this work has been lost to the elements. Harsh light and moisture took their toll.

Fiber art has long been recognized as a springboard for explorations in a variety of media; this is a field that continues to evolve through the use of new materials. Peruse the pages of THE GUILD, and you'll find works in metallic yarns, new lustrous cottons, silk, wools, handmade papers, synthetics,

OVERCOMING GLARE

Artwork that is covered with glass or plastic can reflect light into the eyes of people nearby. The potential for glare can be determined even before the artwork is hung because the angle of light reflection is always the same as the angle of the light on the art.

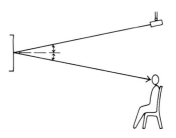

Here are four solutions to the problem of glare:
- Add parabolic louvers to fixture, which provide a 45 degree shielding angle.
- Set the ceiling lights at a sharper angle: move the lights closer to the wall where the art is displayed.
- Use floor canisters that shine light upward.
- Remove the glass or plastic!

Reprinted with permission. Laurence Korwin, *Textiles as Art,* ©1990.

bamboo and wire. Often you'll read in the artists' descriptions of their works, assurances that they are "custom-dyed, lightfast, mothproof, treated with fabric protectant, fireproofing available." Our contemporary fiber artists have become knowledgeable in areas of durability and maintenance. Conservation gets a good start with their expertise, but ensuring textiles a long-term existence takes an ongoing effort, one in which designers and art consultants play an important role. In addition to the advice offered here, there are a number of other resources available regarding the care and conservation of textiles. (See sidebar, Textile Conservation Resources.)

POSITIONING. Safe positioning of a piece of fiber art is very important. In the area of illumination, ultraviolet rays (sunshine) are the most harmful. But incandescent light can also break down natural fibers. Works in fiber should not only be placed out of direct sunlight, but at a safe distance from artificial light where heat can destroy the material. Likewise, heat vents, radiators, and hot wires need to be kept at a distance.

Too-close or too-intense lighting presents not only physical harm to fiber art, but will diminish these works aesthetically as well. Intense bright light destroys the colors of textiles, which have, quite naturally, been painstakingly and masterfully chosen for the ultimate effect. Work lit too brightly can be totally distorted; the colors washed out in the beam. Work with subtle transitions in color

and those in which light plays on fibers, and in which spatial depth are critical, must also be lit very carefully.

Laurence Korwin, in his book *Textiles As Art,* provides an extensive guide to optimum lighting combinations, including suggestions on positioning of lights. (See sidebar, Overcoming Glare.) Korwin presents many lighting solutions for the problems facing the installation of a fiber piece: adding lenses to a fixture to soften potential bright spots; using up-lights from a floor canister; lighting from across the room; choosing between incandescent and halogen bulbs. He also suggests talking to major lighting distributors in your area. Many of them have showrooms where lighting solutions can be tested.

Korwin details the color spectrum enhancement properties of different sources of light. The choice of halogen, incandescent or daylight is critical in preserving the color quality intended by the artist. Cool colors are enhanced by daylight; incandescent lighting is high on the red, or warm, end of the spectrum; halogen light is visually less blue than daylight, less red than incandescent and has a crisp, almost icy whiteness. The lighting should be compatible with the mood of the work. Is it dramatic, moody, romantic, cheery? Choosing the right light source will enhance the aesthetics, not contradict it.

FRAMING. There are many considerations in framing textiles as well. While glass protects against humidity, dust, insects, and touching, it is important, advises West, to allow an air space for the work. It is essential to back with adhesives that won't discolor the fibers. Spacers that keep the glass from coming in direct contact with the material is also critical, since the acidic quality of glass can adversely alter the fibers. While there are plastics on the market today which offer protection from ultraviolet rays, these, as well as glass, may present glare problems.

INSTALLATION. Hanging presents another set of challenges. West says the Center for Tapestry Arts has used the solution of hand-stitching a four-inch wide twill tape (used in upholstering) onto the backs of tapestries. A strip of velcro is attached to the tape and another stapled to a board (shellacked so no acids can leach out) which is covered in muslin. Screw eyes secure the board to the wall, giving the piece adjustability.

While many artists block their work before installation, in some instances gravity can take its toll. The Center solves problems by reshaping works in a squaring up frame. They tack the work down, iron with the use of damp towels, and then let the piece dry overnight. Heavily textured pieces that can not endure the press of an iron are simply wetted down in blocks, squared out, and left to dry.

CLEANING. While the new fabric protectors solve many of the problems associated with soiling, insect infestations and humidity, periodic cleaning may still be needed. Some pieces can be carefully vacuumed, with a mesh screening placed over the work to avoid fibers being either disturbed or extricated from the piece. Dry cleaning though, by anyone other than a well-versed conservator, can be dangerous business.

There are textile conservators around the country who specialize in cleaning. The new fabric protectors are much better, but it's helpful to be aware of these resources should the need arise.

When it is appropriately cared for, contemporary fiber art will endure long after its original purpose. Good care from the beginning will guarantee that the best of our textile treasures will be passed on within the family or to museum archives for future generations to enjoy.

George Alexander

1261 Cerro Gordo Road
Santa Fe, NM 87501
(505) 983-8003
(800) 821-1261

George Alexander's ceramics are unique artistic expressions rooted in the tradition of Italian majolica Richly glazed and exuberantly decorated with fruits, vegetables, flowers and foliage, Alexander's vases bowls, mirrors and architectural elements are imbued with intrigue and whimsy. Crafted in a cone 5 stoneware, they belie their implied fragility. It is his stunning contrasts of forms, colors and textures which delight the senses.

George Alexander is uniquely adept in translating the constraints of specifications into highly original work. Commissions are gladly accepted; additional information available upon request.

Top: *Harvest Mirrior*, 51"H x 31"W x 3 ½"D, *Harvest Bowl*, 8 ½"H x 19"Dia
Bottom Right: *Corn Pilasters, Dancing Corn Series*, 84"H x 16"W x 5"D
Bottom Left: *Bough Mirror*, 50"H x 40"W x 4"D, *Harvest Vases, Dancing Corn Series*, 23"H x 11"Dia

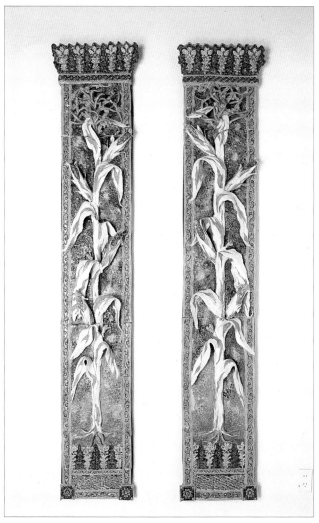

Frank Colson

Colson School of Art/Colson Studio
1666 Hillview Street
Sarasota, FL 34239
(813) 953-5892
FAX (813) 953-5892

Frank Colson has executed numerous major commissions, which include original and unique limited edition sculptures in clay and bronze. His concept of interchangeable modular forms are illustrated on this page.

This *Multiface Panel* (6'W x 3'H) may be re-arranged in groupings suited for large or intimate spaces. Each unit (12" x 12") is in deep relief. Color tones can be utilized to either harmonize or contrast to the site location. Earlier editions of THE GUILD, provide additional illustrations of this established studio.

A portfolio and price list are available upon serious intent of commission or acquisition. Call or FAX for a prompt reply.

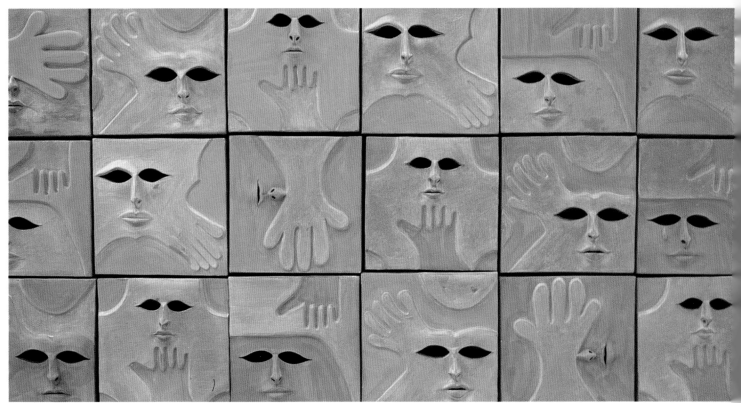

Jamie Fine

1403 Central Parkway, 4th Floor
Cincinnati, OH 45214
(513) 621-5922
FAX (513) 621-5922

Elegant, powerful and subtle are the words used to describe Jamie Fine's ceramic artworks. Ranging in size from intimate table-top screens to multi-story tile installations, the works are suitable for residential, commercial and public spaces.

Using thin sheets of durable stoneware clay, Fine creates textured panels which she airbrushes and paints with multiple layers of richly colored porcelain. These works evoke a sense of the land forms, rivers and sky which inspire her.

This nationally known artist welcomes collaboration with designers and architects. Commissions and collections include IBM, the Chrysler Corporation, and the Detroit Institute of Art.

Call or write for slides and additional information.

Top Left: *Autumn/River*, private commission, 24" x 56"
Top Right: detail, *Autumn/River*
Bottom Left: *Winter*, installation, private commission, 64" x 24"
Bottom Right: *Winter*, private commission 64" x 24"

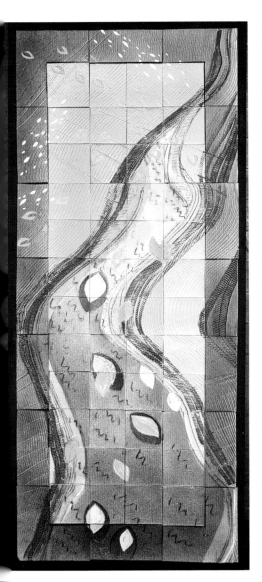

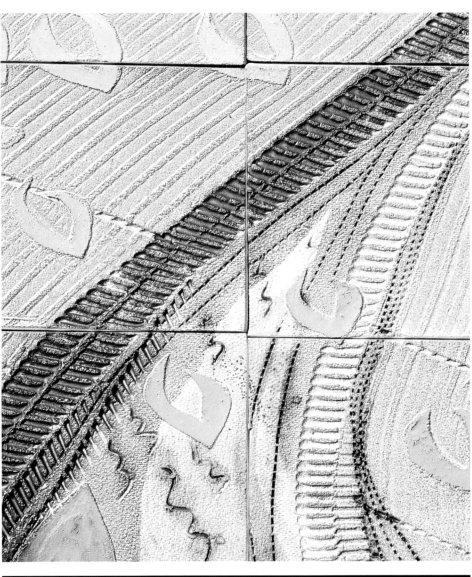

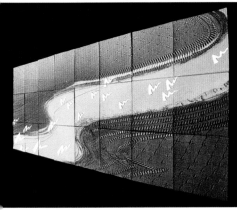

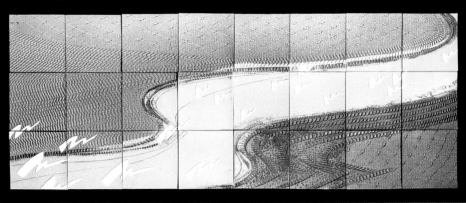

Loraine A. Fischer

406 N. Buffalo
Portland, OR 97217
(503) 289-2510

Loraine Fischer's highly individualized, one-of-a-kind masks enhance public, residential, and commercial settings. High fired in a reduction atmosphere, her ceramic masks are recognized for the superb degree of glaze control, the wide range of colors and the variety of surface textures.

For more than 13 years as a contemporary American ceramic-mask maker, Loraine Fischer's artistry, skill, and alchemy have combined to create masks that elicit the many faces of emotion.

Commissions accepted; personalized collaborative works encouraged. Slides of currently available work on request.

Thomas Lollar

50 West 106th Street, Suite 2A
New York, NY 10025
(212) 864-7973
(914) 964-0812

Tom Lollar builds murals by hand which depict architectural and geographical themes. Subjects depict landmarks in both frontal bas-relief and aerial views. The unique surface color results from applying copper, bronze and platinum metallic paints and glazes. Each rectangular clay construction is approximately 22" x 20" x 3" and may be placed in combinations of unlimited numbers suitable to wall size. Price for each one-of-a-kind section depends on the intricacy of the surface.

Lollar has a Master's Degree in ceramic sculpture from Western Michigan University and has been creating clay murals professionally for ten years.

His murals are in the collections of Hyatt Hotels, Revlon and Steelcase. His work has also been featured in the store windows of Tiffany, Fifth Avenue, New York City.

Top Left: *Manhattan I* (aerial view), 48" x 48" x 6"
Top Center: *Manhattan II* (Central Park), 48" x 48" x 6"
Top Right: *Manhattan III*, (Midtown), 48" x 48" x 6"
Bottom Left: *Albany*, 12' x 8'
Bottom Right : Detail, *Albany*

Elizabeth MacDonald

Box 186
Bridgewater, CT 06752
(203) 354-0594

Elizabeth MacDonald produces tile paintings by layering ceramic powders on thin pieces of textured clay that have been torn into squares. She makes surfaces that suggest either nature's erosion or patinas of age and use. After firing, these tiles are assembled into images, merging the organic into the formality of a grid.

The compositions are suitable for either in- or out-of-doors and they take the form of free-standing columns, wall panels or architectural installations. Attached to ¼" luan with silicone, the tiles (often 3 ½" squares) weigh approximately 1 ¾ pounds per square foot, are durable, and require a minimum of maintenance.

Ms. MacDonald is experienced in working with the client's requirements and can produce either small or large-scale work. Terms and prices are available upon request.

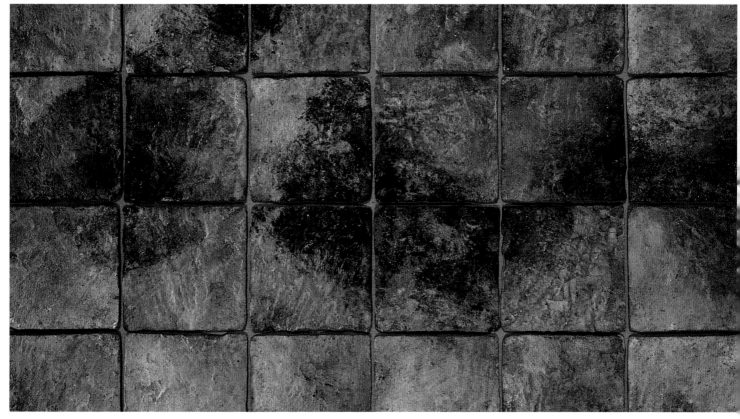

Her work is represented in the collections of Chubb and Sons, Pitney Bowes, The Aetna Life Insurance Company, Miles Pharmaceutical, IBM, The National Conference of Catholic Bishops and the Yale University Medical Center.

Recent commissions include Conrad International Hotel, Hong Kong; St. Luke's Hospital, Denver; ITT Hartford, for the City of Hartford, CT; and the Department of Environmental Protection, Hartford, CT (% for Art)

Left page/Top: *Landscape,* 1992, commissioned by Miliken, Spartanburg, SC, 5 panels, ceramic tile, 56" x 11 ½"
Left Page/Bottom: detail, *Landscape*
Below/Top: Detail, *Quilt,* clay
Below/Bottom: Detail, *Woven Work,* clay,

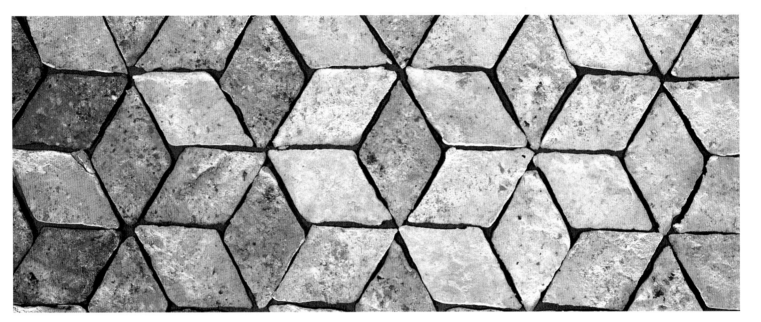

Elizabeth MacDonald, Box 186, Bridgewater, CT, 06752, (203) 354-0594

Richard Thomas
Keit Studios

**1396 Sheffield Place
Thousand Oaks, CA 91360
(805) 495-5032**

Yes, it is tile. In fact, these are authentic RTK Studios reproductions of the Malibu Lagoon Museum's renowned Malibu Tile Persian carpets (circa 1926).

Considered the ultimate in decorative surfaces, Malibu Tile was produced for some of the finest houses in America from 1926 to 1932. Now, with 12 years of experience reviving classic tile making techniques for a myriad of prestigious private and public commissions, RTK Studios has mastered the look and feel of this golden age in hand crafted ceramic art tile.

Suitable for interior and exterior walls, floors and water elements, RTK Studios' carpets, murals, patterns and fields are available from stock in a great variety of styles, colors and sizes.

Custom commissions are available.

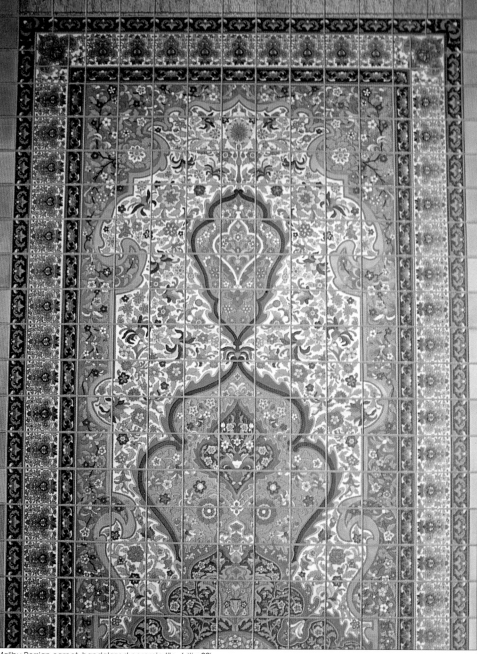

Malibu Persian carpet, handglazed ceramic tile, 6 ½' x 20'

Malibu Persian carpet, handglazed ceramic tile, 3 ½" x 6'

William C. Richards

Clay Canvas Designs
P.o. Box 361
Underwood, WA 98651
(509) 493-3928

William Richards' ceramic work can be found in numerous corporate collections as well as residential environments. He has been working in clay since 1972. His stoneware plates and panels are unique creations that combine textural surfaces and dimensional materials. The bottles and bowls are thrown and hand built to give a casual look. The surfaces are colored with multiple layers of acrylic stain and sealed for longevity. Each plate and panel piece is wired for wall mounting.

He welcomes commissions and custom orders. Plates are sized 11" to 45" in diameter and panels are up to 6' x 3' overall size. Bottles stand 12" to 18" high and bowls are 16" x 6". Professional profile and detailed information is available.

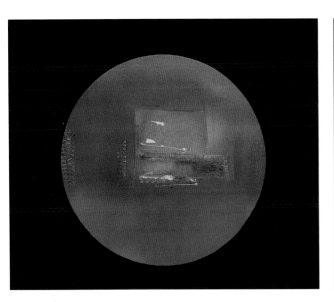

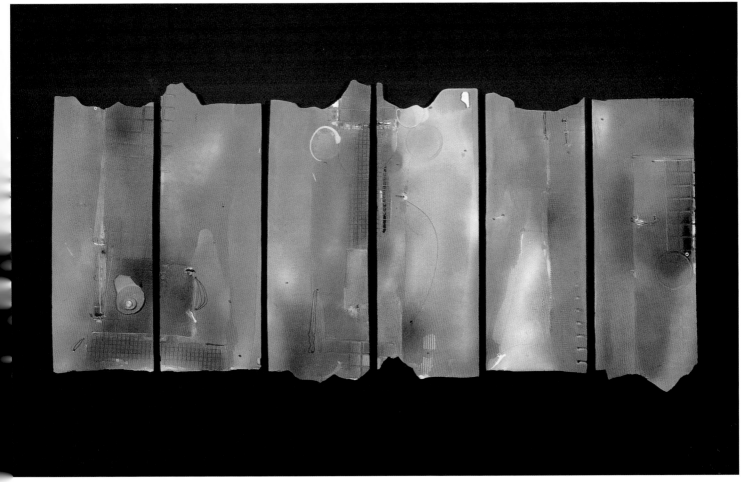

Mathers Rowley

Firedrake Studios
482 Swanton Road
Davenport, CA 95017
(408) 426-5091
FAX (408) 427-1747

Ceramic murals can be functionally integrated into any architectural setting, such as bathrooms, kitchens, fireplace surrounds, floors and counter tops. Firedrake Studio murals are unusual in that the tiles fit together to compose a scene or abstract design without the detracting grid of grout lines seen in most tile murals. The effect is quite striking and has a wonderful organic quality. A wide range of special techniques are employed to make even simple designs uniquely enchanting. Custom and stock designs are available.

Alan Steinberg

c/o Brattleboro Clayworks
R.D. 5 Box 250, Putney Road
Brattleboro, VT 05301
(802) 254-9174

Alan Steinberg's one-of-a-kind wallhangings reflect his sensitivity to the elements of earth, wind and water.

Working from photographs and sketches, he textures and inlays colored stoneware and porcelain clays, often pressing plants directly into the clay gathered at the places portrayed . Stains highlight textures and emphasize forms. The artist calls forth rock formations, cloud patterns and he captures the motion of plants fluttering in the breeze.

Steinberg's wallhangings grace the walls of corporations, professional offices and private residences. Commissions and custom orders are welcome.

Top: *Kauai*, 22"H x 50"W
Bottom: *Acadia*, 18"H x 27"W

David Westmeier

75 Bennett Street
Studio D-1
Atlanta, GA 30309
(404) 351-6724

David Westmeier's ceramic and metal wall reliefs and raku vessel forms enhance corporate offices and private homes throughout the United States and abroad. A selected list of corporate collections includes: Delta Airlines Crown Room, Honolulu, HI; Hotel Nikko, Beverly Hills, CA; McDonnel Douglass Information Systems, New York, NY; P.G.A. Clubhouse, Las Vegas, NV; Unisys Corporation, Atlanta, GA.

Working from more than 20 years of experience, Westmeier draws inspiration from various sources including fossil forms and microscopic observations of plants and aquatic life. His work creates a contemplative mood for the viewer, with each piece possessing a powerful yet serene life force.

Photographer: Kevin C. Rose

Top: *Ancient Koan*, 34"D
Bottom: *Primordial Vestiges #5*, 30" x 96"

Dale Zheutlin

55 Webster Avenue
New Rochelle, NY 10801
(914) 576-0082
FAX (914) 738-8373

Unique site-specific ceramic wall reliefs, hand built in a wide range of dimensions and colors, provide art for public, corporate and residential spaces. Prices vary depending on the size and complexity of the project.

Selected commissions and collections include: Citibank Tower, Phoenix, AZ; Aetna, Hartford, CT; Chase Manhattan Bank, New York, NY; IBM, Armonk, NY; British Airways, Washington, D.C.; Delaware River and Bay Authority, Wilmington, DE; ITT, Hartford, CT.

All photos: *New York, New York*, installed at Pfizer, Inc., New York, NY, ceramic construction, porcelain, 4'W x 6.5'H x 4"D

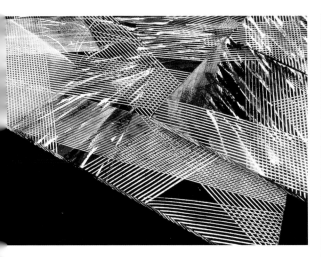

A Conversation with
Elizabeth MacDonald

Elizabeth MacDonald produces tile paintings that are used both as wall panels and architectural installations.

How do you make your tiles?

I start with wet, thin clay tiles, and texture them using a gouged clay rolling pin I made. Then I apply mason stains in powdered form. Experience and trial and error have given me an idea of how much powder of each color to use, yet it's basically a surprise to see what dominant color or hue the tiles will be after they are fired. The tiles go in the kiln damp and I fire them off, which takes about a day. Then they are dipped in an acrylic medium, which glues the color to the tile. I use acrylic because I've found that a glaze will not necessarily go through all the layers of pigment, and the colors can chip off. Plus, the acrylic leaves a less shiny finish.

I take the tiles out of the kiln and lay them out on the floor, and then start picking the tiles I want to use. I describe it as putting a jigsaw puzzle together without looking at the picture on the top of the box. I usually make a third to a quarter more tiles than I will need for the finished piece. I can never intermingle tiles from different projects, because the color system is very complex, but I keep the extra tiles, just in case any repairs ever need to be made. After I've organized the piece, I have wooden boards that protrude an inch off the wall when hung, and I attach the tiles with silicone.

What led you to this technique?

I wanted very much to work with color, but hadn't been satisfied with the results I was getting. I had experimented with weaving and making paper, and I loved the naturalness and roughness of paper, but I didn't want to change my materials. I became intrigued by old painted walls that were peeling and exposing layer upon layer of paint. I loved the subtleness of one color merging out of another, but I knew it would take me years to develop this technique if I tried to get this look from painting.

I happened to have some pigments in my studio that at the time were unfashionable. I started working with them, wedging them into clay. One day some pigment fell on the floor and I hated to throw it away, so I took a hunk of clay, rolled it with a piece of wood, and pressed it into the pigment. Immediately, I thought, "This is what I've been after!"

John Phillips Ashley

6809 Pine Drive
Chattanooga, TN 37421
(615) 899-9861

Ashley's original metalscapes have spawned a new artistic approach that defines the changing convention of the way people perceive sculpture.

Metalscapes are created from fabricated structural wooden designs. These forms are then clad with an anodized aluminum skin. This surface is hand textured and permanently stained with numerous satin overlays, producing the final alluring surface and opalescent colors.

The brunt of Ashley's Metalscapes are wall-mounted sculptures. For larger commissions, a modular system can incorporate multiple, integrated sections, producing a one-unit appearance with unlimited expansion. In addition to the wall-mounted works, monumental Metalscapes sculptures can be created. Unique, functional forms such as tables, desk designs, divider screens, fireplace facades, headboards, door inlay designs and Metalscape tiles can also be produced in this medium.

Maintenance is occasional dusting only.

Brochure and information available upon request.

Top: *Serpentine Table*, 1991, 5'x 28" x 13",
    Sofa Table, 1990, 4'6" x 26" x 18"
Bottom: *Soaring*, 1992, wall sculpture, 52" x
    36 ½" x 4"

Shawn Athari

Shawn Athari's, Inc.
13450 Cantara Street
Van Nuys, CA 91402
(818) 988-3105
FAX (818) 787-MASK

Shawn Athari has become well known for her three-dimensional, fused-glass sculptures (see Sculpture and Objects: Glass). Over the past two years, she has developed a series of larger framed pieces for the wall. Some of these works incorporate styles and patterns of ancient artwork with the color and luster of modern glass, while other pieces are abstract and purely modern in inspiration.

Each piece is original, utilizing glass selected from a large palette of colors, textures and iridescences.

Galleries: Symmetry, Saratoga Springs, NY; Glass Growers, Erie, PA; Carmichael's, Palm Springs, CA; Explore, Quadra Island, BC; 2112 Design Studio, Minneapolis, MN

Top Right: *Star Bowl*, 18" Dia
Bottom Right: *Aten of Egypt*, 38" x 27" x 3"
Left: *Utopia*, 24" x 42" x 5"

Photo: Robert Baumbach

Bruce R. Bleach

229 Coleman Road, RR1
Goshen, NY 10924
(914) 294-8945

Bruce R. Bleach's unique paintings on aluminum are the newest and most exciting work in a career that spans 18 years. These dramatic metal relief paintings are available for wall installation or as free standing sculptures with flat or curved surfaces. The artist combines rich textures and dynamic colors with elegant brushed aluminum or copper areas. Paintings are ready to hang, lightweight, and maintenance free, for corporate, public or residential installations.

Listed in Who's Who in American Art, Bruce R. Bleach is recognized internationally for his etchings, monoprints, cast paper and paintings. Selected collections include AT&T, IBM, Citicorp, Trump Tower and Dupont.

Slides, photos, drawings and color maquettes available.

Installation photos , courtesy of UVW Insurance and Avila Fine Arts, N.J.

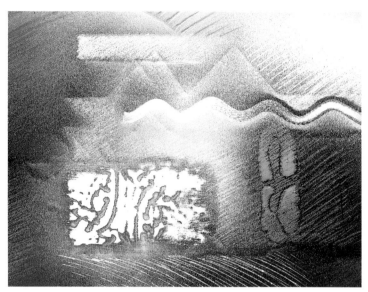

Photos: Nick Saraco

Lucinda Carlstrom

1075 Standard Drive
Atlanta, GA 30319
(404) 231-0227

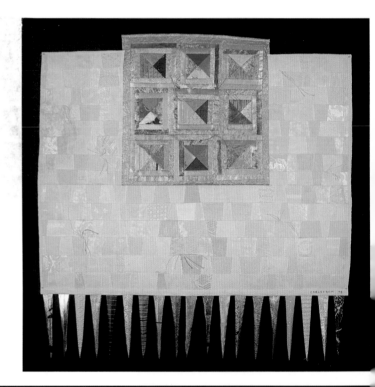

Lucinda Carlstrom's mixed-media constructions and piecework incorporate pure 23K gold leaf, metal leaf, hand-made papers and new and salvaged silks. Current work explores architectural themes of classical temples and contemporary public buildings. Another series of work explores the play of color and reflection of different shades of metals with colors. Different shapes change into different colors as the pieces evolve into larger color areas.

Lucinda Carlstrom welcomes commissions from architects and designers for corporate and personal spaces. Prices are determined by the complexity of the piecework and the materials used. This work is framed under glass for permanent installation.

Photograph books and samples are available.

Recent projects include: Citizens Utilities, Stamford, CT; Walt Disney World Corporate Offices, Lake Buena Vista, FL; Humana Hospitals, Montgomery, AL, Huntington Beach, CA, Abelene, TX and Louisville, KY.

Top: *The Power of Gold - Snow,* 20" x 20"
Bottom: *Architectural Temple Series,* 34" x 44"

Beth Cunningham

32 Sweetcake Mountain Road
New Fairfield, CT 06812
(203) 746-5160

Beth Cunningham creates elegant, ethereal, collaged paintings by airbrushing acrylic paint onto a rough, unprimed canvas background, and overlaying it with a smooth strip or grid surface of muslin, paint and silk tissue paper. Her one-of-a-kind wallpieces are sealed with an acrylic polymer that enables them to be exhibited without additional protection.

Ms. Cunningham has been involved in commission work for 16 years and is experienced in following the client's colors and architectural concepts. She can produce both large and small scale work. Her work is represented in many corporate, public and private collections. Price range is on a per square foot basis.

Top: *Genesis*, 24" x 24"
Bottom: *Catharsis*, 24" x 36"

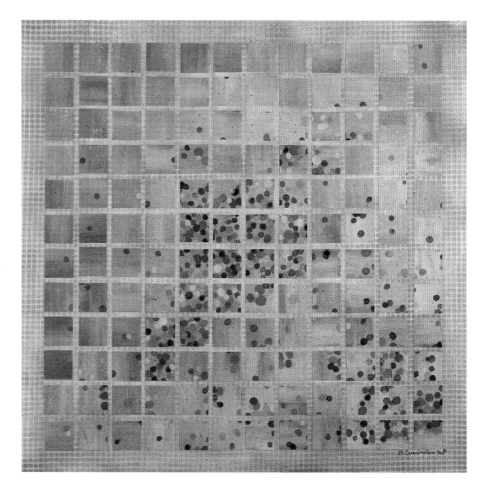

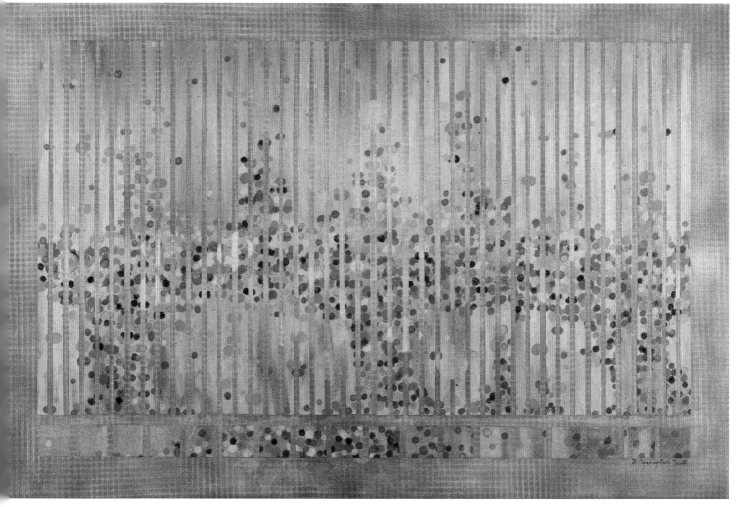

Jeffrey Cooper

Designer of Sculptural Furnishings in Wood
135 McDonough Street
Portsmouth, NH 03801
(603) 436-7945

"The giraffe chairs are a major hit!"
Reba Clark, Interior Designer, Memphis, TN.

The primitive influenced style of Jeffrey Cooper achieves a confluence of design integrity, warmth and charm. Having shown his Animal Chairs in previous editions of THE GUILD, Cooper now introduces high-relief wood carvings that collect into a composite work of art. Working with the artist will make your wall-mounted mural unique and customized for your home, office or corporate lobby.

Contact Jeffrey Cooper to apply his special talents to your design.

Top: A collection of Jeffrey Cooper's work featuring the mural *New Hampshire Forest Animals,* walnut, birch, cherry, mahogany, beech, 4' x 6 ½'
Bottom: Moose from *New Hampshire Forest Animals,* walnut with birch antlers

Barrett DeBusk

DeBusk Art Design
3813 N. Commerce Street
Fort Worth, TX 76106
(817) 625-8476
FAX (817) 625-8476

Barrett DeBusk, a Texas sculptor, illustrates his view of the world in uncomplicated steel-line drawings as well as innovative furniture.

Wall-hanging and free-standing sculptures are available in many sizes, 25" x 22" x 2" to 7' x 5' x 10". Along with limited editions, commissioned pieces are also in this artist's repertoire.

DeBusk's three-dimensional, pictorial stories are made form cold-rolled, hand-bent steel rod. After being welded together and framed, the images are coated with flat black Rustoleum paint, which makes maintenance easy. Not only do the built-in legs make hanging effortless, but they also enable you to see shadowy recreations of the images on the wall behind.

The artist's innovative use of materials and his regard toward the construction process make owning a DeBusk a delight.

Top: *Night of the Iguana*, 48" x 72" x 5"
Bottom: *Lifestyles of the Rich and Famous*,
   24" x 38" x 3"

Katherine Holzknecht

22828 57th Avenue SE
Woodinville, WA 98072
(206) 481-7788

Katherine Holzknecht creates unique mixed-media artworks for architectural spaces. Site-specific art results from collaboration with design professionals to produce innovative artworks that are well suited for the location.

Commissions are welcomed with a design fee. Design work includes scale drawings or maquette and samples. Katherine specializes in full-spectrum colors and visual textures to enhance existing design features. Constructed with dyed and painted wood, metal, wire, fabric and paper, her artworks are ideal for interiors because of their durability and lightfastness. Holzknecht's work has been exhibited extensively in the Northwest and nationally and is included in dozens of corporate, public and private collections.

Top: *Symbiosis Series*, The Corporate Center at Rye, NY
Bottom: *Nu-Wave Navaho*, The Thayer residence in Issaquah, WA

Margie Hughto
Pam Steele

Hughto & Company Studio
6970 Henderson Road
Jamesville, NY 13078
(315) 469-8775

For the past 18 years Hughto has been primarily working in the ceramic medium and Steele has been working in mixed metals and glass. Their wall reliefs are constructed of beautifully colored and textured elements, extremely durable and easy to install and maintain.

In the last three years nationally recognized artists Hughto and Steele have been commissioned to work collaboratively on several projects mixing their clay, metal and glass mediums. Works were created for an airport site, hotel lobby, corporate conference room and several private residences.

Artworks range in size from small intimate pieces to works of architectural scale. Commissions are welcome and existing works are available. Further information furnished upon request.

Hughto, *Westwind*, ceramic, 47" x 38"

Hughto & Steele, collaboration, *Freeze Thaw*, clay and steel, 51" x 41"

Hughto & Steele, collaboration, *Imperial Rule*, clay and copper, 39" x 39"

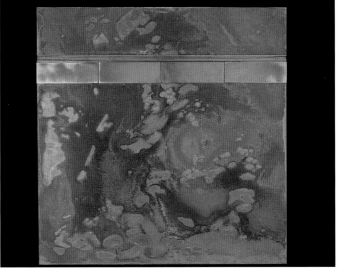

Steele, Foundry Series #10, enamel glass and copper, 24" x 24"

J.E. Jasen

36 East 10th Street
New York City, NY 10003-6219
(212) 674-6113
FAX (212) 777-6375

Unique Lead-free Vitrified Enamel Art!

Investment Quality Art!

Dynamic Designs!

Commissioned Murals and Accessories!
The non-institutional look can be achieved
through the individualized design with an
emphasis on the aesthetic, as well as the
functional aspect of each specific job to
meet the needs of the client.

May be used in interior or exterior public
spaces, such as: lobbies, executive suites,
dining rooms, kitchens, reception areas,
elevator interiors or exterior, recreational
centers, malls, schools, children and adult
facilities, hospitals, health facilities,
spas, etc....

Permanent Colors!

Excellent retention of color and gloss, that
will not peel, blister, and will resist
oxidation so that it will not fade due to
excessive lights, heat, cold, chemicals or
pollution.

Resistant to Weather and Public Elements!

Can be used in the interior or on the
exterior of buildings. Recommended for
high traffic areas because it has
scratch, corrosion and abrasion resistant
qualities. Graffiti resistant.

Durable with Low Maintenance!

If maintenance is necessary it can be
cleaned with water or mild soap and
disinfectant without damaging the
permanent lifetime finish.

Sturdy enough to lean against.

More information available upon request.

Dave Kühn

7601 North C.R. 320 E
Albany, IN 47320
(317) 282-7031

Rich color, texture and humor animate the paintings of Dave Kühn, mixing a contemporary sensibility with echoes of past cultures, animals and nature.

Kühn cuts free-form shapes from thick board, applying modeling paste to create texture, and using dry brush and air-brushed acrylics for depth, both real and illusionary. These lightweight works are often assembled components or groupings, and all have spacers on the backs so they appear to float off the wall.

Kühn's work has appeared in successful gallery shows and has been purchased by residential and corporate collectors. He produces work on commission, as well. Slide portfolio available on request.

Top: *The Wonkees*, 27" x 84"
Bottom Left: *Two for Taos*, 30" x 29"
Bottom Right: *Birdie Rising*, 46" x 36"

George W. Kubiayk

Design Coordinators
W135 N8101 Wood Court
Menomonee Falls, WI 53051
(414) 255-5911

Bronze, aluminum, venetian glass, steel and foundry sand are just a few of the mediums George Kubiayk uses to create works of art of all dimensions for business and industry.

In works ranging from a 24-foot anodized aluminum relief sculpture to a 200-foot supergraphic to a four-foot bronze sculpture, the richness of many types of materials are joined to tell a story in art.

Top Left: *Mayan*, Berlin Foundry, Berlin, WI, sand castings, 6' Dia
Top Right: *Solar*, Custom Products, Butler, WI, mosaic in venetian glass, 8' x 8'
Bottom: *Suns & Earth*, Guhring, Inc., Brookfield, WI, anodized aluminum and foundry sand, 24' x 7'

Trena McNabb

McNabb Studio
P.O. Box 327
Bethania, NC 27010-0327
(919) 759-0640
FAX (919) 759-0641

The unusual work of international artist Trena McNabb is especially adaptable to large commissions and collaborations for specific works. Trena's site-specific works add interesting dimensions to industrial, commercial and public buildings, and private collections, by depicting allegorical ideas, stories, or historical backgrounds.

Trena McNabb's white-on-white style allows the warmth of origional canvas areas to show through surrounding painted surfaces. Color areas appear as transparent collages. Painted scenes overlay one another to form a kaleidoscope of colors.

Different textures are often found on a single painting with unusual materials such as extra canvas, plexiglas, twine, or sawdust sewn or glued to the surface.

Prices and sizes are tailored to fit the scope of the project. Call or write for details.

Reynolds Tobacco Co., Tobaccoville, NC, acrylic on canvas and plexiglass, 4'3" x 19' x 6"

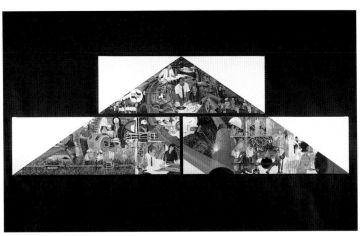

Midcon Corporation, Schaumberg, IL acrylic, 4' x 12' x 2"

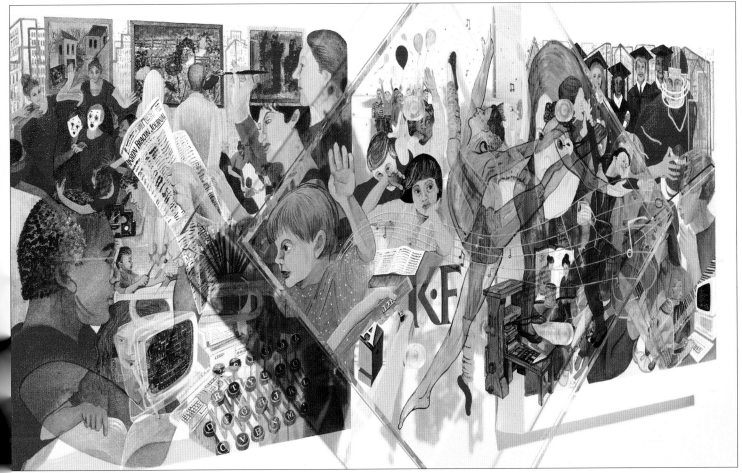

Knight Foundation, Miami, FL, acrylic and plexiglass, 36" x 54" x 6"

Ervin Somogyi

2606 McGee
Berkeley, CA 94703
(510) 524-2227

Ervin Somogyi is a professional luthier and woodworker of more than 20 years standing, whose work is known and respected internationally.

His carving and inlay work arises out of the musical-instrument-building tradition and aesthetic, and includes Japanese, Celtic, Islamic, Judaic and Renaissance designs.

Further information is available on request.

Top Right: *Quilted Maple Shield*, 22"H x 16"W, with inlaid rosewood, maple and ebony
Top Left: Detail, *Japanesque Rosette*, doubled version
Bottom Left: *Celtic Design*, 10" Dia, 20"H x 16"W, in bookmatched Sitka spruce
Bottom Right: *Japanesque Rosette*, 17 ½"H x 23"W, bookmatched red cedar. The rosette is 5" in diameter and has 2,950 cut lines, each requiring one to five cutting strokes.

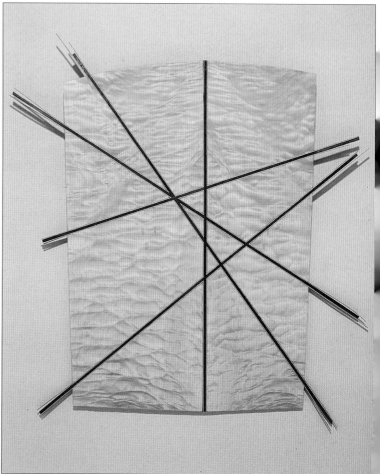

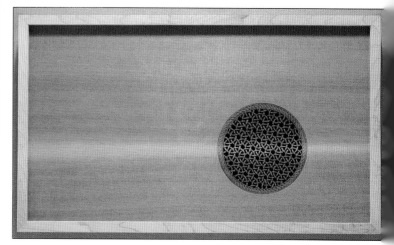

Mike Strohl

11 Schermerhorn Street
Brooklyn, NY 11201
(718) 237-9299

Mike Strohl creates constructions in wood that range from the strong and architectural to the elusive and whimsical. Colors include flat black, solid primaries and coordinated palettes. All are suitable for indoor display.

Strohl's work includes wall hangings, columns, screens, tabletop pieces and full wall installations in all dimensions. He would be pleased to discuss collaborative and commission opportunities.

Collections have been created for display at Tiffany & Company in New York City as well as for gallery showings. Strohl's work is in private collections throughout the country.

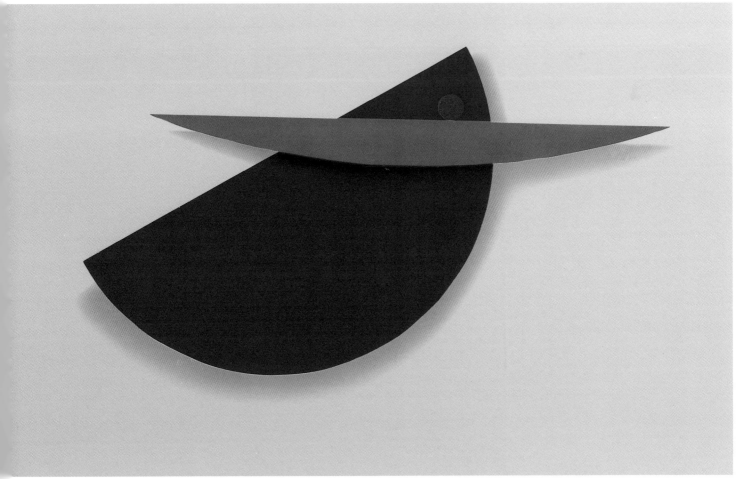

Photos: Larry Smith

Vincent Tolpo
Carolyn L. Tolpo

55918 U.S. Hwy. 285, P.O. Box 134
Shawnee, CO 80475
(303) 670-1733

Since 1981, Vincent and Carolyn Lee Tolpo have created site-specific wrapped fibers, metal and stoneware tile art works for public, corporate and residential spaces. They are collaborative artists who are sensitive to color, concept, space and budget for each project. They provide color drawings and material samples for approval by the client.

Delivery of commissions or available work is within four to ten weeks. Installation is available. Further information is available from the artists or see *THE GUILD 5*, page 252; *THE GUILD 6*, pages 121, 153; *THE GUILD 7: Designer's Reference*, page 99.

Top Left/Right: *Opposition*, wrapped fiber; 6' x 13', *Learning*, suspended sculpture 16' x 6'. Lobby artworks and complimenting floor/wall design, 1800 Glenarm Bldg., Denver, CO.
Bottom Left: *Words & Phrases, Books & Pages*, Co-Visions Sculpture Grant, State of Colorado, 6' x 3' x 3'
Bottom Right: *Above & Below*, Amax Coal Company, brass and stoneware with coal, 4' x 6'

Yoshi Hayashi

351 Ninth Street, 3rd Floor
San Francisco, CA 94103
(415) 552-0755

Yoshi Hayashi's designs range from very
traditional 17th century Japanese lacquer
art themes that are delicate with intricate
detail, to those that are boldly geometric
and contemporary. By skillfully applying
metallic leaf and bronzing powders, he adds
illumination and contrast to the network of
color, pattern and texture. His original
designs include screens, wall panels,
furniture and decorative objects.

Hayashi's pieces have been commissioned
for private collections, hotels, restaurants
and offices in the United States and Japan.
Prices upon request.

FURNITURE

The artists represented in this section of THE GUILD exemplify the world of choices in today's hand-crafted furniture market. In the realms of both beauty and function, there has never been more diversity, more possibilities for satisfying personal tastes.

With limitless imagination, extraordinary talent and skill, these furniture artists contribute lasting monuments to the American studio movement. Here, you'll discover chairs masquerading as sculpture, dressing tables that invoke the reverence of a shrine, a bed that looks like a vessel waiting to take its occupant to sea, cabinets and chests and screens that tilt upward the exotic.

This is furniture that transcends function. Individuals and small teams of artists are working out of their studios to create furniture that heightens the experience of home and workplace.

Here are contemporary artists who have returned to traditional values. They believe in quality, permanence, and the importance of singularity. They pay exquisite attention to detail —to joinery, to finishes, to embellishments. They employ interesting textures and materials. They take great pride in their craft—both structural and artistic, setting their own high standards for workmanship and aesthetics.

Professional in all aspects of their craft, and experienced in commissioned work, these furniture makers ensure integrity of design and materials. They are equally professional in matters of budget and deadlines. They may be contemporary by design, but they still provide old-fashioned, traditional guarantees of quality and performance.

These standards serve them well as more and more people today search for quality, custom-made furniture. In private homes, there is a desire to have furnishings that express personal values, whims, eccentricities. Businesses are eager to convey their corporate image, to establish a relationship with their public even before business in transacted, to project a mood compatible with the organization's mission.

Only artists who "encourage active participation of clients in the design process," "welcome collaboration with design teams," and "invite innovative commissions" are included here. Custom-designed, custom-made furniture brings limitless choices in style, materials, technique, scale, color form and ornamentation.

This is furniture with spirit. You won' find furniture from these pages of THE GUILD in a mainstream furniture showroom or home furnishings store. These furniture makers are creating one-of-a-kind heirlooms of tomorrow. Their clients will be people who care about quality, ingenuity, design singularity and craftsmanship.

FURNITURE

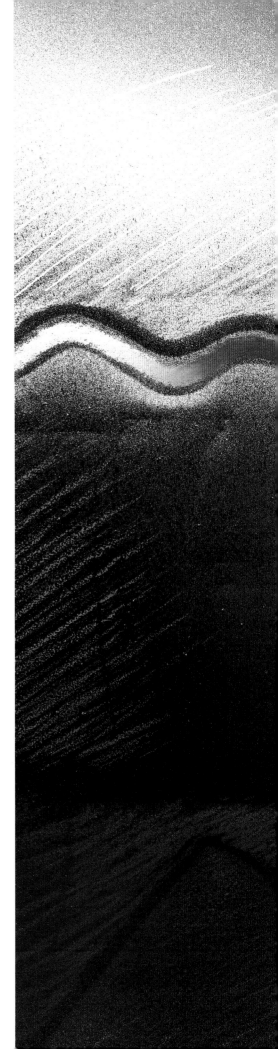

Carter Gustav Blocksma

Designforms
15675 Gorton Road
Grass Lake, MI 49240
(313) 475-8751
FAX (313) 475-0350

Carter Blocksma has been designing and manufacturing fine furniture for 18 years. His company, Designforms, produces custom and limited production pieces for both residential and commercial application nationwide. Blocksma has been recognized by *Fine Woodworking* magazine, included in national collections, exhibited at the International Contemporary Furniture Fair in NY and picked by the Detroit Institute of Arts for a review of his work. His designs show an unusual ability to work with numerous types of materials to achieve the distinctive, flowing style that has attracted such clients as Giorgio Armani in Chicago and Hoffman Jewelers in NY.

Blueprints, models, price quotes and additional information are available. Architectural and interior design collaboration is encouraged.

The Century Guild

Nick Strange
P.O. Box 13128
Research Triangle Park, NC 27709
(919) 598-1612

Since 1982 The Century Guild has specialized in making and designing one-of-a-kind or limited edition furniture for residential, corporate and ecclesiastical settings. This extensive experience produces traditional and contemporary pieces distinguished by well-proportioned design, special materials and time-tested construction techniques. Additional information is available upon request.

Top Right: Altar, Trinity Episcopal Church, Milton, CT; quarter-sawn white oak, designed by Terry Byrd Eason, Chapel Hill, NC
Bottom Right/Left: Details, stereo cabinet, lacewood and ebonized pear veneers with bubinga solids
Middle Left: End table, makore and ebonized cherry (both cabinet and table designed by Samuel Botero, ASID, NYC)
Top Left: Detail, rusticated bed; cherry, cocobolo, designed by Nick Strange

Donald M. De Witt

P.O. Box 62
Southworth, WA 98386
(206) 871-4508

Donald De Witt has been building furniture since 1978. He is known for his ability to create functional works of art from native Northwest materials. Collaboration with designers is welcome. De Witt's works have been commissioned by the creators of the television shows *Twin Peaks* and *Northern Exposure*. Various resorts, including Jasper Park Lodge, use his furniture

Previously commissioned pieces include beds, tables and fully upholstered sofas and chairs. Architectural elements such as handrails are available. Upholstery is available in natural canvas. There is an extra charge for leather, cowhide or customer's choice of fabric. Prices quoted to your drawings or requests. Natural branches can be used to meet your design requirements. Most orders can be met within 90 days after design approval. Inquiries are welcome.

Ron Diefenbacher

Ron Diefenbacher Designs
12132 Big Bend
St. Louis, MO 63122
(314) 966-4829

From design to delivery, Ron Diefenbacher uses a professional approach in assessing clients' needs and developing creative solutions. Combining artistic skill and an ability to work well with architects, interior designers, and private parties, Diefenbacher creates signature pieces which stress the individuality of each new project. These unique designs are placed in many private collections, executive offices, and fine galleries across the country.

Diefenbacher has a Master of Arts in Furniture Design and teaches Woodworking and Furniture Design at Washington University in St. Louis.

Top: *Hall Table*, walnut, maple
Bottom: *Sebastian's Table*, walnut, lacewood

Kevin Earley

1231 E. Wilson St.
Madison, WI 53703
(608) 256-5171

Designs for business interiors are often impersonal, appealing very little to those who use or visit them. Kevin Earley believes that office interiors, where so much time is spent, can be as welcoming as those at home and should display an equal concern for comfort, concept and craftsmanship. He also thinks a well-executed design should reveal something about the designer as well as those who commissioned it.

Projects are designed and built on commission, though preliminary price estimates can often be given. Delivery times of one to six months are common.

Top: club chairs, 1992, lobby area, Neenah
  Paper Company, oak, upholstery
Bottom: reception desk, 1992, lobby area,
  Neenah Paper Company, oak, dyed inlay

The Finished Piece

Frits Maas
R. J. Casey Industrial Park
Columbus and Preble Avenue
Pittsburgh, PA 15233
(412) 321-1701
FAX (412) 321-1701

Working alone, Frits Maas deftly fabricates furniture that is of the highest quality and is guaranteed for life. His work tends to be either modern interpretations of historical styles or unique pieces with minimal historical reference.

He works primarily with domestic hardwoods but will accommodate most materials, including veneer. The type of work includes freestanding furniture and cabinetry. Computer-generated designing is available.

He will also work from drawings supplied by the designer, architect, or residential or commercial client. Close collaboration with clients is the norm.

Frits Maas earned his Bachelor of Fine Arts from the University of Wisconsin-Madison with an emphasis in furniture design, and he has 13 years of experience with the craft.

Call, write or FAX for information folder and references.

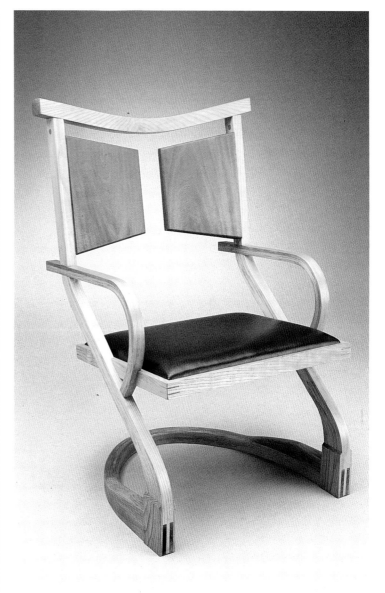

Murray P. Gates

Furniture and Design
14091 Center Road
Clio, MI 48420
(810) 687-1820

Murray P. Gates designs and builds contemporary one-of-a-kind furniture, with careful attention paid to the selection of grain and texture, in both domestic and exotic hardwoods. This allows the design and the wood to speak for themselves creating a unique piece of furniture that evokes a quiet elegance.

Murray P. Gates has over 25 years of experience as both a contemporary painter and furniture designer and maker. His works are in both public and private collections.

A complete portfolio is available. All pieces are guaranteed for the lifetime of the artist.

Top: sofa table, 1992, walnut, curly maple, walnut inlay, 28"H x 60"W x 14"D
Bottom: display cabinet, 1992, padauk, curly maple, glass, 69"H x 32"W x 14"D

Glen Grant

Craft-Wood Products
70 Osgood Street
Andover, MA 01810
(508) 475-6686

Glen Grant continues a family tradition of classical and contemporary fine wood-working. Using personally selected hardwoods, Glen crafts one-of-a-kind and limited editions which are functional and artistic. His specialties include contemporary bombé design, marble and wood inlay, chip and sculptured carving.

Graduate: North Bennet Street School, Boston, MA

Allow one to six months for custom design and production.

Top: *Geese at Rest*, coffee table. Made from select black walnut, the goose heads are dovetailed to base and sculpted to shape, ½" plate glass with polished edges rests on heads.
Bottom: *Night on the Town*, mirrored chest. Hand planed from a single piece of South American mahogany, the kettle shape reveals "hourglass" and "bullseye" grain patterns characteristic of bombé furniture.

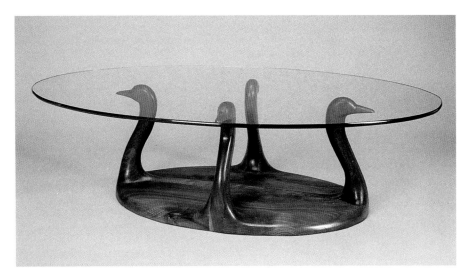

Furniture: Wood   119

William Hewitt

Witticks Design
46 River Road
South Deerfield, MA 01373
(413) 527-5973

William Hewitt has run a custom furniture and cabinet shop for ten years. He is experienced in executing both fine furniture and quality cabinetry of clients' design. His work has generally involved projects designed for existing spaces, while expressing his own solution.

His furniture pieces emphasize solid-wood construction and smoothly working parts. He uses contrasting colors to enhance and balance a design.

He will provide drawings for original projects, for a design fee. Bids are supplied free of charge.

Top: *Bridge Tables*, hallway and coffee tables
Bottom Left: *Skyline Vanity*, 52"L x 60"H x 20"D
Bottom Right: *Castle Fall Front Desk*, 50"L x
   50"H x 20"D

Steven Holman

Holman Studios
P.O. Box 572
Dorset, VT 05251
(802) 867-0131
FAX (802) 867-0255

Since 1980, Steve Holman has designed and built furniture of spirited inventiveness. He offers a wide palate of materials—woods, veneers, metal leaf, solid surfacing, laminates and painted surfaces—coupled with the broad range of finishes possible only with a full spray facility. Bids and drawings are promptly submitted, and difficult schedules are accommodated. Brochures are available.

Top: *Ariodante Chairs*, 1991, ebonized mahogany, ash, gold leaf, 22" x 24"D x 48"H
Bottom: Sideboard, 1990, French walnut solids and veneers, padauk, 16"W x 36"L x 38"H

Peter Maynard

Maynard & Maynard Furnituremakers
P.O. Box 77, Beryl Mt. Road
South Acworth, NH 03607
(603) 835-2969
FAX (603) 835-2969

For 20 years, Peter Maynard has been designing and building classic fine furnishings in a broad range of styles for private individuals and design firms.

His work has been featured in *Architectural Digest, Interior Design* and *Traditional Home* magazines. (Also see *THE GUILD 5* and 6).

Shown here is a sampling of 30 pieces Peter designed and built for an *Architectural Digest* Award Winning House (Special Architecture Issue, 1990).

Top: Pembroke Table in butternut and English Dining Chair in mahogany.
Bottom Left: Triple-pedestal English Dining Table with ten chairs in mahogany.
Bottom Right: Chinese Console Table hand-carved in Indian Rosewood with verde antique marble inset, 36"H x 72"L x 16"D.

Ronald C. Puckett

Ronald C. Puckett & Company
P.O. Box 9549
Richmond, VA 23228
(804) 752-2126

"Classical, yet contemporary and fresh" best describes the furniture of Ron Puckett. Known for its strong architectural and historical influences, Ron's furniture can be found in residential and corporate collections across the country and can be seen in numerous publications such as Patricia Conway's *Art For Everyday*. His pieces are on display in galleries throughout the U.S. He and his staff of craftsmen are available for residential and corporate commissions and are ready to work with architects and designers on all types of projects.

Top Left: *Bench-A-Saurus*, 29"H x 66"W x 26"D, curly maple, lacewood, padouk, silk fabric
Top Right: *Chaps Chest*, 64"H x 44"W x 22"D, bubunga, wenge, holly
Bottom: *O/M Cocktail Table*, 16"H x 60"W x 27"D, curly maple, mahogany, Moabi mahogany, ebony, anodized aluminum

David M. Schiller
Bernice Schiller

Dancing Winds Studio
P.O. Box 617
Chino Valley, AZ 86323
(602) 636-5170

The Schillers draw upon the rich culture and natural elements found in the great southwest. Shape, color and hue born of images both past and present meld into one through the touch of imagination bringing a harmonious existence to form and function.

Custom and commercial commissions and collaborations welcome.

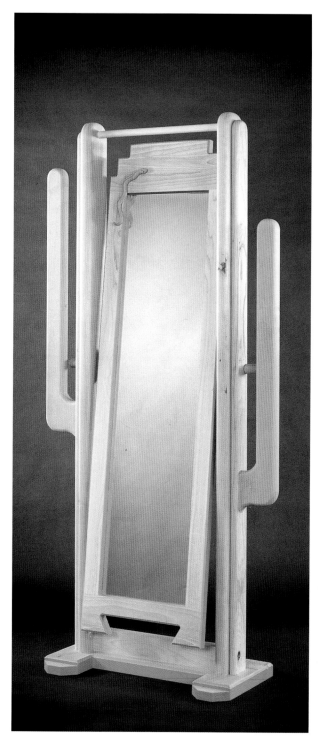

Anne Shutan

RR 1, Box 991
Newfane, VT 05345
(802) 365-7118

Anne Shutan creates one-of-a-kind pieces of furniture and sculpture, affirming the sensuous nature of wood. Through her work, she has discovered that art has as much to do with finesse and taking chances as with intelligence and craft. Anne travels all over the country to discuss projects with her clients. She then returns to her studio to design and create the piece. The process from conception to delivery can take anywhere from one to six months. Please contact the artist for information regarding commissions.

A portfolio is available upon request.

Top: bench, walnut, 16" x 60" x 60"H
Bottom: dining table, walnut, 40" x 40" x 30"H

Thomas Hugh Stangeland

Unique Creations in Fine Woods & Metals
5124 Woodlawn Avenue N
Seattle, WA 98103
(206) 632-2689

Combining beautiful materials and experimenting with pattern and form are the challenges Thomas Hugh Stangeland most enjoys. He strives to create furnishings that will withstand generations of use.

In addition to using environmentally friendly materials and finishes, he has become a pioneer in the use of sustained-yield and rainforest-safe exotic woods.

His goal is to meet the client's needs through site-specific design, appropriate function and aesthetic balance. Slides and scheduling information are available upon request.

Tiger Mountain Woodworks

Barry Jones
Paula Jones
P.O. Box 249, Hwy. 106
Scaly Mountain, NC 28775
(704) 526-5577
FAX (704) 526-2702

Barry and Paula Jones design and produce a variety of furnishings in the "rustic" style. The craftsmanship of the "Arts and Crafts" period and the "Camp" style of the Adirondacks have been the inspiration for their tables, chairs, cabinets, beds, lamps, mirrors and other accessories.

Their work is meticulously crafted using mountain laurel, bent willow and hickory in the rustic pieces along with native and exotic hardwoods in more traditional joinery.

Widely collected by individuals and commissioned by interior designers and architects, their furniture is found in installations throughout the U.S.

Most pieces are custom order and some items are available in limited-production quantities. Completion time is two to six months from confirmation.

G. Whitwell

Gordon Whitwell
8336 Washington Place NE
Albuquerque, NM 87113
(505) 822-8857

The subtle elegance of Gordon Whitwell's *Plains Collection* is the culmination of contrasting materials, historical designs and warm earth tones. His artistic blend of wire-brushed oak and patined steel creates this characteristically unique furniture style. *The Plains Collection* is available in limited editions or custom commissions.

Gordon Whitwell's pride and integrity as a furniture maker is drawn from more than 20 years of experience. Specializing in country furniture styles, he welcomes collaboration with design professionals and discriminating collectors.

Additional information is available upon request.

The Studio Furniture Movement

In this article, the term "studio" differentiates the furniture created by artists in their studios from that made by factories.

Since the late 1940s, something momentous has been brewing in the universe of American studio furniture makers. It started haphazardly, just a few individual woodworkers setting up shops where they could produce furniture completely by hand that transcended the genre's functional goals, They used furniture to explore the nature of their materials, the techniques that would help them achieve new kinds of designs and, finally, to explore the ability of furniture to powerfully convey emotion and ideas the way painting and sculpture have for centuries. Over the years, their one-of-a-kind works have caused a massive accretion, drawing new talents to the field from areas as disparate as architecture and jewelry-making. The gathering momentum has reached its climax in this decade. It is clear today that the American studio furniture movement has arrived at its Big Bang.

Without a doubt, contemporary studio furniture enjoys the cultural status of being a bona fide artistic movement. Its history was carved out by the movement's progenitors; seminal figures like Wharton Esherick, George Nakashima, Wendell Castle, and Tage Frid became respected and well-known figures in the 1960's. Since then the movement has spawned a sophisticated body of writings and criticism. And it has demanded attention as an independent art form in the art departments of American colleges and universities.

At the center of this movement is the artist/craftsperson whose creativity and imagination have been able to summon new concepts out of the aesthetic and philosophical repertoire of fine and decorative art history. What most sets today's studio furniture artists apart from the early practitioners is formal education. Some of the best-known furniture makers producing work now were students of the university programs established first by Tage Frid in the '50s, then later by Jere Osgood, Dan Jackson, Alphonse Mattia, Wendell Castle and others. They have been dubbed the "second generation" furniture makers by Edward S. Cooke Jr. in his influential essay for the "New American Furniture" exhibition at the Museum of Fine Arts, Boston (1989). The new academic environment, as well as the liberal social and political climate during which it took root (in the '60s and '70s), resulted in work that was daring and confrontational.

Yet much of the early furniture from this period was primarily concerned with technical bravura and the exploration of artistic ideas. It was esoteric and inaccessible to many and had little to do with function and comfort. "I knew many woodworkers who would throw everything they knew into one piece," recalls the metal artist Peter Handler. "It showed their virtuosity, almost to a baroque extent. But, many times, it went beyond good taste and comfort."

Gradually, however, these artists matured and moved away from shock value toward more livable designs. As they left this early period of experimentation, they became, in the words of woodworker Kevin Earley, "ready to explore the functional aspects of furniture, to look at it as furniture first, then, secondarily, as sculpture." What's more, he adds, "Over the last ten years, we've seen the functional aspects of furniture being accepted, in and of themselves, as artistic."

con't on page 146

Joseph A. Bonifas

Black Oak Forge
9090 Spencerville Road
Spencerville, OH 45887
(419) 647-6598

The range of possibilities afforded by shaping metal under the powers of heat and force is infinite. This unique characteristic of forged metal has enabled Joseph Bonifas to produce a wide range of architectural embellishments, sculptural and site-specific pieces. His work includes railings, gates, furniture, lighting fixtures, wall and freestanding sculpture.

Only an idea is necessary, as Bonifas will work with potential clients to develop design possibilities for site-specific commissions. Given the limitless potential of forged metal, Bonifas believes that if an idea is conceived it can be developed and created in his studio.

Top: *King Size Bed*, 7'H x 7'W x 7'L
Bottom: *Jack in the Beanstalk Table*,
   29"H x 33"W x 29"L
Below: *Vase Stand*, 54"H x 30"W x 28"L

George Gradzki

Gradzki Hand Forged Metal Arts
206 Greenfield #F
Elcajon, CA 92020
(619) 444-2904

George Gradzki is a European master of artistic craftsmanship in metalwork. Museums, monasteries and great homes across Europe feature his art. He has won numerous awards and medals.

Gradzki designs and creates "usable sculpture". He fashions elaborate light fixtures, such as candelabra and chandeliers, and custom furniture, including consoles and dining and coffee tables. He also tailors entry gates and railings to enhance the natural beauty of each property.

George Gradzki fabricates artwork to your individual taste out of many mediums: iron, copper, silver, steel and gold. He utilizes fifteenth-century methods of the masters, molding the distinctive look of the Old World artistry with the contemporary look desired by today's clients.

His unique drawing skills bring to life your wildest artistic fantasy. You may choose the medieval look, European contemporary, or whimsical variations of any style. Traditional works are, of course, a staple of his craft.

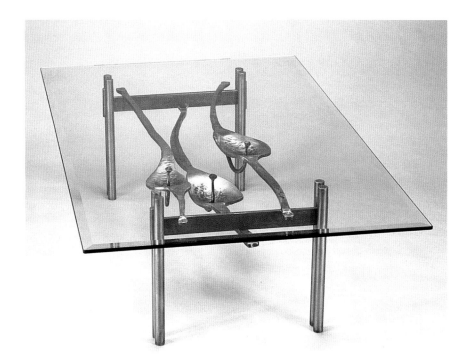

John Kennedy Studios

996 Tuxedo Circle
Palm Springs, CA 92262
(619) 320-9205

John Kennedy was born in Burma of Scottish descent and now works in his studios in Palm Springs, California and Oxford, England. Although his earlier work was purely sculptural, recently he has been exploring a new world of figurative functional art in bronze and steel. Bending and painting steel or casting bronze using the lost-wax method, Kennedy creates objects that also function as benches, tables and chairs. Many of his recent works incorporate the female human figure.

His works are shown in galleries around the world and are collected by internatioal art connoisseurs. Kennedy's sculptures have also been installed in such public settings as hotels and hospitals.

After a recent exhibition in London, Max Wykes-Joyce of Arts Review commented, "I much approve of this utilitarian sculpture which is too well crafted as pure artwork to dismissed as gimmicky or effete."

Top Left: *Meditation* , painted steel, 58" x 29" x 28 ¾"H
Middle Left: *Tranquillity II*, bronze, 13" x 28 ¾"H
Bottom Left: *Dancers*, bronze, 34" x 29"H
Top Right: *Friendship Bench*, bronze, 42" x 28" x 47"H
Bottom Right: *Sun Girl*, steel, 82" x 19" x 25"H

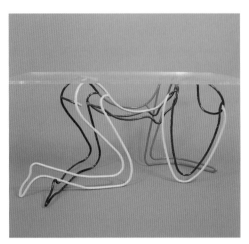

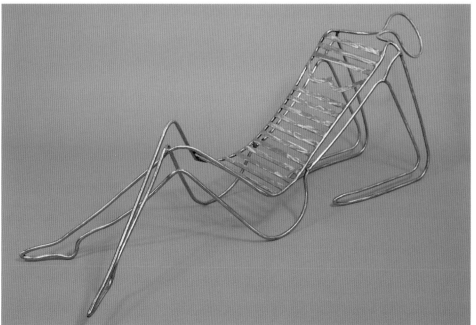

Marsha Lega

Marsha Lega Studio
1819 N. Center Street
Joliet, IL 60435
(815) 727-5255
FAX (815) 727-5255-*0

Marsha Lega's furniture bridges the gap from functional to sculptural. Her interest in metal began with a Master's Degree in three-dimensional design and her work as a jewelry designer.

She loves the stability of metal and the intrinsic beauty that waits inside ready to be translated into many needs. She believes that the beauty of metal is a door to good design. Her interests in furniture, sculpture, functional artifacts and jewelry are all facets of one artist's work. Marsha Lega's work funtions in both residential and corporate settings.

Selling her work nationwide through galleries, shows and designers, Lega has exhibited both nationally and internationally. Custom orders are welcomed. A catalogue is available.

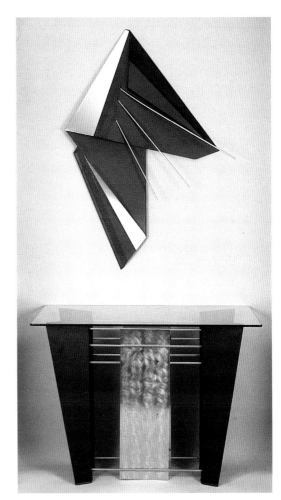

George F. Martell

Martell's Metal Works
36 Maple Avenue
Seekonk, MA 02771
(508) 761-9130

Designer metalsmith, George F. Martell, displays his creativity in a wide variety of forms: furniture, accessories, aviaries, room dividers, weathervanes and more. He collaborates with designers, architects, individuals, and corporations to create one-of-a-kind and limited-edition pieces. His own designs range from old world styling to contemporary to whimsical. Yet Martell's work is clearly recognizable for both design and craftsmanship.

Top: *Newburyport Rose*, oval dining table, polished steel with brass roses, 36" x 48" base for 48" x 60" glass top
Middle: *Woodland Rose*, cocktail table, black lacquered steel, brass wild roses, steel vine painted Verde, walnut top, 24" x 48". The hand-raised brass bowl contains forged steel fruit and vegetables, painted with acrylic.
Bottom: Child's Sleigh features hand forged steel bells and runners with a maple deck. Numbered limited edition.

Doug Weigel

P.O. Box 92408
Albuquerque, NM 87199-2408
(505) 821-6600

Weigel designs and produces in steel two and three-dimensional sculptures and furniture. Styles include Southwestern, Western, art-deco and client-commissioned ideas.

Allow four to eight weeks from design approval and contract to completion. Shipping and handling, FOB Albuquerque.

Selected commissions include the collection of President George Bush, Petrified National Forest, Scottsdale Airport, Sandia Laboratories, and the Hyatt Aruba.

Top: Steel Petroglyph and Glass Coffee Table, 1992, 18"H x 36"W x 36"D
Bottom: *Steel Petroglyph Bench with Navajo Rug,* 1992, 24"H x 36"W x 16"D

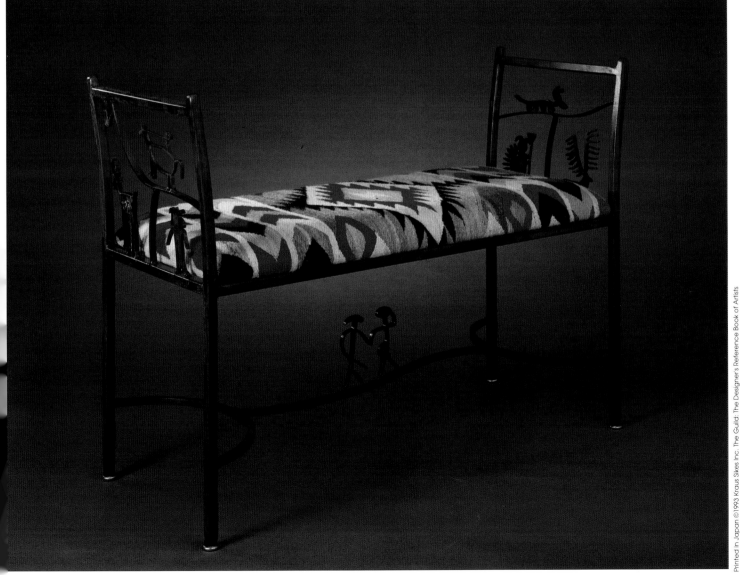

Printed in Japan ©1993 Kraus Sikes Inc. The Guild: The Designer's Reference Book of Artists

A Conversation with
Kevin Earley

Kevin Earley is a furniture maker in Madison, Wisconsin whose work is distinguished by the use of inlays and the reliance on veneers.

Where do you find the wood you use?

Much of it comes from local lumberyards that stock native hardwood. Veneers come by mail from all over the world. I did one project with English sycamore. Another project used birds-eye maple veneer from northern Wisconsin. The wood comes as flitches, sequentially cut layers of veneer in a stack or bundle.

I don't use very much tropical wood. Native hardwoods have grains and features that are just as interesting without being environmentally questionable. Part of the reason for using veneer is that it is a way to conserve natural wood.

I have also begun recycling wood from old buildings. I have gotten very good cypress from some old wooden water towers. Old wooden tanks that were used in wine making are another source of vintage lumber.

Why do you use veneers?

There are aesthetic reasons for using veneers, of course, but there are also some very sound construction reasons. Solid-wood lumber tends to swell, shrink and warp as humidity changes. Substrate such as birch plywood or medium-density fiberboard is more stable. Casework made from veneered substrate is beautiful and retains its shape.

Most importantly for me, I use a variety of veneers for inlay, and I am now using dyes and paint as accents as well. I use inlay to bring color and liveliness to a piece.

How do you design a piece for a client?

I talk to the client about their functional needs and look at the physical space in the room. I also look at the other furniture in the room. Beyond the functional considerations, I try to determine what my client expects from the process itself. I like someone with definite ideas about what they want but who is flexible enough to permit some experimentation. Most people like the idea of having something special made for them by an artist.

Larry Benjamin

The Glass Silo
215 Glen Ridge Road
Tobyhanna, PA 18466
(717) 894-9001

Larry Benjamin designs and creates a wide variety of sculptural furniture, lighting and accessories using techniques he developed for texturing, laminating and sandblasting heavy glass.

He specializes in limited-edition and commissioned work for residential and corporate applications.

Top: End table, laminated glass,
    26" x 20" x 24"
Bottom: Cocktail table, multi-level
    laminated-glass, 54" x 48" x 17"

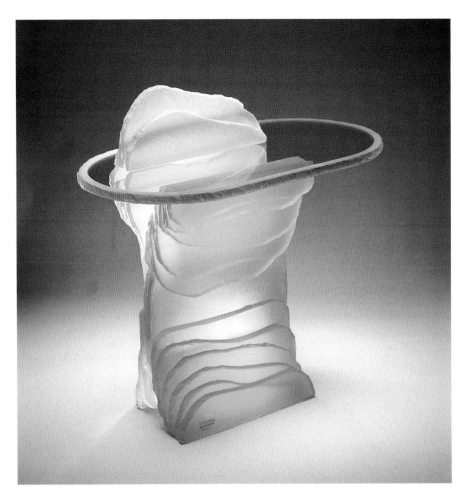

John Blazy

John Blazy Designs
P.O. Box 364
11729 Peckham Avenue
Hiram, OH 44234
(216) 569-7134

Using a vast array of visual references and design influences, from cooling fins on engines to Oriental architecture, John Blazy creates limited production furniture using wood, glass and man-made materials to exactly fulfill the vision of the client/designer.

John will be glad to collaborate with design professionals on work normally installed within one to two months.

Top: *The Orient Goes Modern*, ebonized oak, 60" x 19" x 17"
Bottom: *Crimson Tunnel Syndrome*, neon, walnut veneers, ABS pipe, mirrors and melamine, 43"Dia x 18"
Inset: *Crimson Tunnel Syndrome*, overhead view shows inter-reflective effect of neon and mirror

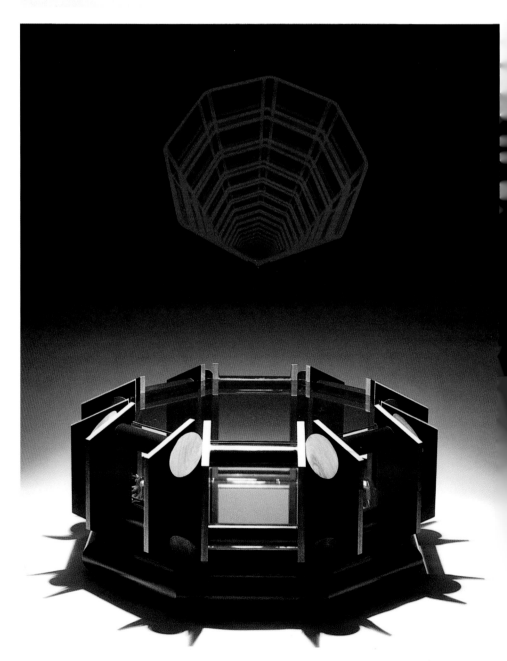

Larry Raymond Brown

5201 Aveneida Del Mare
Sarasota, FL 34242
(813) 364-8099

Unrestricted movement and dynamic balance are two concepts that describe Larry Brown's work. Ethereal forms that move in space, attempting to defy the essence of function, these pieces are made to stand alone as sculpture.

A graduate of R. Buckminster Fuller's School of Design, Southern Illinois University, Brown has spent the last 18 years producing works that are represented in both public and private collections.

Using solid hardwoods that have been carefully stack laminated and precisely carved to shape, the signed pieces are meticulously finished. One-of-a-kind and limited-edition pieces are available.

Designs range from unique tables to individual artistic pieces specifically created for the client. Comfortable working with designers, architects and clients, the artist welcomes collaborative projects in both private and commercial applications.

Slide portfolio available on request.

Carlton Cook

1715 West 26th
Houston, TX 77008
(713) 880-1122
(713) 880-5744

Carlton Cook uses unique solutions, unusual detailing and various materials in producing his work. He has been producing furniture for 20 years and offers complete design, fabrication, finishing and installation services.

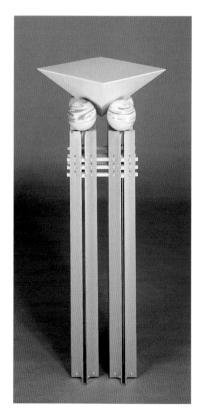

Joseph I. Galván

Joseph Galván Studio
3533 Kelton Avenue
Los Angeles, CA 90034
(310) 390-7940
FAX (310) 391-0961

A sculptor and designer for nearly 20 years, Joseph Galván conceives and executes art objects and sculptural furniture in acrylic and mixed media. Joseph Galván's creations are inspired by the enduring beauty of Rene Lalique's artistry and are characterized by luminosity, exquisitely detailed handcarved motifs and unparalleled craftsmanship. (See Lighting section for more of Galván's work.)

Joseph Galván welcomes challenging requests from architects, designers and gallery owners for one-of-a-kind commissions and limited editions for furniture, screens, architectural installations, sculpture, or recognition awards for corporate and residential clients.

Brochure and information available upon request.

Victoria, console table, handcarved design in acrylic, neon lighted, 60"W x 34"H x 18"D

Marine Serenity, handcarved acrylic screen and dining table, both neon lighted; dolphin chairs in ¾" acrylic

Johanna Okovic Goodman

Goodman Associates, Inc.
718 S. 22nd Street
Philadelphia, PA 19146-1105
(215) 546-1448
(215) 546-8048

"Chairs designed to upgrade craft to the status of Art," London Independent, June 1, 1992.

Goodman's innovative, sculptural chairs are show stoppers. She was trained as a fine artist and her chairs combine both painting and sculpture. Real clothes, fabric, stuffed leather, and acrylic transform the chair into a witty sculpture. The integrity of the chair is kept intact.

Clients delight in the way Goodman's chairs take art off the walls. Stars, famous or historical figures, or clothing chairs add humor to the home decor.

Johanna Okovic Goodman works directly with clients and is also represented by galleries across the country.

Top Left: *Marie Antoinette*, 1992, red dress, stuffed arms, acrylic on found wooden chair, functional chair

Top Right: *Bill Clinton*, 1992, real suit and tie, painted leather head, collection of President Clinton

Bottom Left: *Gold Tux*, 1991, real suit and tie, gold powder, polyurethane, on found wooden chair

Bottom Right: *Toga*, 1991, fabric, wood, acrylic on found wooden chair

Greg Sheres Studio

Gregory D. Sheres
P.O. Box 2409
Coeur d'Alene, ID 83816
(208) 773-8180

Greg Sheres brings fine art to furniture. Experienced as a painter and sculptor, the artist designs and creates innovative furniture. Sheres is internationally renowned for his hand-painted granite and marble tables. All of these tables are done to the client's custom specifications. In addition, the artist is now designing a striking line of stainless-steel table bases accented with gold-plated brass. These sculptural pieces take glass tops.

Lead time is two to three months. A catalog is available.

Top: *Ponte d'Oro,* dining table base, polished stainless steel with gold-plated brass ribbons,
Bottom: Blue pearl granite dining table on stainless-steel base, 10' x 5'

Joan Irving

Joan Irving Glass Design
710 13th Street #216
San Diego, CA 92101
(619) 232-3007
FAX (619) 232-3046

Joan Irving has been creating unique and contemporary glass sculptures, furniture and accessories since 1978. She is recognized as an inventor in technique, concept and design. Her work is extensively exhibited and collected internationally, and is included in the permanent collection of the Corning Museum of Glass. She received the 1989 American Craft Awards grand prize for functional art. Joan Irving continues to break ground in the 90's with bold, new functional and sculptural works that explode with color and imagery.

Spiral, circle accent table, 20"H x 19"Dia

Console table, 30"H x 47"W x 16"D

Slateworks

Christina
P.O. Box 77
Cave Junction, OR 97523
(503) 592-3867

Natural, enduring slate serves as the canvas for Christina's carving, which artfully blends sculptural beauty with architectural function. Her one-of-a-kind stone creations range from lustrous patio and furniture inlays to elegant cornerstones, mantelpieces and wall hangings.

Pieces are based on the size, design, intricacy and finishing techniques.

Top: *Egyptian Figure*, black slate, 24"H x 16"W x 1"D

Bottom: *Calla Lillies*, coffee table inlay, three sections (18"H x 15"W each), in collaboration with woodworker Lance Logan

The Studio Furniture Movement

con't from page 129

The ascendance of Post Modernism during the '80s also had a huge impact on the second generation furniture makers. It not only brought a renewed appreciation of classical proportion and form to their work, but it opened up the whole vocabulary of art and design history to the modern artist/craftperson's interpretation.

This is not to say that the avant-garde impulse among furniture makers is dead. But, as Cooke states in his essay, by the early '80s in the worlds of art, architecture, design, music and literature, "The need to constantly invent an avant-garde position had become self-absorbed, circular, and, therefore, alienated from normal activity." The most successful work today fuses the rigorous technique of craft with the functional problem-solving approach of design and the intellectual and creative conceptualization of art.

When artists like George Nakashima, Art Carpenter and Sam Maloof began exhibiting their designs in the late '40s and early '50s, the buying public was not thinking about furniture as art. The importance of the academic landscape during the '60s and '70s cannot be understated. Places like Boston University's Program in Artistry, the Rochester Institute of Technology, and the Rhode Island School of Design changed the conceptual development of studio furniture in America. Also in the 1970s, museums began acquiring and exhibiting studio furniture, and galleries began to specialize in it as the commercial value of the work became apparent. Places like Workbench Gallery (New York), Pritam & Eames (East Hampton, NY) and Snyderman Gallery (Philadelphia) can be credited with vigorously promoting the furniture of the emerging movement among the art-buying public and, with adding momentum to the movement's growth.

The prosperity of the 1980s brought a whole new dimension to studio furniture. People began to travel and see the work of Italian, Scandinavian and Japanese furniture designers which made the mature American work — with its clean, classic lines and solid construction — seem comfortable and familiar. The sophistication of American studio furniture appealed to what these consumers perceived to be their own newly acquired sophistication and worldliness.

Marianne McNamara, director of the International Contemporary Furniture Fair (ICFF), which has become one of the most influential commercial venues for furniture makers who seek larger markets, admits, "One of the things that made it easier for us to set up ICFF in 1989 is that more and more Americans were going to the fairs in Europe and were being exposed to the type of furniture that they couldn't see here because there was no commercial arena to see it in." And Ilene Shaw, a design consultant who was instrumental in creating the concept behind ICFF, points out that one of the main reasons for the creation of the show was to give these emerging furniture makers a voice to effect change in the sedentary world of American commercial furniture design. (ICFF, now in its fifth year, showcases work that is about 40 percent one-of-a-kind or limited-production.)

Whereas the Arts and Crafts movement arose as a well-defined social and philosophical force, the modern studio furniture movement is highly idiosyncratic — for most, a very personal solitary pursuit.

These are the antiques of tomorrow, as prized for their beauty as they are for the way they changed cultural and aesthetic attitudes at every level of art and design.

Visibility — in museum exhibitions, design magazines, galleries — gave the American furniture-buying public a new way to see the work of the second, and by now an emerging third, generation of American furniture makers. But there were several other social factors that conspired to enhance the allure of American studio furniture. Primarily, the materialism and excess of the '80s made it clear that Americans had lost their connection to what was really important. Even worse, the belief that technology would improve our quality of life suddenly seemed more the cause for the erosion of that quality than its betterment.

This manifested itself in a desire to reconnect with the earth and with products that did not exploit it. A rejection of industrialism gave way to a yearning for something machines could not offer —beautifully detailed handwork. Like the initiators of the Arts and Crafts movement at the turn of the century, many modern furniture makers believe in the virtue of the craftsperson's lifestyle. But there the similarity ends. Whereas the Arts and Crafts movement arose as a well-defined social and philiosophical force, the modern studio furniture movement is highly idiosyncratic — for most, a very personal, solitary pursuit. And collectors buy the work precisely because of its individualism.

People are looking for a product that's not just functional, but that also hits an emotional chord," explains Shaw. Studio furniture "gives us a sense of humanity because it is handmade. But, also, you're buying a piece of an artist — that person's craft, that person's touch, that artist's vision, point of view and expression. And that's what

you get from art. You get an emotional, as well as an aesthetic, punch."

The new political climate that we have entered in 1993 holds great promise for studio furniture makers. As the society continues to reassess the "traditional values" that were touted as idyllic in the '80s, its aesthetic appreciation is bound to evolve as well.

"Socially, I think on a global scale there's a lot of change taking place," adds Gary Upton, another furniture maker. "People are taking a look again at their perceptions. They're questioning those perceptions politically, environmentally, in terms of design."

Whatever the future holds in terms of new designers however, it seems clear that studio furniture has definitely passed a point of no return. It is evident not only in the prices it commands, but also in the general acknowledgment that it is an art form unto itself. It does not need to be compared in any way to painting and sculpture or even to other traditional craft media like clay and glass. And, now that it has reached aesthetic independence, studio furniture's place as an art historical movement will continue to fuel the market, increasing the work's monetary and emotional value. These are the antiques of tomorrow, as prized for their beauty as they are for the way they changed cultural and aesthetic attitudes at every level of art and design. ◆

Susan J. Brasch

S. J. Brasch Studio
719 P Street #9
Haymarket District
Lincoln, NE 68508
(402) 474-4080

Using birch hollow-core doors these folding
screens are cut to size, carefully finished,
and painted with acrylic or oil paint to suit
the client. A special feature is the innovative
double-acting canvas hinge countersunk
into the sides and painted so the motif is
continuous.

The standard is 5'8" in height with (three to
seven) 18" panels, however, different sizes
are available. Designs other than gardens
are also available. Please inquire.

Commissions welcomed.

Top: *Treehouse*, 4-panel screen, acrylic
Bottom: *Geske Garden*, 5-panel screen

Uli Kuess

Uli Kuess Studio
2106 Flamingo Drive
San Antonio, TX 78209
(210) 826-3013
FAX (210) 826-0997

Uli Kuess' commitment to quality craftsmanship and her vast array of designs and specialty effects are evident in commissions from many private and public clients.

This European-trained artist has 15 years of experience in the field of painted furniture, frescos, large-scale murals, trompe l'oeil and architectural decorative painting.

She has command of all styles and periods and her expertise encompasses all of the decorative painting techniques, including marbleizing, glazing, graining, ragging, gilding and grisaille.

Uli Kuess has successfully collaborated with individual clients, designers and architects to produce the finest quality pieces available today. Please call for additional information and a portfolio.

Fiorenza, table top, Faux Pietra Dura painting, 72"Dia

Granada, handcarved and painted headboard

Palladian Screen, 1990, fresco finish on wood panels, 7' x 12'

Christian Thee

49 Old Stagecoach Road
Weston, CT 06883
(203) 454-0340

Using his talents as a theatrical designer, Christian Thee has focused his talents towards residential trompe l'oeil, hotel and restaurant murals as well as fine art for galleries.

A brochure is available upon request and project discussion is invited. Clients include: Trump's Taj Mahal Hotel and Casino, Atlantic City; Buccelatti Jewelers; Tiffany and Co. and Bergdorf Goodman's, NYC; Merridien and Hilton Hotels; The Spoleto Festival USA and the Joan Rivers residence.

Top: *Midieval Mouse*, created for Tiffany and Co.
Bottom Left/Right: *Space Bridge's 11 and 12*, This name refers to the combining of two-dimensional paintings with three-dimensional objects, creating functional tromp l'oeil.
Opposite Page: A trio of screens, inspired by French terra-cotta garden sculpture, created for Bergdorf Goodman NYC

Christian Thee, 49 Old Stagecoach Road, Weston, CT, (203) 454-0340

ACCESSORIES

Contemporary artists who create textiles, floor coverings, lighting, sculpture and objects have found the last decade to be an immensely exciting and gratifying period in their professional lives. They have been inspired by the new appreciation for their crafts as art, and by a growing market for art in corporate spaces.

An artist who creates turned wood vessels says that this area is one of many that have gained new status in recent years. Once deemed pure craft, it has in the last five years been elevated to art. Likewise, glass has gained new stature and baskets are in increasing demand in art circles. We are also witnessing a new wave of artists working in neon, metal, wood, stone and textiles. Curators of museums around the country are seeking them out, and this new exposure continues to enhance their visibility and popularity among the art-buying public.

Many traditional crafts are also getting a new look. One of THE GUILD's rug makers talks about using new tools and materials to revitalize an old craft. She is free in today's design movement to make bold personal statements, because designers, and art lovers in general, are looking for something special.

If you're furnishing an existing space, commissioning custom-made art means finding an uncompromising match for your needs. Clients won't have to alter their colors, space, lighting or materials to fit the work; these artists specialize in making their creations fit the space. Most offer not only a portfolio of their work but will accommodate clients with drawings, color renditions, samples of materials, even models. It's the zenith of custom design.

These are artists who know the art of give and take; artists who choose to work with interior designers and art consultants because they enjoy the synergy generated by the collaborative process.

Designers benefit in extra ways when they bring an artist into the process before all the details of a building project or renovation are settled. It is at this point that spaces can be designed with the art in mind. Accessories can become dynamic focal points, animating a room, and elevating its aesthetic quality.

Designers find that working with these savvy, immensely talented, professional artists is extremely satisfying. They can be counted on not only to present solutions to design problems, but to do it on time and within the budget.

From hand-woven rugs to candlesticks and vases, freestanding sculptures, baskets and ceramic vessels, the work in this section resonates with today's design freedom—new images, new language and new ideas. Individualization and personalization have become not only acceptable by desirable.

ACCESSORIES

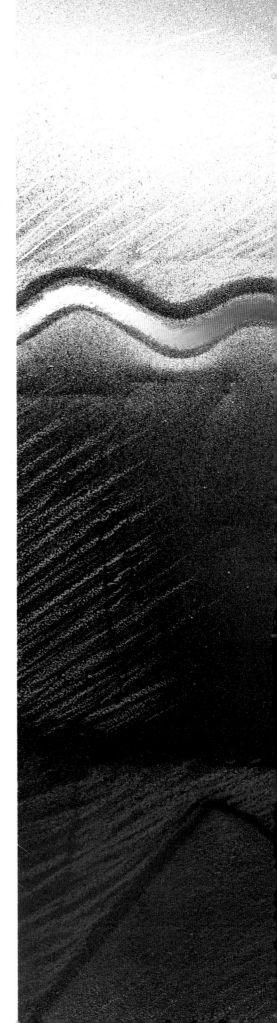

Bob Brown
Judy Dykstra-Brown

Brown Studio
1060 Nina Court
Boulder Creek, CA 95006
(408) 338-7505

Bob Brown and Judy Dykstra-Brown strive for a fusion of nature and function in one-of-a-kind lamps and ikebana vases that express a quiet, elegant simplicity. A sculptor for 30 years, Bob Brown works with hand carving tools as well as the oil and water cooled diamond saws, grinders and core drills required for working the granite river boulders that are an integral part of their art. Judy Dykstra-Brown, a jeweler with wide experience of many world cultures, collaborates in the designs, adds embellishments, and builds lamp shades when necessary. Each piece they create is unique.

A portfolio of currently available pieces will be mailed for a small fee which is refundable with a purchase.

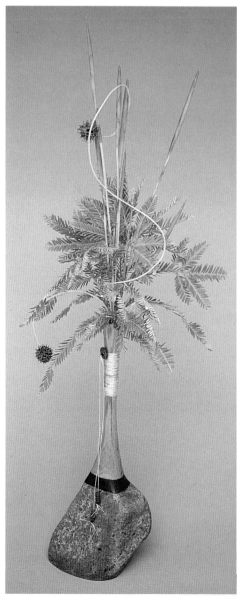

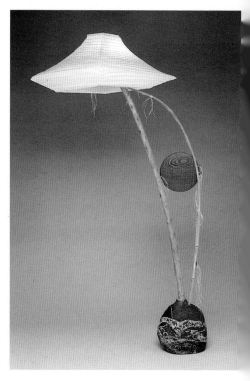

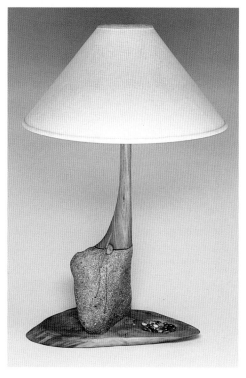

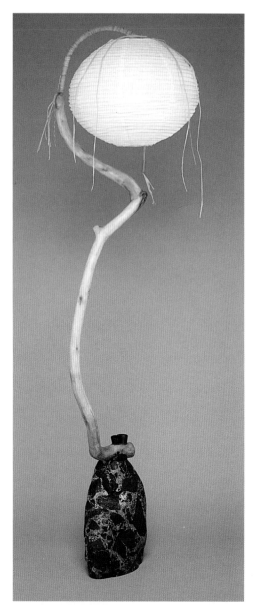

Christopher Thomson Ironworks

P.O. Box 578
Ribera, NM 87560
(505) 421-2645
FAX (505) 421-2618

Christopher designs home furnishings and creates them directly in steel with hand-forging techniques. Steel is heated in the forge to red-hot, then the pliable steel is hammered into the desired shape. These elegant furnishings, pictured here, complement various decor. Full catalogue and video are available for $15.

At Christopher's studio, larger architectural works can be executed. Recent projects include the Red Sage Restaurant in Washington, D.C. and the Seret and Sons Galleries in Santa Fe.

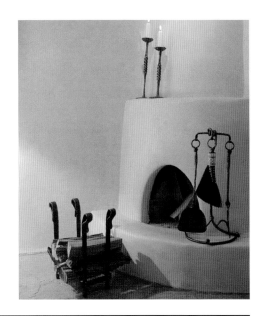

Joseph I. Galván

Joseph Galván Studio
3533 Kelton Avenue
Los Angeles, CA 90034
(310) 390-7940
FAX (310) 391-0961

Our sculptural lighting is inspired by love of ancient art and the influence of Frank Lloyd Wright. These designs harmonize traditional and contemporary media—art glass and acrylic—and are a collaborative invention of master glass artist John Michael Citrino, who brings 20 years of experience to crafting each shade, and sculptor Joseph Galván, who, for more than 18 years, has created acrylic sculpture and art furniture . (See Furniture section for more of Glaváns work.)

Art glass is American-made and selected for its richness of color, texture and iridescence. Copper-foil and soldering techniques insure strength and elegance. Columns are fabricated of crystal-clear Plexiglass and feature handcarving that complements the glass shade. Bases are of black acrylic (also available in Corian colors).

For dramatic indirect lighting two sources of illumination are incorporated. Halogen quartz is used in the shade and incandescent lighting in base, with our patented 'invisible' wiring from base to shade.

More information is available on request.

Magnifica, floor lamp, 26"W x 67"H;   *Columna*, table lamp, 10"W x 40"H;   *Columna*, floor lamp, 10"W x 72"H

Brian McNally

3236 Calle Pinon
Santa Barbara, CA 93105
(805) 687-7212

Brian McNally, an MFA graduate of the Rhode Island School of Design, has been working at his Santa Barbara studio since 1976. Using the finest rolled glass and original designs he creates one-of-a-kind pieces for corporate and private clients. In addition to his original work he does design consulting and restoration.

Areas of Specialty: scenic windows, doors and entryways, screens and dividers, skylights, lighting and view enhancements.

Top: Tulip shade on Japanese bronze base, 1991, copperfoil technique, 20"D x 20"H
Bottom: Magnolia screen, 1990, mahogany frame, copperfoil technique, 52"W x 68"H

Photo: Bruce Burkhardt

Cathy Richardson

Nature's Image Studio
1201 Airport Road, Suite D
Ames, IA 50010
(515) 232-4529

Cathy Richardson combines a flair for contemporary images with traditional fine craftsmanship to create colorful and dynamic work in glass. Her lamps contain strong moving forms in colored glass, combined with precise and delicate etched or painted areas. Special handblown glass, faceted jewels or bevels are often used to create stunning surface effects.

Richardson also makes fine stained or etched glass screens (see page 158 in *THE GUILD 7: Designer's Reference*), leaded windows, etched and carved bowls and vases, and other sculptural items.

Commissions are welcomed. Richardson is happy to work with other artists and design professionals.

Left: cylindrical lamp, 7" x 7" x 13"
Right: cylindrical lamp, 8 ½" x 8 ½" x 15"

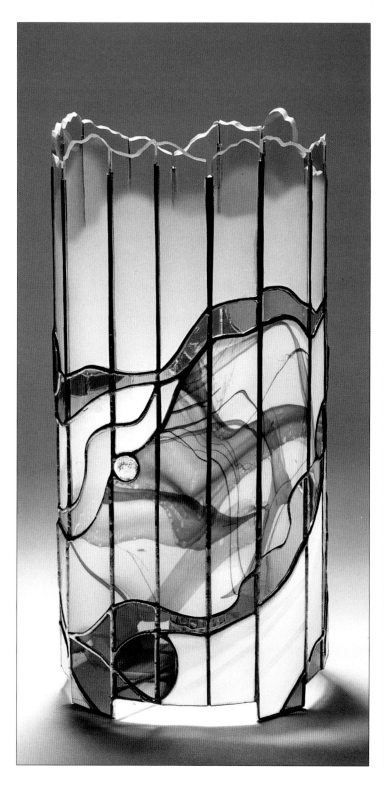

Bruce Siegel

ILLUMIN8
3332 N. Humboldt Boulevard
Milwaukee, WI 53212
(414) 964-7336

Bruce Siegel has been producing unique 'Prairiental' lighting and furniture since 1976. His attention to detail and materials incorporate the use of Japanese laminated papers which are not only strong but retain the look of handmade paper. Siegel's limited-edition and custom work can be seen in the Frank Lloyd Wright designed Wingspread Conference Center and *Design Book 6*.

Limited-edition pieces and site-specific design are available. Please call or write for additional information.

Angelika Traylor

100 Poinciana Drive
Indian Harbour Beach, FL 32937
(407) 773-7640

Specializing in one-of-a-kind lamps, autonomous panels and architectural designs, Traylor's award-winning work can be recognized by its intricate, jewel-like composition.

This exquisite lamp and charming autonomous panel (shown) reflect an original and intensive design process implemented with meticulous craftsmanship and an unusually beautiful selection of glass.

Traylor's attention to detail and vibrant colors have resulted in her work being eagerly sought by collectors.

Please inquire for more specific information on available work, commissions and pricing.

A Conversation with
Angelika Traylor
Angelika Traylor makes leaded glass
in her Florida studio

How does living in Florida influence your work?

Most of my inspiration comes directly from the flowers and trees that surround my home and studio. In the morning, I will take a pad of paper and colored pencils to my garden or neighboring parks to sketch a new flower or palm frond. Back in the studio, I make a second drawing, incorporating the imagery of my initial sketch. It is then time to select and form the glass I will use.

I start with pieces of hand-rolled, colored glass. But that is only the beginning. To obtain the variety of color and shape I need to recreate the beauty of a flower, I enamel the glass, fuse pieces of glass together, refire glass with thin strands of glass of a different color, or slump the glass over a mold to achieve a desired form or contour. Only then are the pieces ready to be hand-cut, foiled, and soldered into a shade or window.

Could you describe the type of work you do?

Lamps and panels make up the greatest portion of my work, although I find that the portion of each varies from year to year. Generally, I avoid very large commissions, and my largest panels are almost never bigger than 6 feet by 8 feet. I never do reproductions, and I refer those inquiries to other artists. Most of the imagery I use is botanical or from nature.

How do you sell your work?

I sell most of my work directly to clients, and client referrals have been important to me. I also try to take in several fine craft shows each year, but I favor the retail rather than wholesale shows. Acquiring my leaded glass is a lot like acquiring an oriental rug. It is a very personal acquisition.

Marjorie Atwood

First Hand Studio
11 East Brady
Tulsa, OK 74103
(918) 583-0886
(800) 484-9174 PIN# 5096

Trained in faux finishes in New York and
San Francisco, Marjorie Atwood creates
distinctive floor and wall art that is meticulously crafted using high-quality paints and
various metal finishes, including gold and
silver leaf. A protective sealer ensures easy
cleaning, maintenance and durability.

Commissions and collaborations are
welcome. Designs can complement fabrics,
wallpaper and artwork. Any size or shape is
available. Atwood has had solo shows in
California and her work has appeared in
several national publications.

Prices and slides are available.

Carl T. Chew

Mia Gallery
536 First Avenue S
Seattle, WA 98104
(206) 467-8283

Carl Chew's love of textiles and his desire to create a new kind of work from his computer graphics led him to Kathmandu; where in 1983 he began making luxurious rugs. He now collaborates with weavers in his own factory to produce these magical pieces.

The rugs are handwoven from colorfast woolen yarn, and are available in limited editions or as commissions.

Carl Chew's rugs reside on the floors of private homes, and in numerous public and corporate collections.

Top: *Zena Sees a Hoopoe*, 1992, wool rug,
  6 ½' x 9 ½'
Bottom: *Koi 8*, 1992, wool rug, edition of 10,
  9 ½' x 14'

Susan Eileen Burnes

6980 Mill Road
Brecksville, OH 44141
(216) 838-5955

Inspired by artifacts of other ages and cultures, Susan Burnes interprets their features into today's decorative accents. Her enchanting creations embody the artistry and skills of three generations of needlewomen.

These refreshing and unexpected compositions of color and pattern may be crafted in needlepoint or in counted thread embroidery, utilizing fine wool, silk or cotton fibers.

Completed works are available and commission inquiries are welcome.

Design patterns and materials may be furnished for clients interested in completing the needlework project themselves.

Natalie Darmohraj

Natalka Designs
P.O. Box 40309
Providence, RI 02940
(401) 351-8841

From luxurious hand-dyed, handwoven blankets to sophisticated upholstery and drapery, Natalie Darmohraj's unique fabrics enrich any interior space.

Using the finest fibers, including wool, silk and mohair, the artist creates abstract images and patterns through the juxtaposition of textures and colors. Fabrics are suitable for both functional use or hanging on the wall. They are designed for both durability and aesthetic appeal, appropriate for residential as well as commercial spaces. Commissions of all sizes are welcome.

Natalie Darmohraj holds a B.F.A. in Textile Design from Rhode Island School of Design.

For further information please contact the artist.

Photography: Cathy Carver

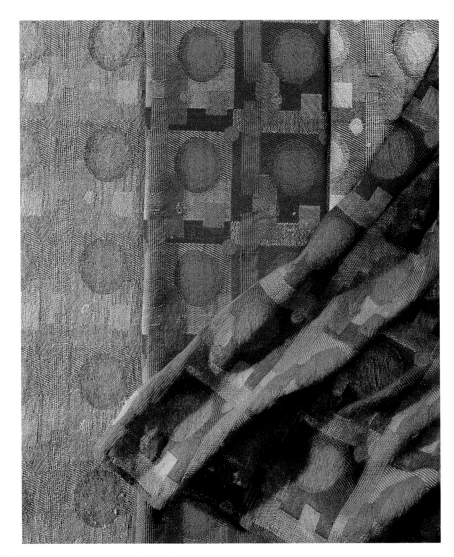

Sue Harmon

Sue Harmon Studios
2688 Brentwood Road
Columbus, OH 43209
(614) 231-9223

Sue Harmons' creative use of color and texture are captured in every one-of-a-kind, hand-knit designer throw. The unique combination of yarns, ribbons and metallic fibers, many imported and hand-dyed, always achieves an unusual and impressive work of art.

Sue Harmons' designs are considered "art for furniture" and will complement any and all interiors. Selected throws are being shown in designer showrooms across the country.

Sizes are approximately 48" x 78" with a 12" fringe. Harmon designs for specific settings and she welcomes collaborations. Private and corporate commissions are invited. A limited inventory is available. Brochures upon request.

Helio Graphics

Dawn Wilkins
P.O. Box 6213
Key West, FL 33041
(305) 294-7901

The vibrant colors and ambiance of the tropics are captured in the design work Dawn Wilkins has been creating professionally in Key West for more than 12 years.

Paintings, canvas pillows, floor cloths and canvas furniture are available for galleries and by custom order.

Using textile inks and acrylics handpainted with bristle brushes, vivid shading is emphasized with attention to detail. Works also incorporate graphic design and variations of ancient printing techniques. Pigments are permanent and pieces are cleanable.

Photos and prices are available upon request.

All photos: Deb Gilmore

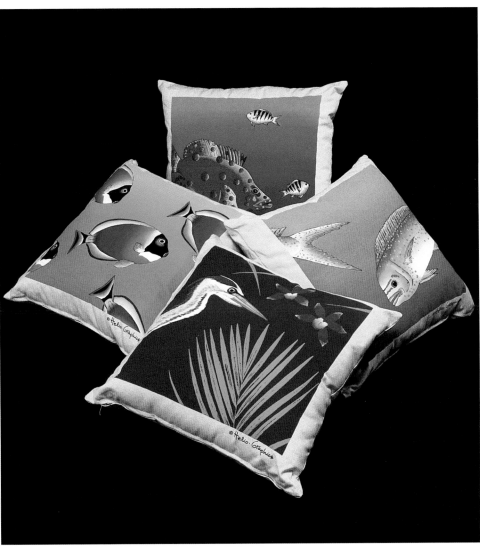

Assorted canvas pillows, 22" x 22"

Going Bananas, floor cloth, runner, 22" x 55"

Spotted Dolphin and Moons, painting, 34" x 45"

A Conversation with Gloria Crouse

Gloria Crouse works in the historic tradition of rug-hooking, but has added new techniques and materials to create a contemporary look and feel to her pieces.

How does your work fit into the history of textiles?

In the eighteenth and nineteenth centuries, warm and decorative rugs were needed to cover wooden plank floors. Farmers and village people alike made hooked rugs from recycled cloth. As cloth and rugs became cheaper, however, and everyone became relatively more wealthy, rug hooking nearly died out, like other textile skills. What I have tried to do is preserve the ethic of craftsmanship embodied in the hooked rug, but to make it contemporary by incorporating new materials and techniques.

Are your hooked rugs functional?

Some of my rugs using contemporary techniques have a much greater texture of pile than traditional hooked rugs, and are designed specifically for the wall. Others, however, are made for the floor and use materials and techniques that are very durable.

What are your ideas about color?

I love color! Some of my work is very colorful, with all the colors of the spectrum set next to each other. But I also like monochromatic work, and have done some pieces in all white, all black, or all gray. In that work, It is the texture of the fiber that becomes the exciting feature. I make these changes partly to achieve a fun-loving, creative spirit. Making transitions between color pathways, textural features, design concepts and materials keeps the work fresh and exciting.

How do you divide your work between commissions and made to sell?

Actually, I find that I am doing fewer commissions now than five or ten years ago. With the publication of Hooked Rugs: New Materials, New Techniques (a book by Crouse recently published by Taunton Press), I feel a strong obligation to promote the book and the art of rug hooking. I travel to workshops and lectures throughout North America. Much of my current hooking is either exper-imental, samples for workshops, or pieces intended for publication. So commissions have been limited to two or three a year. But these may be as large as 10' x 13'.

Boots Culbertson

Culbertson Pottery
4844 Brywill Circle
Sarasota, FL 34234
(813) 355-3604

Boots Culbertson's unique stoneware fountains bring special energy to any environment, indoors or out, corporate or residential. Elegant nature-inspired forms are animated by moving water, which adds the dimension of pleasant, peaceful sound. Fountains pictured here range from one- to four-feet tall.

Individually thrown and constructed, each fountain has a recirculating pump and is easy to maintain. Design, dimension and glazes are carefully combined to suit client and setting. All pieces are high-fired and very durable.

For more than 20 years Boots Culbertson has also designed and produced stoneware lamps, garden pieces and other accessories. Production time is four to eight weeks, depending on size and type of commission.

For further information, please contact the artist.

Linda Dixon
Drew Krouse

LDDK Studios
5741 Erect Road
Ramseur, NC 27316
(919) 879-4200
FAX (919) 879-4200
After 1993: (910) 879-4200

Linda Dixon and Drew Krouse produce contemporary architectural installations, commissioned sculpture and a collection of functional and decorative pottery. They combine their love for glaze, form and texture to interpret ancient forms in classical glaze colors.

Both artists are master-level craftsmen and terra cotta experts with a decade of experience in architectural restoration.

Wholesale inquiries are welcome.

Top: *Lizard Temple*, 1992, installed at Moffitt Mill House, N.C., terra cotta sculpture, 48"H
Bottom: pottery, 3" to 28"

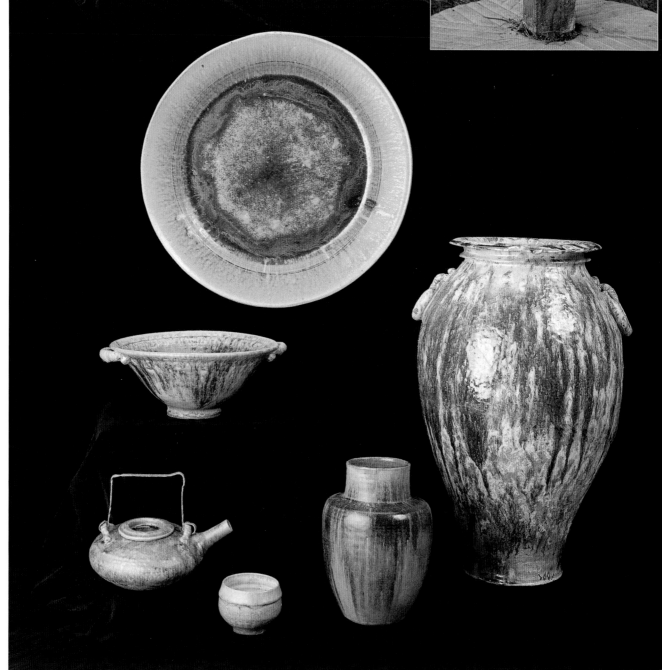

Edith A. Ehrlich

1070 Park Avenue
New York, NY 10128
(212) 534-0732

Influenced by the timelessness and symbolism of primitive art, Edith Ehrlich's ceramics invoke the same spirit of creativity that has existed since artisans began making objects essential to their well being. These objects relate to nature and to man's place in the universe.

Her particular interest is in the vessel as a container for anything, physical or spiritual. Often her work has a "dug up look". Often it portrays the eternal impulse to decorate, through surface incisions, adornment and color.

Her pieces, exhibited in museums and galleries, are also in many private collections. More examples can be seen through slides that are available upon request.

Top: *Lucifer I and Lucifer II*
Bottom: *Broom Sprouting Vessel*

Joshua Horn

225 W. 34th Street
New York, NY 10122
(212) 594-1150
FAX (212) 695-4581

Joshua Horn's work is from his "D.R. Arizona Series". The work is meant to be direct and strong, but yet, still impart simplicity and beauty without compromising the integral beauty in the clay.

In six years of working with clay, he has had the honor of working with several internationally ranked artists. In addition, Joshua Horn has to his credit several public commissions and inclusions in private collections. Information regarding commissions, prices, and slides are available upon request.

Right: *The Four Elements, Earth Wind Fire Water*, 32" x 20" x 2"

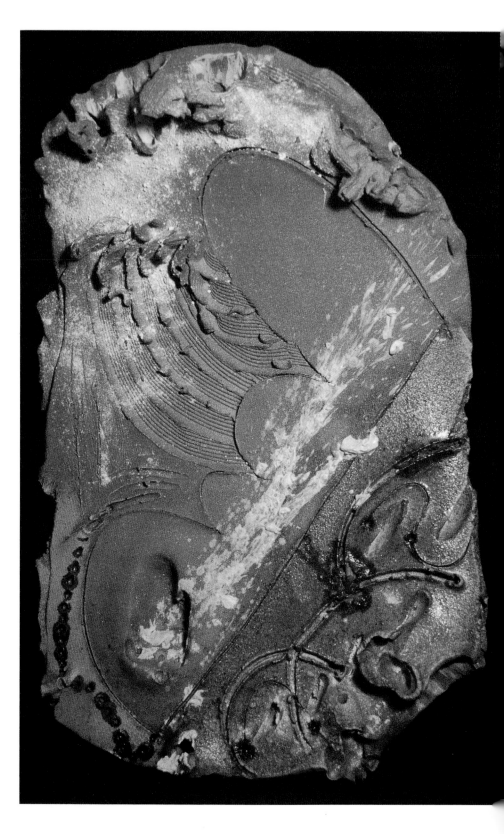

Claudia Hollister

1314 NW Irving Street #206
Portland, OR 97209
(503) 228-7648
FAX (503) 226-0429

Known for their vibrant color and whimsy, Claudia Hollister's hand-built vessels and teapots are created from inlaid, colored porcelain. Limited hand-painting enhance the surfaces that are made tactile by embossing. The richly patterned pieces have glazed interiors and selectively glazed exteriors. Delicate in scale but bold in presence, these limited-edition collections range in height from 8" to 12".

Claudia's new work includes framed, miniature-scale porcelain stamps created as intricate variations on her original technique.

Price list and slides are available upon request.

Top Left: *Still Lifes*, 1993, wallpiece, inlaid colored porcelain, frame 8" sq., stamps vary from 1 ¼" x 1 ¾" up to 2 ¾" x 4"

Top Right: *Enchanted Evening*, 1993, teapot, hand-built colored porcelain, 9"H x 9"W x 1"D

Bottom: *Still Lifes*, 1993, teapot, vase and pitcher, hand-built colored inlaid porcelain, 9"H x 9"H x 1"D, 11"H x 11"W x 2"D, 10H x 8"W x 1"D

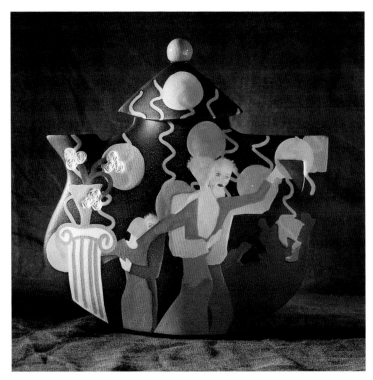

Tom Neugebauer

RD 2 Box 8990 Sawkill Road
Milford, PA 18337
(717) 296-6901

"Movement of forms in space...the motion of spirit in growth."

Tom Neugebauer's sculpture is widely exhibited and is represented in many private and corporate collections. He produces one-of-a-kind and limited-edition works, and he invites cooperative efforts with designers, architects, or individual clients for site-specific commissions (indoor or outdoor). The scale of his sculpture ranges from intimate pieces for the home collection to those suitable for office and corporate settings.

Although he produces sculptures in both clay and metal, he is known for his unique combination of the two media, frequently drawing inspiration from the human form, and often emphasizing dynamic, dance-like movement.

Additional information, slides or photos are available on request.

Top Left: *Lifedance II*, from a series, private collection, brushed steel (lacquered) and clay, 48"H x 22"Dia base

Right: *At the Center is Strength*, 1992, Marsh Co., Belleville, IL, steel (ground, lacquered) and clay, 28"H x 16"W x 14"D, variations available 2' to 10'

Bottom Left: *The Appeal II*, from a series, 1992, private collection, clay and copper (ground and lacquered), 38"H x 20"W x 14"D

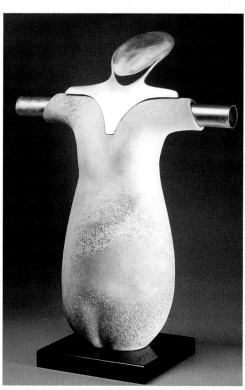

Charles Pearson
Timothy Roeder

Whitehead Street Pottery
1011 Whitehead Street
Key West, FL 33040
(305) 294-5067

Charles Pearson and Timothy Roeder collaborate to produce large hand-thrown and slab-built Raku-fired vessels.

The forms have a visual strength that demands a response while maintaining the traditional subtleties of color by reduction in a post-firing of seaweed.

Commissions include the Southern Progress Corporation, Rath Manufacturing Co., Inc., Demille Corporation, and various other public sites.

Slides ($3 refundable) and additional information can be obtained by writing directly to their studio.

Represented by:
The Signature Shop and Gallery, Atlanta, GA
Acropolis Now, Santa Monica, CA
The Red Lion Gallery, Vero Beach, FL
The Bell Gallery of Fine Art, Memphis, TN

Top: *Monolith #32*, 1992, Raku-fired clay,
  14"W x 5"D x 19"H
Bottom: *Rose Snapper*, 1992, Raku-fired clay,
  18"W x 14"D x 19"H

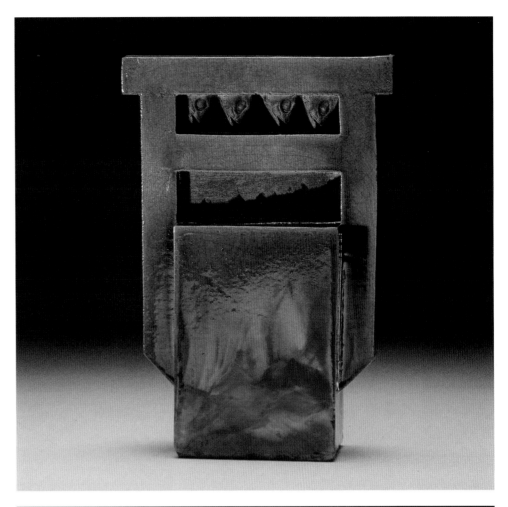

Betsy Ross

1160 Fifth Avenue
New York, NY 10029
(212) 722-5535
(914) 679-7964

Betsy Ross' earthenware vessels incorporate wheel-thrown and hand-built components. Her forms evoke traditional feelings, combined with a modern alternative to glazing. The surfaces are embellished with lusters, creating rich metallic-like patinas.

Complementing her larger vessels, 24"-29"H (Bottom) are a series of mini-vessels, 3"-6 ½"H (Top), which maintain the same infinite attention to detail.

Her works are exhibited in galleries throughout the United States and are represented in the Far East. She continues to enjoy collaborating with architects and designers in creating site-specific commissions.

Linda Bruce Salomon

Librus Studio
3920 Country View Drive
Sarasota, FL 34233
(813) 921-5421
FAX (813) 922-2367

Enchanting ceramic creatures serve a double purpose. As figurines on vessels they are functional as jars, vases, decanters and bowls. At the same time they are sculptural pieces to be appreciated as fine art and as an important detail in interior design.

Porcelain animal dolls have rich fabric, leather or beaded bodies. Each comes with its own accessories such as a chair, table, instrument, game, mirror, clock or box. Each one creates a scene. Dolls range in size from 10" to 30".

Lois S. Sattler

3620 Pacific Avenue
Marina Del Rey, CA 90292
(310) 821-7055
FAX (310) 305-9229

In the past two years Lois Sattler has collaborated with a metal artist, Stephen Thompson. Together they have designed and produced large wall pieces, wall sconces, screens, and free standing containers. All work is one of a kind and can be custom ordered. There is no limit to size or color.

Lois Sattler's work is handbuilt and sculptural in form. Her work appears in design studios and galleries throughout the United States and she has clients in Canada and Europe. Sattler's work can also be seen in THE GUILD 2, 3, 4 and 6.

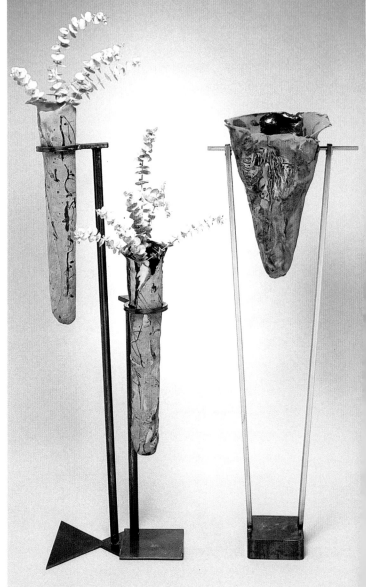

Robert C. Shenfeld

5093 Skyline Drive
Syracuse, NY 13215
(315) 492-0702

Robert Shenfeld's ceramic vessels are wheel-thrown, some with hand-built lids. His recent work incorporates rich, deep tones of slips and underglazes sprayed and brushed onto the surface. Copper fibers melted onto the clay transform into matte black veins imbedded into the high-gloss surface. The pieces possess elegant simplicity in form and expressive decoration; unique in their individuality.

Bowls are available from 8" to 27" in diameter; lidded vessels up to 24" high.

Slides are available upon request; commissions welcome.

Michelle Svoboda

Red Top Design
P.O. Box 213
Laguna Beach, CA 92652
(714) 494-6151

Michelle Svoboda produces hand-built earthenware dinnerware and larger one-of-a-kind pieces. Many coats of glaze give an appearance of intensely colored embossing. Dinnerware varies in shapes, colors and patterns. Sets can be complemented with any accessory piece.

Michelle's ceramics have been featured in galleries nationally, *Ceramics Monthly, Bon Appetite, Los Angeles Times Magazine, Designers World Magazine* and collections including McDonald's Corp. and that of President Bush.

Slides and prices available upon request. Commissions welcome.

Top Left: *Alice in Wonderland Teapot & Teacups*

Top Right: *Dalmatian Dinnerware;* All pieces are a solid color with a contrasting colored edge. The underneath of all pieces are white with black dots.

Bottom: *Fruit & Vegetable Bowls,* approx. 20"W x 6"D

David Westmeier

75 Bennett Street
Studio D-1
Atlanta, GA 30309
(404) 351-6724

David Westmeier's ceramic and metal wall reliefs and raku vessel forms enhance corporate offices and private homes throughout the United States and abroad. A selected list of corporate collections includes: Delta Airlines Crown Room, Honolulu, HI; Hotel Nikko, Beverly Hills, CA; McDonnel Douglass Information Systems, New York, NY; P.G.A. Clubhouse, Las Vegas, NV; Unisys Corporation, Atlanta, GA.

Working from more than 20 years of experience, Westmeier draws inspiration from various sources including fossil forms and microscopic observations of plants and aquatic life. His work creates a contemplative mood for the viewer, with each piece possessing a powerful yet serene life force. Photographer: Kevin C. Rose

Below: Charger, 22"D, lamp, 28"H, vessel, 15"H

Conversation with Nina Paladino and Michael K. Hansen

Nina Paladino and Michael K. Hansen have created blown glass during a 16-year collaboration.

Nina, how do you and Michael collaborate?

Michael is in charge of the equipment, studio production and inventory. I handle employees, marketing and the everyday running of the business. We both work in design. Occasionally we disagree on a design, but generally we work it out. After 16 years of collaboration, we have learned to trust each other's creative intuition. We both produce glass, with the assistance of one other studio glass blower. Glass is an immediate art form, like dance. It is fluid glass, fluid motion, instantly frozen in time.

Do you have other employees?

Two employees do etching, grinding, polishing and other finishing. Another two take orders and do packing, shipping, invoicing, office accounting, and production scheduling. It is a very dedicated group, almost like a family.

What are the special production aspects of producing blown glass?

We have a multi-step production process, with specialized work assignments, and we also produce multi-media sculpture that incorporates metal and glass. Since we keep our furnaces going 24 hours a day, it is imperative that we use them efficiently. Effective furnace utilization and efficient work flow means that production scheduling is a very critical aspect of our business planning.

Where could we see your work?

We test-market our work in our gallery in Sacramento, but do our major sales through wholesale craft shows. For retail buyers, our work is carried in more than 1,000 galleries nationwide, including many in popular resort areas, and the museum shops of Corning Glass and The Smithsonian. Some people see our work first as gifts produced under special corporate gift orders. As an example, last year we received a major order for holiday gifts from Southwest Airlines.

Shawn Athari

Shawn Athari's, Inc.
13450 Cantara Street
Van Nuys, CA 91402
(818) 988-3105
FAX (818) 787-MASK

Shawn Athari combines various techniques of glassmaking and occasional metalwork and fuses them into one another to recreate ancient artifacts in a contemporary form. The resultant pieces are evocative of cultures long since diminished or extinct.

Each sculpture is original and an accumulation of extensive research and glass-making expertise acquired throughout the last 18 years. Shawn Athari's excellent sense of color harmony combined with her study of many ancient cultures results in a unique sculpture that preserves its ancient heritage, yet complements modern interiors.

Galleries: See listings under Work for the Wall: Other Media

Top Right: *Nigerian 2*, Yoruba, Africa, 12" x 16" x 3"
Middle Right: *Bobo Fing*, Africa, 21" x 9"x 2"
Bottom Right: *Dual*, Equatorial Africa, 18" x 24" x 2 ½"
Left: *Baule*, Ivory Coast, Africa 15" x 33" x 5"

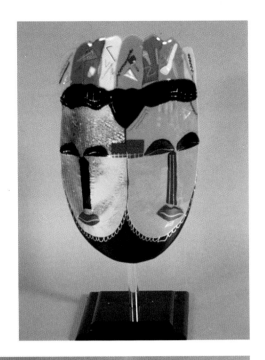

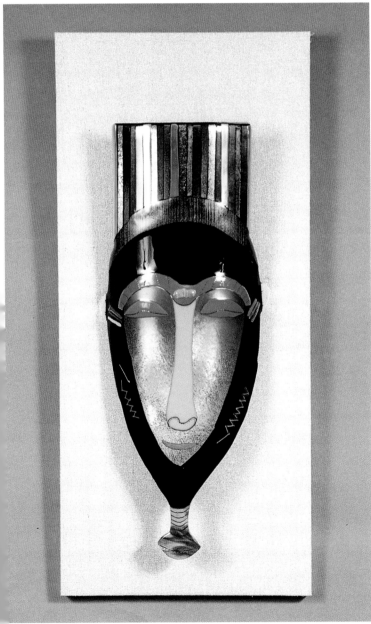

Photo: Robert Baumbach

Sandra C.Q. Bergér

Quintal Unlimited
100 El Camino Real #202
Burlingame, CA 94010
(415) 348-0310
FAX (415) 340-0198

GLASS SCULPTURE CAPTIVATES – in any scale!

Depicted here is a small-scale, limited-edition series, *Mayan Ice.*

Nearly black, precision-glass planes slice through solid cast-glass, punctuated with a tiny sphere in *Column of Ice* (Top).

God of Light and *Temple Spirit* (Below) consist of symmetrical units of custom-cast glass, capturing a Mayan belief in the powerful force of light.

EXCEPTIONAL custom works and limited editions.

EFFECTIVE responses for large environments or small-scale interiors.

EXPERIENCED. Professional. International. Worldwide service. Delivery 3-6 months.

GLASS art installations work everywhere!

Quintal's installations include: cast sculptures, wall reliefs, floor pieces, window treatments, textured panels and luminous sculptures.

All Photography by William A. Porter.

Column of Ice, 10"H x 10"W x 5"D

God of Light, 11"H x 5"W x 4"D

Temple Spirit, 10"H x 8"W x 4"D

Cohn-Stone Studios

Michael Cohn
Molly Stone
5755 Landregan Street
Emeryville, CA 94608
(510) 654-9690

Michael Cohn and Molly Stone are internationally acknowledged by museums, corporate and private collections for their unique sculptural works of art.

Ms. Stone's limited-edition "Reflecting Bowl Series" (pictured) incorporates the age old arts of blown, cut and polished glass with metallic leafing in gold, copper, silver or brass.

Cohn-Stone Studios also produces a wide variety of functional forms in hand-blown art glass: vases, bowls, paperweights and perfume bottles.

Brochure available upon request.

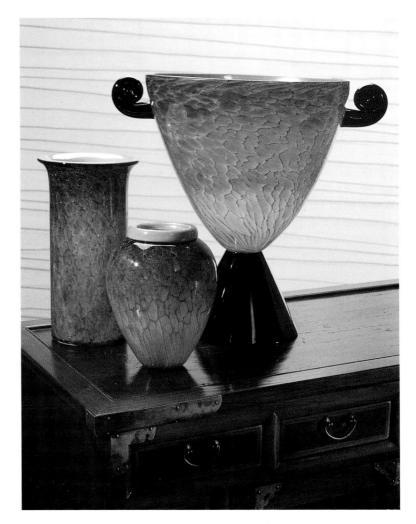

Dale R. Eggert

Eggert Glass
1918 E. Beverly Road
Shorewood, WI 53211
(414) 962-0808

Glass and metal combine in dramatic sculptures for residential and business interiors.

By sandblast etching and painting on half-inch or thicker plate-glass panels, mounted in simple and elegant wrought iron frameworks, Dale Eggert creates distinctive contemporary sculpture. His work has been exhibited in galleries and juried exhibitions in both the U.S. and Japan.

These one-of-a-kind pieces are available in floor standing and table top sizes. Delivery in 30 to 90 days for custom commissions.

Left: glass 5'H x 14"W each panel (overall height 6')
Top Right: glass 24" Dia (overall height 3')
Bottom Right: glass 30"W x 24" H (overall height 5')

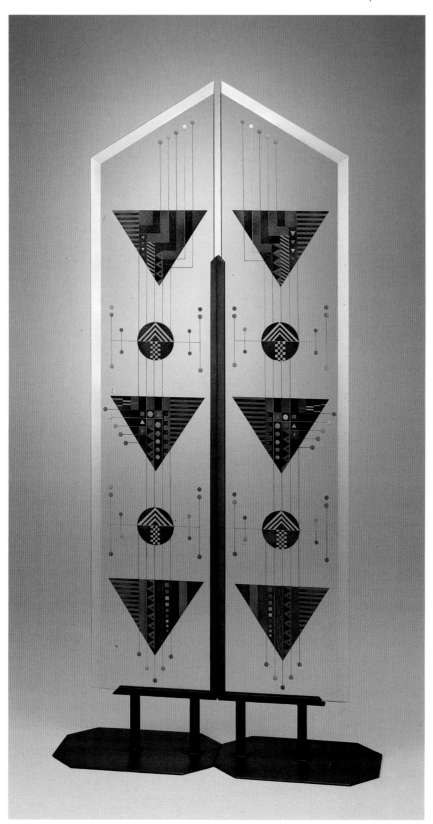

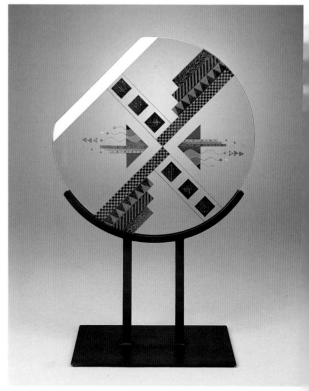

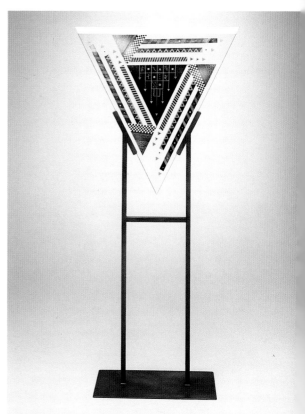

Michael K. Hansen
Nina Paladino

California Glass Studio Inc.
P.O. Box 215786
Sacramento, CA 95821
(916) 925-9322
FAX (916) 925-9370

Michael Hansen and Nina Paladino have been working together for 16 years. Their glass is represented internationally in galleries and in private and corporate collections.

Pictured are handblown glass vessel forms.

A complete catalog is available upon request.

Left: *Feathers Series*, three-sided free-form vessel with optically polished opening
Top Right: *Feathers Series*, one-of-kind, carved, disk-shaped bowl
Bottom Right: *Feathers Series*, free-form bowl

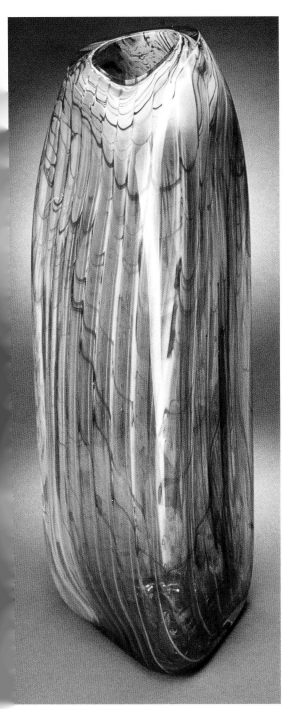

J.C. Homola

The 3 of Swords Rt. 1 Box 395
Ava, MO 65608
(417) 683-3460

J.C. Homola is a self-taught artist working in kiln-formed glass.

Innovative design and color use distinguish J.C.H omola's work from the commonplace.

The pieces shown here are part of her "color in the round" series, each measuring 18" in diameter. Other work is presented in low relief flat panels suitable for display in shadow boxes, under Plexiglass or installed as permanent architectural light sources.

Collected in the United States and Japan, J.C. Homola has many corporate acquisitions to her credit.

The raw materials used are manufactured primarily from recycled glass goods.

Site-specific and customized commissions are welcome. Call or write for additional information.

Available mid-1993: glass tiles for home use.

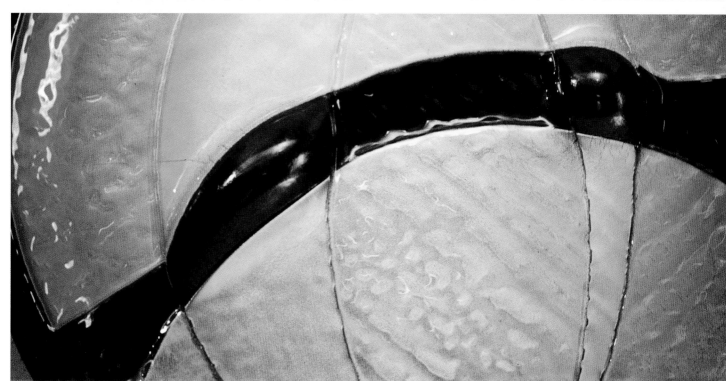

Christine E. McEwan

Verre Visage, Inc.
294 Clinton
Elmhurst, IL 60126-2404
(708) 941-7884

Christine McEwan creates imagery on glass. Her background in architectural glass has enabled her to develop fused glass ensembles that enlighten many interior design applications. Christine McEwan maintains a unique style of controlling the fusing temperature, that transcends the boundaries of glass. Her complete understanding of color transforms glass to life. Designs are both inspirational illusions as well as illustrious abstract arrangements.

Verre Visage, Inc. produces a line of limited-edition plates, tiles and decorative accessories.

Photos: Christopher Kean

David Jaworski

Sunesis
11 Clerbrook Lane
Ladue, MO 63124
(314) 994-9820

David Jaworski has been producing fine gold jewelry and sculptural works since 1981. His sculptural works are best known for their unique blend of metal and glass in energetic and flowing studies of form optics and color.

Jaworski is comfortable collaborating with other designers on site-specific installations. Previous projects range from small to medium-scale works for residential, to large-scale, free-standing works as well as wall-hung installations for public spaces.

Corporate clients include AT&T, Monsanto, Max Plank Institute, Carboline, St. Louis Arts & Education Council, Washington University, St. Louis Centre for Holistic Healing, and many others.

Slides of portfolio are available.

Top: *Quest,* 1993, bronze, glass, 26"H x 21"L x 16"D
Bottom: *Cirrus,* 1993, private residence, St. Louis, bronze, glass, 5'H x 6 ½"L x 6'D

Elizabeth R. Mears

Windy Hill Glassworks
10160 Hampton Road
Fairfax Station, VA 22039
(703) 690-2545

Flat or sculptured, colored glass or clear, leaded or laminated—Elizabeth Mears uses all in her site-specific and autonomous creations. In both public and private spaces, she collaborates with clients to fulfill their needs with her visions. She often incorporates sandblast carving, painting, and neon in her completed works.

Inquiries are invited.

Commissions include:
St. Andrews Episcopal Church, Burke, VA, windows
Montgomery County, MD, Kaleidoscope, hanging sculpture, 17' x 24' x 10'

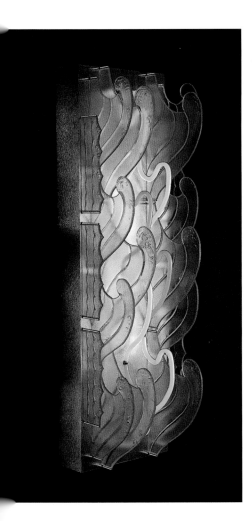

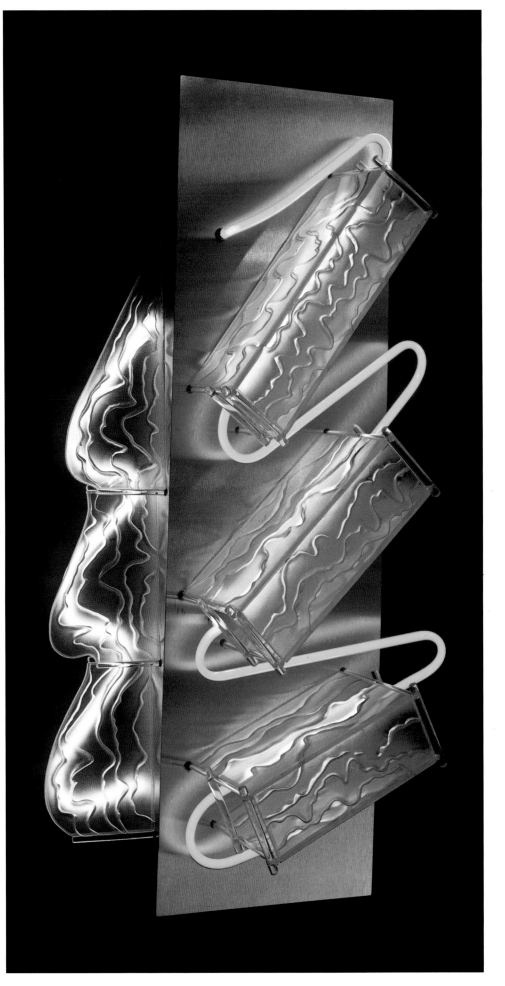

Mesolini Glass Studio

Gregg Mesmer & Diane Bonciolini
13291 Madison NE
Bainbridge Island, WA 98110
(206) 842-7133
(206) 587-0275

Gregg Mesmer and Diane Bonciolini combine extensive backgrounds in art glass production to create award-winning dishware that is both beautiful and practical. Each signed and dated piece in this collection is created from hand-rolled iridescent, transparent, or opalescent glass that is "slumped" into molds during a kiln firing.

Additional examples of their work can be seen in *THE GUILD 5*, page 99, *THE GUILD 6*, page 248 and T*HE GUILD 7*, page 209. Color sample kit available for fifteen dollars, including shipping. Call or write for current catalog.

Orient & Flume
Art Glass

2161 Park Avenue
Chico, CA 95928
(916) 893-0373
FAX (916) 893-2743

Internationally acclaimed, the artists of Orient & Flume specialize in one-of-a-kind, handblown vases, perfumes and paper-weights. Using only "off-hand" blowing tech-niques, each piece is individually designed and created. Motifs range from traditional to contemporary.

Orient & Flume Glass Art can be found in the permanent collections of the following museums: The Metropolitan Museum, The Smithsonian Museum, The Chrysler Museum, The Steuben Glass Museum and the Chicago Art Institute.

Top Left: Winter Woods, cased vase
Bottom Left: Square 1, glossy vase
Top Right: Cherokee Rose, cased cabinet vase; Bamboo Bud, cased cabinet vase; Blue Orchid Bud, cased cabinet vase; Rose, cased vase; Rosebuds, cased vase; Pilsner, iridescent vase/blue threaded rim; Pilsner, malachite; Winter Bamboo, cased vase; Santa Fe, glossy vase; Dove, Pink Waterlily, cased bowl; Toucan, cased egg; White Asiatic Lily, cased cabinet vase; Harbor Seal, cased egg; Cactus Garden, cased cabinet vase

Bottom Right: Nature Series. Left bowl: Plum, amethyst; Apple, gold speckled; Apple, blue cloud; Pear, blue iridescent; Pear, gold iridescent; Pear, blue cloud; Right bowl: Apricot, Pear, gold speckled; Mini Apple, clear crackled; Pear, Cypriot; Mini Apple, black glossy; Pear, blue iridescent; Apricot; Table top: Pear, gold speckled; Mini Peach, pink glossy; Apple, green glossy; Peach, pink iridescent; Apple, gold iridescent

Rupama

Kroma
1420 Fourth Street
Santa Fe, NM 87501
(505) 989-1744
(800) 345-7662

Rupama creates masterful and meticulously designed glass objects by fusing numerous layers of exotic glasses. She was an original member of the Bullseye Glass Co. fusing group which pioneered this contemporary specialty and her Kroma studio was and is the original source of decorative products made of the multiple colored "dichroic glass". This engaging mirrored material has the unusual ability to change color when viewed from different angles. In addition to the masks and platters shown, the studio work also includes jewelry, mobiles, windows and furniture.

Wendy Saxon Brown

341 West Saugerties Road
Saugerties, NY 12477
(914) 246-4673

Wendy Saxon Brown sandblasts her artwork in full relief into ¾" glass. The lifelike contours and graceful detail are accented with laminations of anodized and airbrushed aluminum. These unique standing or wall-hung pieces range in size from 6" x 12" to lifesize installations. Wendy Saxon Brown is presently showing her work in museums and galleries both nationally and internationally.

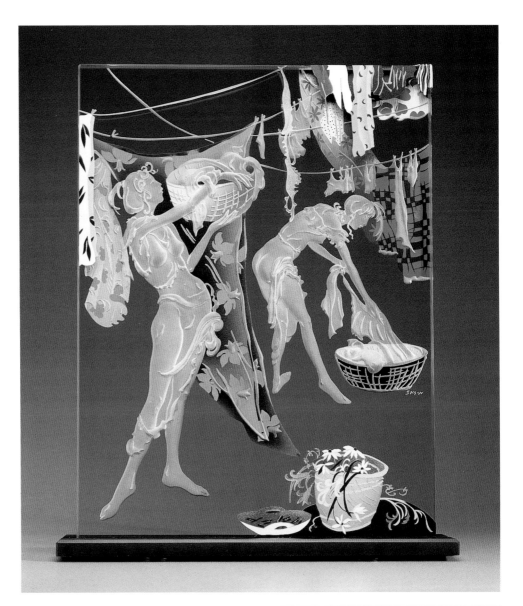

Patricia Weyer

Lake Studio
414 Lakeside Avenue S #13
Seattle, WA 98144
(206) 329-2880

Patricia Weyer's sculpture integrates the optic qualities of sand-etched and sand-cast glass with structural elements of welded steel. These mythical narratives evoke an underwater realm of dappled light, and explore the expressive power of human and animal figuration. As a Pilchuck scholar, Weyer's facile rendering of form in glass has earned nominations for the Corning Prize, and has been installed in numerous private, public and corporate collections. Commissions are accepted.

Top Left: *Portal*, 18"Dia
Top Right: *Threshhold*, 18"Dia
Bottom: *Free of the Freize*, 20"H

Jonathan Winfisky

Potter Road/Legate Hill
Charlemont, MA 01339
(413) 339-8319

Jonathan Winfisky has been designing and producing unique and original blown and cast sculptural glass vessel forms since 1976.

The "Sculptural Design Series" and the "Cast Design Series" are examples of forms which are designed to work collectively or individually when displayed in private residences and public spaces.

Larger pieces are available by commission and all designs can be produced in a wide variety of sizes and colors. Please call or write for further information.

Top: *Cast Design Series*, 1991, bowl 15", vase 14", vial 6", bud vase 8", ming vessel 8"
Bottom: *Sculptural Design Series,* ©1991, bowl 15", vase 12", fluted vase 8", perfume vial 5 ½", tapered vase 10"

A Conversation with Nancy Moore Bess

Nancy Moore Bess maintains a studio in New York City, where she creates basket forms.

What kinds of markets do you approach with your baskets?

Basket making is highly competitive, largely because of imports from the Pacific Rim. It is absolutely essential that my product be unique. I often design site-specific baskets, taking into account the size of the space, surrounding color, traffic patterns, direction of approach, height of installation, lighting and touch factors. I also produce work for advertising stylists. They will have very decided ideas about the commission, right down to the number of apples and pears a basket will hold. I have also worked with theatrical prop masters to produce baskets for the Covent Garden scene of "My Fair Lady", which was being staged by the Minnesota Opera Company. Working in multiple markets, and with galleries as well, keeps my creative fires burning.

How does a basket maker find herself in New York City?

The cultural expectation may be that basket makers live and work in the country, but having a studio in New York City makes a great deal of sense for my business. Not only do I have all the cultural advantages of living here, but my studio is very accessible to and convenient for my clients, many of whom have other business in the city. I am within walking distance north of Soho, right off Fifth Avenue.

Will you tell us about your studio?

I am part of a cooperative studio in New York's photography district. There are several jewelers on my floor, a ceramic artist, a toy designer, a display designer, and an architect, among others. We share heat, light and kitchen facilities. Sharing space in this way stimulates creative energy, and also opens up the opportunity for collaboration. In working on one recent project, for example, I sought help from one of the jewelers who works with leather to find the right creative solution for a client's needs.

Nancy Moore Bess

5 East 17th Street, 6th FL
New York, NY 10003
(212) 691-2821
Messages (212) 388-0511

Influenced strongly by Japanese folk art and packaging, Nancy Moore Bess relies on the traditional basketry techniques of twining, coiling and plaiting to create her non-functional basket forms and fiber constructions. Some pieces are mounted on lucite for easy installation and maintenance, others rest on Japanese river stones or bamboo. Display elements are included in pricing.

Bess will collaborate with art consultants and designers on custom work for private collections and corporate installations. Her expanded studio allows for prompt attention. Inquiries are invited

Top Left: Vessel grouping, 11"H
Top Right: Black Jar with Bamboo Cover, 6"H
Bottom: Private Armor, U.S. Embassy
    commission, 19" x 48"

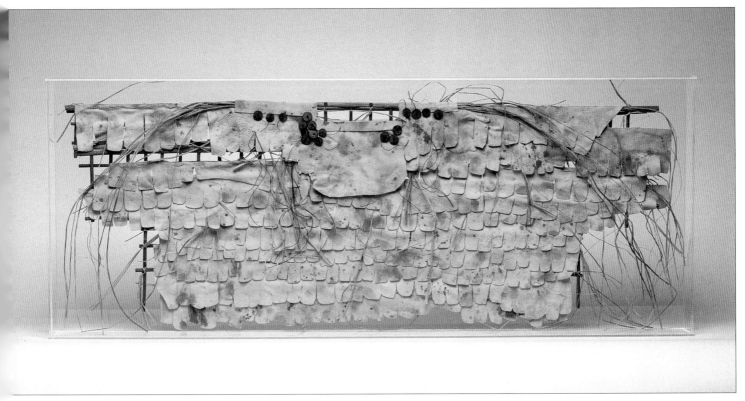

BIP'S Translucent Collection

Ingemar Persson
Star Route 2
P.O. Box 264
La Honda, CA 94020-0264
(415) 949-1437

Ingemar Persson's specialty is very thin, translucent, spalted, vessels. These turned, one-of-a-kind vessels are made from roots, crotches and burls. The vessels' variegated colors and patterns are due to nature's spalting process. Each piece is individually designed then turned on a lathe. Completion can take up to three years.

Ingemar Persson's pieces are included in private collections in the United States, Latin America and Europe. He has been a featured artist in many architectural and international craft magazines.

Slides and additional information are available upon request.

Top: *Syzygy*, vessel, translucent spalted Monterey pine, 6 ¾"H x 9 ½"W
Bottom: *Vespers*, vessel, translucent spalted Monterey pine, 13 ½"H x 10"W

Eva S. Walsh

P.O. Box 2266
Winter Park, FL 32790
(407) 628-0422

Eva Walsh's one-of-a-kind sculptures, fashioned from gourds, provide a dramatic focal point for home and office. Their glowing colors are produced by leather dyes, and are sealed and protected by satin finish. She has created over a dozen designs and a number of larger pieces. They are exhibited in private collections, in galleries and home furnishings showrooms. Private and corporate commissions are welcome.

Top (left to right): *Birds on a Nest*, *Birds*, and *Turtle*, gourds, edged with palm bark, broomcorn and palm ribs
Bottom Left: *Spirits Rising*, 11" gourd cut into sections and rebuilt with palm ribs, reed and twisted paper stand
Bottom Right: *My Cup Runneth Over*, gourd adorned with a beaded bib, *Captured Spirit*, gourd with twined pine needles

Sydney K. Hamburger

466 Washington Street #2E
New York, NY 10013
(212) 219-2109

Sydney K. Hamburger's sculptures are modern versions of traditional "Safe Spaces": caves, cathedrals, and places of sanctuary in which people have traditionally sought refuge for comfort, inspiration and vision.

Scale has been designed into Hamburger's art thus allowing her clients the widest possible range of flexibility in terms of size and materials for either in or out-of-doors installations.

The studio provides engineering and installation supervision.

Hamburger has been: visiting artist at the American Academy in Rome, Fellow at the Macdowell Colony and the Wurlitzer Foundation. Her works have been installed at the Washington County Museum of Fine Arts, the Baltimore Museum of Art, and at homes and corporations throughout the country.

Brochure available on request.

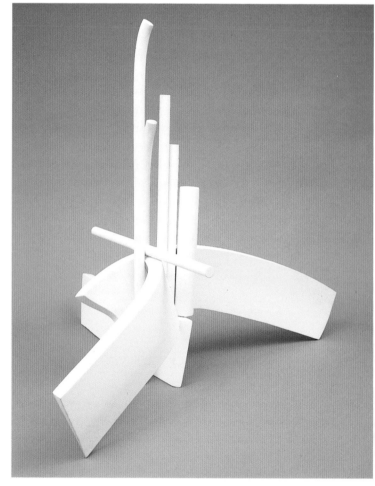

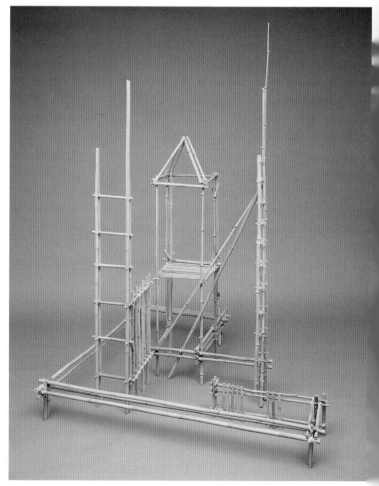

Robert Hargrave

P.O. Box 116
Middle Falls, NY 12848
(518) 692-7283

For the past 20 years Robert Hargrave has been laminating and carving Birch and Luan plywoods into fluid forms, contradicting the negative image of ordinary plywood.

Robert produces a unique line of mirrors and sculptural accessories, as well as more limited art pieces such as furniture, wall-relief and in-the-round sculpture.

Many of the designs have a figurative emphasis and create a sense of movement by using the black glue lines to enhance form.

His work is sold nationally in many galleries, as well as purchased by collectors, corporations and interior designers.

A complete catalogue and photos are available upon request.

Right: *Life Size Standing Figure,*
 60" x 18"x 12"D
Below: *Triple Mirror with Shelf,*
 37" x 25" x 10"D

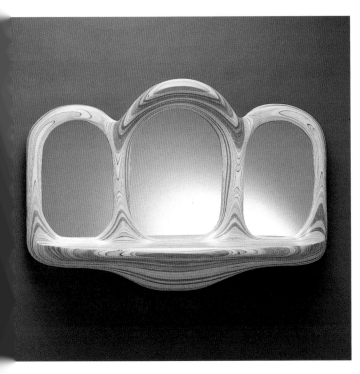

Pamela Joseph

Metal Paintings, Inc.
R.R. #3 Box 140
Pound Ridge, NY 10576
(914) 764-8208
FAX (914) 764-8215

Pamela Joseph has designed numerous painting/sculptures for both natural and architectural situations. This series of maquettes created in 1991-92, based on a pyramidal theme, explores the concept of a shelter or an oasis for public space. Materials include aluminum, paint, wood, glass and stone aggregate.

Commissions include the General Services Administration, Embassy of the Hungarian People's Republic, Allied Services for the Handicapped, Schein Pharmaceutical and the Philadelphia Commission on the Arts. Selected exhibitions have been at The Katonah Gallery, Hudson River Museum, Vassar College, Fairfield University, and the Everhart Museum.

Top Right: *Cosmic Blue Crystal Bottom*
Right: *Red River Schist*
Top Left: *Golden Pyramid Middle*
Left: *Green Mineral Mountain*
Bottom Left: *Shelter Dome,* in collaboration with Martin Kryska

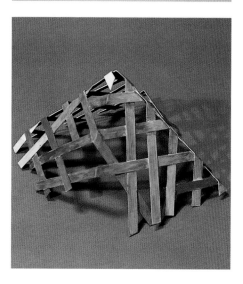

Carol Kropnick

135 Eastern Parkway
Brooklyn, NY 11238
(718) 638-4909

Whimsical, provocative, mystical, and sensuous, the masks of Carol Kropnick represent a singular art form. Shaped from such diverse materials as antique textiles, leather, exotic feathers, bone and vintage beads, these works take one month to finish and are surprisingly durable.

Kropnick has created her masks for more than 15 years. They have been exhibited in national museums and galleries, displayed in art books worldwide, and commissioned for theater, film, interior design and by private collectors.

More examples of her work can be seen in *THE GUILD 5* and *THE GUILD 7: The Designer's Reference*. A brochure and slides are available upon request.

Below: *Mask for Winter Solstice*, leather, bone, horse hair, paint, 14"W x 14"H x 7"D

Photo: Maje Waldo

Anne Mayer Meier

Creative Textures
169 Sandalwood Way
Longwood, FL 32750
(407) 332-6713

Anne Mayer Meier has been creating a broad range of contemporary art to complement residential and corporate settings since 1979. Meier's "Ancestors"© and "Old Souls"© are mixed-media figures that evoke man's primitive past, using original design and fabrication. Often, found objects are included to enhance the magical qualities of the pieces. At times Meier will complete the "Ancestor" with one of her unusual story baskets. Although fictional in nature, each one-of-a-kind "Ancestor" or "Old Soul" explores cultural, spiritual and folkloric concepts.

Contact artist for further information.

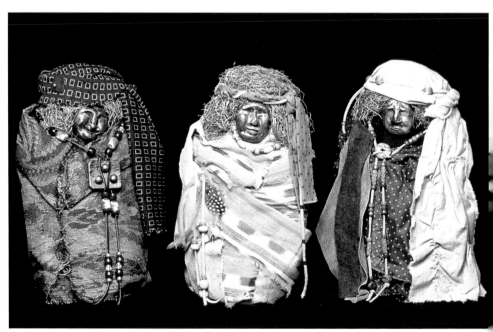

Old Souls©, clay, fabric, found objects, 12"

Clan of Wisdom, wood, clay, fabric, found objects, hand woven and painted basket, 45"

Ancestor©, clay, fabric, found objects, 22"

Susan M. Oaks

6581 Fox Run
San Antonio, TX 78233-4706
(210) 656-8440

Susan Oaks, a longtime artist, exhibits nationally. Her one-of-a-kind vessel forms are made from wool, silk or cotton. She also constructs individual collages, always using an element of fiber—silk or ultrasuede or a special thread—in the finished composition. Information regarding prices and slides is available on request.

Right: *Containment,* goat hair and silk over sisal, 7 ½"H x 3 ½"Dia
Bottom Left: *The Meditative Aspect of Process,* wool over sisal, 5 ¾"H x 13"Dia
Bottom Right: *Being,* angora over rush, 3"H x 6"Dia

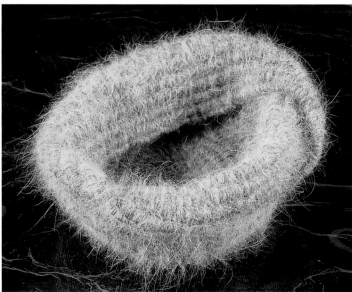

Lori A. Paladino

700 Fairview Avenue
Fairview, NJ 07022
(201) 945-9525

Lori Paladino's unique dramatic wood designs add a fashionable touch to any public/corporate space or residential dwelling. Clients may choose from various woods and color combinations or stains.

Each piece is an original—hand cut and hand painted in acrylics giving an almost animated effect, finalized with the date and Lori's insignia. Lori offers a variety of dramatic designs which will excite a feeling of enchantment into any surrounding.

Lori's line also includes switch plates, jewel boxes, picture frames, sconces and floor screens.

Prices vary according to size, intricacy and finish.

Top: wall mirror, 4'Dia x ¾"D
Bottom Left: clock, 19" x 19" x 1 ½"
Bottom Right: hand mirror, approx. 16" x 8" x ½"

George Radeschi

P.O. Box 1498
Doylestown, PA 18901
(215) 348-5208
FAX (215) 348-4113

George Radeschi has developed a unique technique through which he captures the spirit of native American and ancient Egyptian and Grecian art in wooden vessels. Internationally recognized, George is a frequent award winner. The one-of-a-kind vessels are in museum, corporate and private collections nationwide.

Top Left: carved basswood, mahogany, padouk, 15" x 12"
Top Right: purpleheart, zebrawood, 26" x 19"
Bottom: carved basswood, rosewood, 17" x 17"

Judy Stone

25A Mirabel Avenue
San Francisco, CA 94110
(415) 285-0572

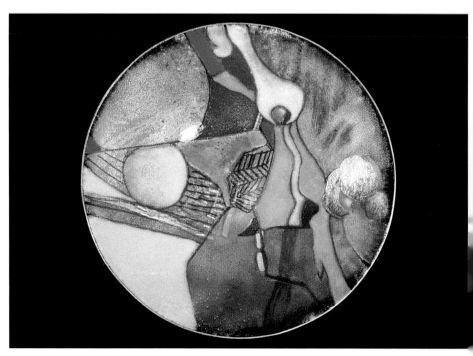

Judy Stone approaches enameling with technological skill and fearless expression. Using both traditional and innovative techniques gleaned from art and industry, she enamels two-dimensional and three-dimensional pieces for interior and exterior spaces.

Judy's enameled light switch covers can transform a mundane place on the wall into beautiful and subtle art.

She works with architects, designers and home owners. More information is furnished upon request.

Top: bowl, enameled copper, 4" Dia
Bottom: light switch cover, enameled
   copper, 10"W

S.M. Warren

Vermont Paperworks
Box 7, Middletown Road
Grafton, VT 05146
(802) 843-2369
FAX (802) 843-2585

Sculptures such as these seductively textured, organically shaped crowns have been exhibited across the country in juried shows as well as private galleries for the past 20 years. While the sculpture shown here is suitable for a pedestal or desktop, other pieces from this series range in size from six-inch-high sculptures to 15-foot wallpieces and mobiles.

Resume and slides available upon request.

Top: *Crown with Grapevine, Archaeological Artifact Series,* mixed media, 12"Dia x 9"H
Bottom: *Metal Crown, Archaeological Artifact Series,* handmade paper and copper, 3"H x 6 ½"Dia x 11"L

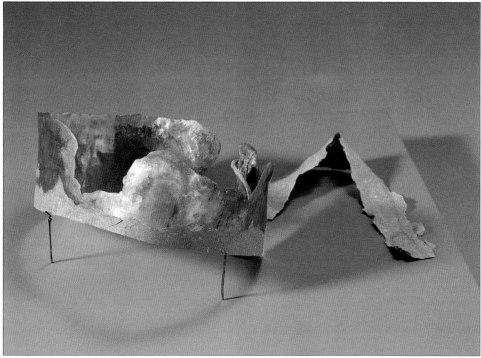

Photos: Greg Bolosky

Nancy J. Young
Allen Young

11416 Brussels NE
Albuquerque, NM 87111
(505) 299-6108

The Youngs design and produce original two- and three-dimensional works. Sculpture is available for exterior pieces. Interior pieces include free-standing or mixed-media wall pieces. Color preferences and commissions accepted.

Prices depend on size and complexity. Allow 4-8 weeks from design approval and contract to completion. Shipping and handling FOB Albuquerque.

Selected commissions include IBM, American Express and AT&T.

Top Left: Sturdy handcast paper vessels, 1992, from 3"H x 4"Dia to 13" H x 18"Dia
Bottom Left: Wall sculpture, 1992, 4'H x 3'W x 4"D
Right: Free-standing sculptures, 1992, ranging from 5'6"H x 8"W x 3"D to 8'H x 16"W x 3"D. Wall pieces range from 24"H x 5"W x 2"D (not shown) to 54"H x 11"W x 3"D.

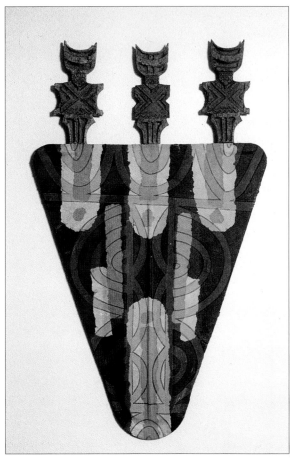

A Conversation with Don Drumm

Don Drumm uses industrial metal techniques to produce both one-of-a-kind sculpture and limited-edition pieces in cast aluminum.

How did you begin working in metal?

My grandfather was a blacksmith and carpenter. My father was a mechanic, an inventor, and ran a GMC truck dealership. I learned metal processes at an early age from them. When I graduated from Kent State University, my first job was at an industrial design firm where I introduced a line of aluminum gift items for them. When they later dropped the business, I apprenticed myself to a retired sand-caster who had made aluminum molds for the tire and rubber industry. In 1960, I set up my first foundry in a rented space. Ten years later I had my own foundry.

What kind of materials do you use?

I use between six and 12 tons of aluminum a year, depending on a number of cyclical factors. I usually buy it in the form of ingots, about one ton at a time. Early on, I experimented with several different aluminum alloys, and found one that was entirely safe for cookware. It is a very high-quality alloy and ideal for all other types of sculptural casting as well.

Could you describe your workshop?

Because I am industrially oriented, I attempt to apply the best available industrial tools and techniques in my work. I employ a full-time foundry man and two finishers. My foundry foreman was a music major at Akron University. I also have a network of friends who can do specialized tasks, like water-jet cutting, sand-blasting and anodizing. For some of my multiples, such as dinner plates or small decorative items, I work with two other foundries. In addition to commissions, I supply 30 to 50 galleries with my own work.

Do you do commissioned work?

Yes! I recently received a call from an interior designer who was redoing an embassy in Central America for the State Department: "Would I like to submit a proposal?" I like doing birds in my work, so I sent a sketch and proposal to do the eagle in our American seal. It was to be eight feet tall and six feet wide. She liked the proposal, and commissioned the piece. It was made for the U.S. Embassy in Tegucigalpa, Honduras.

Joseph L. Brandom

1802 Landry Drive
Baker, LA 70714
(504) 775-4037

Joseph L. Brandom has been creating functional and sculptural objects in metal since 1970. His work is in public, private and corporate collections in the United States and Europe.

Brandom's one-of-a-kind pewter vessels range in size from 8" to 24" in diameter. The vessel pictured is 14"W x 9"H.

The figurative sculptures are life sized, one-of-a-kind pieces, cast in pewter. Sculptures of specific individuals may be commissioned.

More information is available upon request.

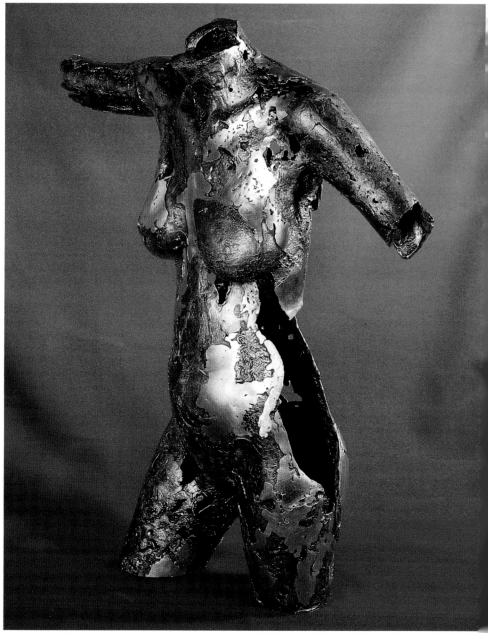

David M Bowman Studio

P.O. Box 738
Berkeley, CA 94701
(510) 845-1072

David Bowman has been working with metal for more than twenty years developing his own idiosyncratic method of construction of holloware. His vases are fabricated from pieces cut from brass sheet, hammered or bent and then brazed together. Some vases are etched to provide a surface texture. After testing for water-tightness the completed vase is patinaed using durable sculptural patina techniques.

Candlesticks, candelabra and wallpieces are also available. Please call for slides of current work.

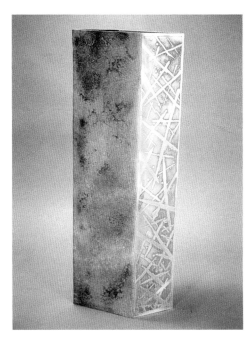

Don Drumm

Don Drumm Studios and Gallery
437 Crouse Street
Akron, OH 44311
(216) 253-6268
FAX (216) 253-4014

Don Drumm, a pioneer in the use of cast aluminum as a sculptural medium, maintains his own foundry where he produces a wide variety of work, including limited-edition sculpture, one-of-a-kind sculpture, architectural commissions and craft objects.

During his 30 years of doing commissions, he has produced work ranging from ten-story murals in sandblasted concrete, to monumental, free-standing steel sculptures, to wall reliefs in applied cement or cast aluminum for corporate and private homes. In addition, the small sculptures have been used worldwide by executives, government officials and individuals as gifts, awards and honorariums.

Catalogs and slides of architectural work, sculpture and crafts are available. Please indicate your interest. Call to discuss projects.

Top: *Stallion*, sculpture multiple, cast
  aluminum, 15" x 14½"
Bottom: *Chief Joseph's Last Ride*, sculpture
  multiple, cast aluminum, 18" x 11" x 4"

J. Dub's

Jerry Wayne Bement
Jill Voss
115 West 4th
Ellensburg, WA 98926
(509) 925-9401

Jerry Wayne Bement, a former Farrier, has been working from his home in Ellensburg, WA, creating these unique silhouettes since 1980. Jerry's particular style in carving true-to-life images gives his two-dimensional art a three-dimensional feeling. This transformation of raw steel produces a classical yet delicate work of art.

A nationally recognized artist, Jerry torch cuts his images by hand from mild plate steel. Most of the art work is then incorporated into functional items such as weather vanes, coat racks, signs and furniture. Hundreds of detailed patterns are at hand. However, commissioned work is encouraged.

A complete catalogue is available upon request.

Craig Lauterbach

The Inquisitive Eye
526 Loma Alta
Carmel, CA 93923
(408) 375-3332

Working in hardwoods for 20 years has inspired Craig to venture into the medium of bronze. Like his wood sculptures, there is a combination of function and abstraction, a sweeping motion that flows in all of his creations.

In The Curl (Top) is a collaboration with internationally renowned marine artist, Randy Puckett.

A portfolio and price list is available upon request.

In the Curl, issued 1991 in an edition of 150, 20"H x 16"W x 14"D

Trumpeter, issued 1991 in an edition of 50, 16"H x 20"W x 9"D

Courtship, issued 1990 in an edition of 50, 10"H x 17"W x 9"D

Andrew Moritz

Special Creations in Metal
550 SW Industrial Way, Suite T
Bend, OR 97702
(503) 389-1107

Andrew Moritz has been creating sculptures in steel and bronze for private collections (as shown in *THE GUILD 5* and *6*) as well as corporate and public installations since 1971. The care in planning and detail of execution is reflected in every commission accepted and has helped gain Moritz an international following. In addition to satisfying the aesthetic requirements, practical aspects such as shipping, installation and lighting are always considered and discussed before work begins.

Both Photos: *Ndovu*, 1992, table, bronze, steel, African woods, 6'W x 26"H x 24"D

Martin Sturman

M. Sturman Steel Sculptures
20412 Roca Chica Drive
Malibu, CA 90265
(310) 456-5716
FAX (818) 905-7173

Martin Sturman creates original steel sculptures in floral, figurative, and abstract designs.

His sculptures range from table-top to free-standing indoor and outdoor pieces, including sculptured tables and entry gates. These beautiful sculptures are executed in stainless steel, weathered (rusted) steel, powder-coated carbon steel and acrylic-painted carbon steel.

Martin Sturman frequently has sculptures available for immediate delivery, but he encourages site-specific and collaborative efforts. Depending upon complexity, most sculptures can be shipped within 10 to 12 weeks of commission. Sizes range from 12 inches to ten feet high.

Top Left: *Dancers,* 1992, acrylic on steel, 22" x 29" x 11"
Bottom Left: firescreen, 1992, acrylic on steel, 48" x 32" x 16"
Right: *Adam & Eve,* 1992, stainless steel, 56" x 46" x 19"

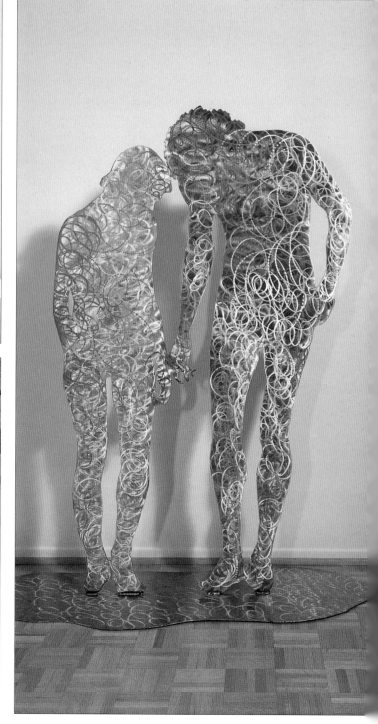

Wasserman Studios

Myron Wasserman
1817 North 5th Street
Philadelphia, PA 19122
(215) 739-5558
FAX (215) 739-5558

Myron has for more than three decades been an award winning artist, art director and designer.

Individuals and corporations have been attracted to his mobiles and stabiles. They have an interactive quality that lends them to an elegant atrium setting as well as a desk top.

Myron personally designs the single and multiple axis mobiles to fit into any size, space or environment. Constructed of various metals, they can be ordered in a variety of colors and finishes.

Slides and details are available upon request.

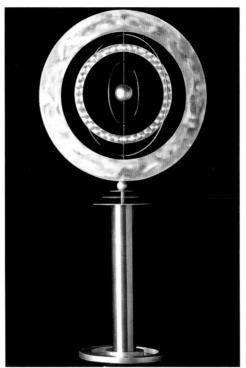

Stabile, metal and wood, 56" x 27"

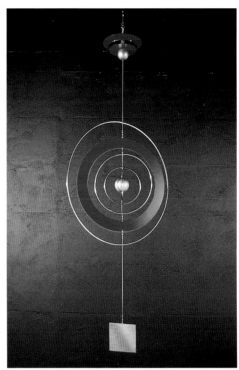

Single Axis Mobile, metal, 50" x 20"

Multiple Axis Mobile, metal, wood and crystal, 98" x 98"

Doug Weigel

P.O. Box 92408
Albuquerque, NM 87199-2408
(505) 821-6600

Weigel designs and produces in steel two
and three-dimensional sculptures and
furniture. Styles include Southwestern,
Western, art-deco and client-commissioned
ideas.

Allow 4 to 8 weeks from design approval
and contract to completion. Shipping and
handling, FOB Albuquerque.

Right: *Steel Hopi Diety*, 6'H x 3'W x 2'D

Jamie Davis

1239 Mile Creek Road
Pickens, SC 29671
(803) 868-3302

Lightweight, wall-mounted personal
"theaters", each signed and dated, involve
the viewer through layers of detail. Garden
and family themes. Irreverent techniques
and materials.

Right: *Men Who Dance*, 1993,
   20"W x 20"H x 6"D

9   Paul Schraub
10   Kimball/Nanessence
12   David Belda
13   Charles Mode
14   Ray Andrews
15   David Gleghill (Top)
     Aiden Bradley (Bottom)
16   Frank Pronesti
17   Ron Schwager
19   Alex Hughes
21   Herb Lotz
23   Chip Yates
25   James D. Toms
26   Jon Reis Photography
27   Paul Hester (Top)
     J.W. Nave (Bottom Left/Right)
28   Bill Bachhuber
29   Robin Miller
30   Sharon Risedorph
33   Breger and Associates
35   Peter Lee (Bottom)
36   Roger Schreiber
37   Ron Breland
39   Jeremy Harris
44   Michael Tropea
46-47 Renny Mills
49   Michael Harrison
50   Mark Frey (Bottom)
51   Sharon Risedorph
54   Albin Dearing
82   Dennis Maxwell
83   James Dee
84-85 Bob Rush
86   D. Sands (Top)
88   Alexis Andrews
89   Jay Carrol
90   Kevin C. Rose
91   Andrew Bordwin (Left)
     Nick Saraco (Right)
94   Robert Baumbach (Bottom Right)
95   Nick Saraco
97   Dave McCaughan/Images
100 Moy Wong (Top Right/Left)
     Jim Mannino (Bottom)
101 Anthony Potter
103 Tony Frederick/C.S. Kern & Assoc.
104 John Buckaklian
105 McNabb Studio
106 George Post
107 Larry Smith
115 Pelafos/Grace
116 Lois Stauber
117 Capitol Hill Photographers
         (Top/Bottom Left)
     William Lemke (Right)
118 Ron Lazarus
119 Spectrum Photography
121 Cook Nielson
123 Richard Larimer
124 Keith Perry
125 Steve Heller
126 Gregg Krogstad
128 John Yost
133 George Post (Top)
     Sam Wilcoxen (Bottom)
137 Glenwood Jackson
139 Peter Turo

141 Mathew Fried/Photovisions
142 Robert M. Goodman
143 Rick Bassett (Top)
     Jonathan Rachline (Bottom)
144 Alan Watson
148 John Nollendorfs
149 Swain Edins (Top/Bottom Left)
     Albert Photography (Top Right)
154 George Post
155 Herb Lotz
156 Mathew Freid/Photovisions
158 Peter Krumhardt
159 Michael Scheafer
160 Randall Smith
162 Scott Miller
164 Kurt Miller
165 Cathy Carver
166 Robert Cole (Top/Detail)
     Jerry Anthony Photography (Bottom)
167 Deb Gilmore
169 Don Hall
170 Paul Dodge (Bottom)
171 John Schwartz
174 Bob Barrett (Right/ Bottom Left)
     Ralph Gabriner (Top Left)
177 Greg Wilson
178 George Post
179 Gary A. Stanko
180 Claire Curran
181 Kevin C. Rose
183 Robert Baumbach (Left)
184 William Porter
186 William Lemke
187 Rick Waller
190 Rudy Ershen (Top)
     Carl Bartz (Bottom)
191 Eric Long
193 Jeff Teeter
196 Ken Wagner (Top Left/Bottom)
     Roger Schreiber (Top Right)
197 George Erlich (Top)
     Tommy Elder (Bottom)
200 George Post
203 Hartford Photo
205 Maje Waldo
206 Richard Rosetto (Top)
     Gary Warnimont (Bottom Left/Right)
207 Diane Kelly Pierce (Right/Bottom Left)
     Photographs by Sally (Bottom Right)
208 Brian Lacey
209 Stephen Barth
210 Scott Braley
211 Greg Bolosky
216 Jeff Corbett
217 Debbie Storlie
218 Bob Western
219 Indivair Sivanathan
220 Neil Nissing
221 Michael Furman (Top Left)
     Steve Coan (Top Right)
     Robert Hakalski (Bottom)

Gallery Resources

• Alabama

JEFFERSON STREET GALLERY
313 E Jefferson St
Montgomery, AL 36104
(205) 263-5703

MAIN AVENUE POTTERY &
GALLERY
503 Main Ave
Northport, AL 35476
(205) 758-5002

MARALYN WILSON GALLERY
2010 Cahaba Rd
Birmingham, AL 35223
(205) 879-0582

NEW DIRECTIONS GALLERY
111B First St NE
Cullman, AL 35055
(207) 737-9933

THE KENTUCK MUSEUM
3500 Hwy 82
Northport, AL 35476
(205) 333-1252

• Alaska

KIKO B FIBERARTS
411 Fourth Ave
Fairbanks, AK 99701
GUILD Artist: Ruth Gowell, see
page 39.

OBJECTS OF BRIGHT PRIDE
165 S Franklin St
Juneau, AK 99801
(907) 586-4969

• Arizona

ART AMERICA GALLERY
OF ART
9301 E Shea Blvd
Scottsdale, AZ 85260
(602) 951-9000

ARTISTIC GALLERIES
7077 E Main St
Scottsdale, AZ 85251
(602) 945-6766

BENTLEY TOMLINSON
GALLERY
4161 N Marshall Way
Scottsdale, AZ 85251
(602) 941-7800

BERTA WRIGHT GALLERY
260 E Congress St
Tucson, AZ 85741
(602) 742-4134

EL PRADO GALLERIES, INC
P.O. Box 1849
Sedona, AZ 86336
(602) 282-7390

EVERY BLOOMING
THING, INC
2010 E University
Tempe, AZ 85281
(602) 921-1196
GUILD Artists: David M. Schiller and
Bernice Schiller, see page 124.

GALLERY TEN
7045 Third Ave
Scottsdale, AZ 85251
(602) 994-0405

GALLERY THREE
3819 N Third St
Phoenix, AZ 85012
(602) 277-9540

GIFTED HANDS
Tlaquepaque Center #221
Hwy 179
Sedona, AZ 86336
GUILD Artist: Don Drumm, see
page 216.

IMAGINE GALLERY
34505 Scottsdale Rd #E7
Scottsdale, AZ 85262
(602) 488-1161
GUILD Artists: Bob Brown and Judy
Dykstra-Brown, see page 154.

LA FUENTE GALLERY
Box 2169
Sedona, AZ 86336
(602) 282-5276
GUILD Artist: Nancy J. Young and
Allen Young, see page 212.

OBSIDIAN GALLERY
4340 N Campbell Ave #90
Tucson, AZ 85718
(602) 577-3598

PEARSON & COMPANY
7022 E Main St
Scottsdale, AZ 85251
(602) 840-6447

RAKU GALLERY
250 Hull Ave
P.O. Box 965
Jerome, AZ 86331
(602) 639-0239

SKY FIRE GALLERY
39 Main St
Jerome, AZ 86331
(602) 634-8081

THE HAND AND THE SPIRT,
JOANNE RAPP GALLERY
4222 N Marshall Way
Scottsdale, AZ 85251
(602) 949-1262
GUILD Artist: Elizabeth MacDonald,
see pages 84 and 85.

THE MIND'S EYE CRAFT
GALLERY
4200 N Marshall Way
Scottsdale, AZ 85251
(302) 941-2494

TOTALLY SOUTHWESTERN
GALLERY
5575 E River Rd #131
Tucson, AZ 85715
(602) 577-2295
GUILD Artists: David M. Shiller and
Bernice Schiller, see page 124.

• Arkansas

CONTEMPORANEA
GALLERY
516 Central Ave
Hot Springs Nat Park, AR 71901
(501) 624-0516

• California

A GALLERY OF FINE ART
73-580 El Paseo
Palm Desert, CA 92260
(619) 346-8885
GUILD Artist: Marsha Lega, see
page 133.

A NEW LEAF GALLERY
1286 Gilman St
Berkeley, CA 94706
(510) 525-7621
GUILD Artist: Martin Sturman, see
page 220.

ACROPOLIS NOW
2510 Main St
Santa Monica, CA 90405
(213) 396-7611
GUILD Artists: Charles Pearson and
Timothy Roeder, see page 175.

AGNES BOURNE, INC
2 Henry Adams St #220
San Francisco, CA 94103-5024
(415) 626-6883

ALLEN FINE ART GALLERY
73-200 El Paseo Dr #4B
Palm Desert, CA 92260
(619) 341-8655
GUILD Artist: Martin Sturman, see
page 220.

ALLRICH GALLERY
251 Post St #400
San Francisco, CA 94108-5004
(415) 398-8896

AMBIANCE
405 Second St
Eureka, CA 95501
(707)445-8950
GUILD Artist: Victor Jacoby, see
page 25.

APPALACHIA
14440 Big Basin Way
Saratoga, CA 95070
(408) 741-999

ARCHITECT'S INTERIOR
1300 N Santa Cruz Ave
Los Gatos, CA 95030
(408) 354-1020

ART BY DESIGN GALLERY
5889 Oberlin Dr #103
San Diego, CA 92121
(619) 452-8586

ART COLLECTOR'S GALLERY
4151 Taylor St
San Diego, CA 92110
(619) 299-3232
GUILD Artist: Martha Chatelain,
see page 10.

ART OPTIONS
1935 Divisadero
San Francisco, CA 94131
(415) 567-8535

ART OPTIONS
2507 Main St
Santa Monica, CA 90405-3517
(213) 392-9099
GUILD Artist: Michelle Svoboda,
see page 180.

ART WORKS
1250 Prospect St
La Jolla, CA 92037
(619)459-7688
GUILD Artist: Michelle Svoboda,
see page 180.

ARTIFACTS GALLERY
3024 Fillmore St
San Francisco, CA 94123
(415) 922-8465
GUILD Artist: David M. Bowman,
see page 215.

ARTIFAX INTERNATIONAL
GALLERY & GIFTS
148 E Napa St
Sonoma, CA 95476
(707) 996-9494

ARTWORKS GALLERY
15 Helena Ave
Santa Barbara, CA 93101
(805) 966-9832

BANAKER GALLERY
1373 Locust St
Walnut Creek, CA 94596
(510) 930-0700

BANAKER GALLERY
251 Post St #310
San Francisco, CA 94108
GUILD Artist: Nancy Moore Bess,
see page 199.

BAY ARTS
309 Sutter St
San Francisco, CA 94108
(415) 399-9925

Gallery Resources

BAYSIDE GALLERY
Seaport Village
867-C W Harbor Dr
San Diego, CA 92101
(619) 233-4350

BENDICE GALLERY
380 First St W
Sonoma, CA 95476-5631
(707) 938-2775

BETH CHRISTENSEN FINE ART
538 Silverado Drive
Tiberon, CA 94920
(415)435-2314
GUILD Artist: Karen Davidson, see
page 11.

BOB LEONARD, INC.
2727 Main Street
Santa Monica, CA 90405
(310) 399-3251
GUILD Artist: Lois Sattler, see
page 178.

BRAVO GALLERY
302 Island Ave #101
San Diego, CA 92101
(619) 232-0396

BRENDAN WALTER GALLERY
1001 Colorado Ave
Santa Monica, CA 90401
(213) 395-1155

BRONZE PLUS, INC
6790 Depot St
Sebastopol, CA 95472-3452
(707) 829-5480

BRUCE BROWN ORIGINALS
680 Eighth St
San Francisco, CA 94103
(415) 252-9667

CALIFORNIA
CONTEMPORARY CRAFTS
109 Corte Madera Town Center
Corte Madera, CA 94925
(415) 927-3158
GUILD Artist: Ingemar Persson,
see page 200.

CEDANNA GALLERY
400 Main St
Half Moon Bay, CA 94019
(415) 726-6776

CEDANNA GALLERY &
STORE
1925 Fillmore St
San Francisco, CA 94115
(414) 474-7152

CELEBRATE LIFE
28 E Colorado Blvd
Pasadena, CA 91105
(818) 585-0690

CHAPSON ARTSVISION, LTD
2 Henry Adams St #489
San Francisco, CA 94103
(415) 863-2117

CHRISTINE OF SANTA FE
220 Forest Ave
Laguna Beach, CA 92651
(714) 494-3610

CLAUDIA CHAPLINE
GALLERY
3445 Shoreline Hwy
P.O. Box 946
Stinson Beach, CA 94970-0946
(415) 868-2308

CLYDE STREET GALLERY
34 Clyde St
San Francisco, CA 94107
(415) 546-5185

COAST GALLERY
P.O. Box 223519
Carmel, CA 93922-3519
(408) 625-3575

COLLAGE GALLERY
1345 18th St
San Francisco, CA 94107
(415) 282-4401

COMPOSITIONS GALLERY
The Cannery
2801 Leavenworth
San Francisco, CA 94133
(415) 441-0629
GUILD Artist: Joan Irving, see
page 144.

CONCEPTS GALLERY
Sixth St (at Mission)
Carmel, CA 93921
(408) 624-0661

CONTEMPORARY IMAGES
GALLERY
14027 Ventura Blvd
Sherman Oaks, CA 91423
(818) 783-2007

COUTURIER GALLERY
166 N La Brea Ave
Los Angeles, CA 90036
(213) 933-5557

CRAFTSMAN'S GUILD
300 De Haro
San Francisco, CA 94103
(415) 431-5425

CROCK-R-BOX
El Paseo Village
73-425 El Paseo
Palm Desert, CA 92260
(619) 568-6688

DAVID AUSTIN
CONTEMPORARY ART
355 El Portal
Palm Springs, CA 92264
(619) 322-7709

DE NOVO
250 University Ave
Palo Alto, CA 94301
(415) 327-1256

DE VERA
384 Hayes St
San Francisco, CA 94102
(415) 861-8480

DEL MANO GALLERY
11981 San Vicente Blvd
Los Angeles, CA 90049
(213) 476-8508
GUILD Artists: Martha Chatelain,
see page 10. Claudia Hollister,
see page 173. Tom Neugebauer,
see page 174. Ingemar Persson,
see page 200. George Radeschi,
see page 209.

DEL MANO GALLERY
33 E Colorado Blvd
Pasadena, CA 91105-1901
(818) 793-6648
GUILD Artist: Martha Chatelain,
see page 10.

DISCOVERIES
CONTEMPORARY CRAFT
17350 17th St #E
Tustin, CA 92680
(714) 544-6206

ECLECTIC GALLERY
Kasten & Ukiah St
Mendocino, CA 95460
(707) 937-5951

EDITIONS LTD. GALLERIES
625 Second Street,
Suite 400
San Francisco, CA 94107
(415) 543-9811
GUILD Artist: Joan Schulze, see
page 51.

EILEEN KREMEN GALLERY
619 N Harbor Blvd
Fulleron, CA 92632
(714) 879-1391

ELEGANT EARTH GALLERY
13148 Central Ave
Boulder Creek, CA 95006
(408) 338-3646
GUILD Artists: Bob Brown and Judy-
Dykstra-Brown, see page 154.

ELIZABETH FORTNER
GALLERY
100 W Micheltorena St
Santa Barbara, CA 93101
(805) 969-9984

EUREKA ART CENTER
211 G St
Eureka, CA 95501
(707) 443-7017

FAITH NIGHTINGALE
GALLERY
535 Fourth Ave
San Diego, CA 92101
(619) 236-1028

FEINGARTEN GALLERIES
P.O. Box 5383
Beverly Hills, CA 90209-5383
(310) 274-7042

FERRARI OF CARMEL
San Carlos 5th & 6th
P.O. Box 3273
Carmel, CA 93921
(408) 624-9677

FILLAMENTO GALLERY
2185 Fillmore St
San Francisco, CA 94115
(415) 931-2774

FINE WOODWORKING
GALLERY
1201C Bridgeway
Sausalito, CA 94965
(415) 332-5770

FLUSH
245 11th St
San Francisco, CA 94103
(415) 252-0245

FOLLOWING SEA
8522 Beverly Blvd
Los Angeles, CA 90048
(310) 659-0592

FONG & SPRATT GALLERIES
383 S First St
San Jose, CA 95113
(408) 298-4141

FREEHAND GALLERY
8413 W Third St
Los Angeles, CA 90048
(213) 655-2607

FRESNO ART MUSEUM SHOP
2233 N First St
Fresno, CA 93703
(209) 485-4810

FURNITURE FUNCTIONAL &
ESSENTIAL
437 Hayes St
San Francisco, CA 94102
(415) 703-0718

GALLERY ALEXANDER
7850 Girard Ave
La Jolla, CA 92037
(619) 459-9433

GALLERY EIGHT
7464 Girard Ave
La Jolla, CA 92037
(619) 454-9781

GALLERY FAIR
P.O. Box 263
Mendocino, CA 95460
(707) 937-5121

GALLERY FOURTEEN
947 61st St
Oakland, CA 94608
(510) 547-7608

GALLERY JAPONESQUE
824 Montgomery St
San Francisco, CA 94133
(415) 398-8577

GALLERY MILLIEU
3835 Cross Creek Rd
Malibu, CA 90265
(310) 456-7664
GUILD Artist: Martin Sturman, see
page 220.

GALLERY OF
FUNCTIONAL ART
2429 Main St
Santa Monica, CA 90405-3539
(213) 450-2827
GUILD Artists: Johanna
Goodman, see page 142. John
Kennedy, see page 132.

GALLERY ONE
32 Liberty St
Petaluma, CA 94952
(707) 778-8277

GARRETT & WHITE GALLERY
664 S Coast Hwy
Laguna Beach, CA 92651
(714) 494-4117

GOOD DAY SUNSHINE
29 E Napa St
Sonoma, CA 95476
(707) 938-4001

GUMP'S GALLERY
250 Post St
San Francisco, CA 94108
(415) 982-1616
GUILD Artist: George Radeschi,
see page 209.

HANDMADE GALLERY
12169 Ventura Blvd.
Studio City, CA 91604
(818) 752-4383
GUILD Artist: Martin Sturman, see
page 220.

HANK BAUM GALLERY
P.O. Box 26689
San Francisco, CA 94126
(415) 752-4336

HARLEEN AND ALLEN
FINE ART
427 Bryant Street
San Francisco, CA 94107
(415) 777-0920
GUILD Artist: Susana England, see
page 12.

HENLEY'S GALLERY
On the Sea Ranch
1000 Annapolis Rd
The Sea Ranch, CA 95497
(707) 785-2951

HIGHLIGHT
45052 Main St
Mendocino, CA 95460
(707) 937-3132

HUMANARTS
310 E Ojai Ave
Ojai, CA 93023
(805) 646-1525

I WOLK GALLERY
1235 Main St
St Helena, CA 94574-1902
(707) 963-8801

IMAGES OF THE NORTH
1782 Union St
San Francisco, CA 94123
(415) 673-1273

INTERIA
11404 Sorrento Valley Rd
San Diego, CA 92121
(619) 455-7177

INTERNATIONAL GALLERY
643 G St
San Diego, CA 92101
(619) 235-8255

INTERSIA GALLERY
155 Camino Del Mar #308
Del Mar, CA 92014
(619) 792-5000

JAPONESQUE, INC
50 Post St
San Francisco, CA 94114
(415) 398-8577

JOANNE CHAPPELL GALLERY
625 Second St #400
San Francisco, CA 94107
(415) 543-9811
GUILD Artist: Rebecca Bluestone,
see page 21.

KALEIDOSCOPE GALLERY
3273 Rogers Ave
Walnut Creek, CA 94596
(510) 210-1336

KILIM FLAT WOVEN RUGS
8675 N Lake Blvd
Kings Beach, CA 95719
(916) 546-4011

KIMBERLEY'S
25601 Pine Creek Lane
Wilmington, CA 90744
(310) 835-4169

KIYO HIGASHI GALLERY
8332 Melrose Ave
Los Angeles, CA 90069
(213) 655-2482

KOKOPELLI'S
1010 El Camino Real #120
Menlo Park, CA 94025
(415) 328-6472

KURLAND SUMMERS GALLERY
8742-A Melrose Ave
Los Angeles, CA 90069
(310) 659-7098
GUILD Artist: Cohn-Stone Studios,
see page 185.

L.H. SELMAN, LTD
761 Chestnut St
Santa Cruz, CA 95060
(800) 538-0766

LA QUINTA GALLERY
La Quinta Hotel
La Quinta, CA 92253
GUILD Artist: John Kennedy, see
page 132.

LAISE ADZER GALLERY
401 N Maple Dr
Beverly Hills, CA 90210
(310) 274-5018

LANE GALLERY
173 Horton Plaza
San Diego, CA 92101
(619) 234-4234

LEGENDS GALLERY
483 First St W
Sonoma, CA 95476
(707) 939-8100

LOS GATOS COMPANY
17 1/2 N Santa Cruz Ave
Los Gatos, CA 95030
(408) 354-2433

MADE IN MENDOCINO
13500 S Hwy 101
Hopland, CA 90024
(707) 744-1300

MANDEL & CO.
8687 Melrose Ave.
Los Angeles, CA 90069
(310) 652-5025
GUILD Artist: Greg Sheres, see
page 143.

MANY HANDS GALLERY
1001 Center St
Santa Cruz, CA 91350
(408) 429-8696

MARTIN LAWRENCE
GALLERIES
16250 Stagg St
Van Nuys, CA 91406
(818) 988-630

MASTER'S MARK GALLERY
3228 Sacramento St
San Francisco, CA 94115
(415) 885-6700

METAL SMYTHE
152 Sacramento St
Auburn, CA 95603
(916) 823-9776

MICHAEL HIMOVITZ GALLERY
1020 Tenth St
Sacramento, CA 95814
(916) 448-8723

MODERN LIFE DESIGNS
682 Post St
San Francisco, CA 94109
(415) 441-7118

MODERN LIVING
8125 Melrose Avenue
Los Angeles, CA 90046
(213) 655-3898
GUILD Artist: Anne Shutan, see
page 125.

MOONSTONES GALLERY
4070 Burton Dr
Cambria, CA 93428
(805) 927-3447

NADEL PHELAN GALLERY
1001 Center St
Santa Cruz, CA 91350
(408) 426-4980

NADEL PHELAN GALLERY
3555 Clares St #10
Capitola, CA 95010
(408) 464-9120

NEW STONE AGE
8407 W Third St
Los Angeles, CA 90048
(213) 658-5969

OFF YOUR DOT
2241 Market St
San Francisco, CA 94114
(415) 252-5642

OLIVE HYDE ART GALLERY
123 Washington Blvd
P.O. Box 5006
Fremont, CA 94537
(415) 791-4357

OPUS III
1835 Newport Blvd
Costa Mesa, CA 92627
(305) 568-9153

OUT OF HAND GALLERY
1303 Castro St
San Francisco, CA 94114
(415) 826-3885

P R COONLEY GALLERY
325 Stanford Shopping Ctr
Palo Alto, CA 93921
(415) 327-4000
GUILD Artist: Karen Adachi, see
page 9.

P.R. COONLEY–HANDWORKS
Delores and Sixth Street
Carmel, CA 93921
(408) 624-6400
GUILD Artist: Karen Adachi, see
page 9.

PALM SPRINGS DESERT
MUSEUM
101 Museum Dr
Palm Springs, CA 92262
(619) 325-7186

PATRICIA CORREIA GALLERY
1355 Abbot Kinney Blvd
Venice, CA 90291
(310) 314-2626

Gallery Resources

PAUL LUSTER GALLERY
6517 Dry Creek Rd
Napa, CA 94558
(415) 431-8511

PAZAR GALLERY
23561 Malibu Colony Dr
Malibu, CA 90265
(310) 456-1142

PERIWINKLE PRINTS & GIFTS
88 Eureka Square
Pacifica, CA 94044
(415) 359-4236

PLUMS CONTEMPORARY ART
2405 Capitol St
Fresno, CA 93721
(209) 237-1822

POT-POURRI GALLERY
4100 Redwood Rd
Oakland, CA 94619
(510) 531-1503

PRIMAVERA GALLERY
214 E Ojai Ave
Ojai, CA 93023
(805) 646-7133

PUBLIC ART SERVICES
1242 Crescent Heights #20
West Hollywood, CA 90046-5037
(213) 650-3709

RANDOLPH & HEIN, INC
8687 Melrose Ave #310
Los Angeles, CA 90069
(310) 855-1222

RESOURCE FOR ART
200 Kansas St
San Francisco, CA 94103
(415) 864-2787

ROOKIE-TO GALLERY
P.O. Box 606
14300 HWY 128
Boonville, CA 95415
(707) 895-2204

RUTH BACHOFNER GALLERY
926 Colroado Ave
Santa Monica, CA 90401
(310) 458-8007

**SANTA BARBARA STYLE
AND DESIGN**
**137 E. Dela Guerra
Santa Barbara, CA 93101
(805) 965-6291**
GUILD Artist: Brian McNally, see
page 157.

SCHWARTZ CIERLAK
GALLERY
26106 Paulino Pl
Valencia, CA 91355-2039
(213) 396-3814

SCULPTURE TO WEAR
8441 Melrose Ave
Los Angeles, CA 90069
(213) 651-2205

SEEKERS COLLECTION &
GALLERY
**2515A Village Lane
P.O. Box 521
Cambria, CA 93428
(805) 927-8626**
GUILD Artists: Wendy Saxon
Brown, see page 139. Jonathan
Winfisky, see page 197.

SHERWOOD GALLERY
460 S Coast Hwy
Laguna Beach, CA 92651-2404
(714) 497-2668

SHIBUI HOUSE
630 Cliff Dr
Aptos, CA 95003
(408) 688-7195

**SHO-EN OUTDOOR
SCULPTURE CENTER**
**P.O. Box 1210
Ramona, CA 92065
(619) 789-7079**
GUILD Artist: Gradzki Hand Forged
Metal Arts, see page 131.

SIGNATURE GALLERY
3693 Fifth Ave
San Diego, CA 92103
(619) 297-0430

SILICA GALLERY
460 N. Canon Drive
Beverly Hills, CA 90210
(310) 550-5987

SIMPSON HELLER GALLERY
2289 Main St
Cambria, CA 93402
(805) 927-1800

SMILE GALLERY
1750 Union St
San Francisco, CA 94123
(415) 771-1901

SMITHEREENS
250A Magnolia
Larkspur, CA 94939
(415) 924-5093

SPECTRUM CONTEMPORARY
FINE ART
72-785 Hwy 111
Palm Desert, CA 92260
(617) 773-9281

STEVE'S GALLERY
**9630 Santa Monica Blvd
Beverly Hills, CA 90210
(310) 274-6567**
GUILD Artist: Lois Sattler, see
page 178.

STILLWATER GALLERY
**1228 Main St
St Helena, CA 94574
(707) 963-1782**
GUILD Artist: J. Dubs, see
page 217.

STUDIO FORTY TWO
42 Elm St
Los Gatos, CA 95030
(408) 395-3191

SUMMER HOUSE GALLERY
14 Miller Ave
Mill Valley, CA 94941
(415) 383-6695

SUSAN CUMMINS GALLERY
32 Miller Ave
Mill Valley, CA 94941-1904
(415) 383-1512

TAFOYA GALLERY
**Lincoln Court Bldg #110
2105 S Bascom St
Campbell, CA 95008
(408) 559-6161**
GUILD Artist: Marjorie Tomchuk,
see page 18.

TAKADA FINE ARTS GALLERY
**251 Post St, Sixth Floor
San Francisco, CA 94108
(415) 956-5288**
GUILD Artist: Joan Schulze, see
page 51.

TAKE A SECOND GALLERY
38 Petaluma Blvd N
Petaluma, CA 94952
(707) 763-7560

TAPESTRIES GALLERY
145 Hamilton Ave
Palo Alto, CA 94303
(415) 324-1908

TARBOX GALLERY
1202 Kettner Blvd
San Diego, CA 92101
(619) 234-5020

TEN DIRECTIONS GALLERY
723 Santa Ysabel
Baywood Park, CA 93402
(805) 528-4574

TERCERA GALLERY
24 N Santa Cruz Ave
Los Gatos, CA 95030
(408) 354-9482

TESORI GALLERY
**30 E Third Ave
San Mateo, CA 94401
(415) 344-4731**
GUILD Artists: Vincent Tolpo and
Carolyn L. Tolpo, see page 108.

TESORI GALLERY
**319 S Robertson Blvd
Los Angeles, CA 90048
(213) 273-9890**
GUILD Artist: Michelle Svoboda,
see page 180.

TEXTURES GALLERY
550 Deep Valley Dr #135
Rolling Hills Ests, CA 90274
(213) 541-1943

**THE AESTHETICS
COLLECTION, INC.**
**1060 17th Street
San Diego, CA 92101
(619) 238-1860**
GUILD Artist: Alexandra
Friedman, see page 23.

THE ART COLLECTOR
**4151 Taylor St
San Diego, CA 92110
(619) 299-3232**
GUILD Artist: John P. Ashley, see
page 93.

THE ARTFUL EYE
1333A Lincoln Ave
Calistoga, CA 94515
(707) 942-4743

THE BERNARD GALLERIES
1489 E Newell Ave
Walnut Creek, CA 94596
(510) 932-2738

THE COBWEB COLLECTION
83 Main St
Sutter Creek, CA 95685
(209) 267-0690

THE COURTYARD GALLERY
1349 Park St
Alameda, CA 94510
(415) 521-1521

THE CRAFT & FOLK ART
MUSEUM
5800 Wilshire Blvd
Los Angeles, CA 90036-4500
(213) 937-9099

THE GALLERY
329 Primrose Rd
Burlingame, CA 94010
(415) 347-9392

THE GALLERY AT LA QUINTA
**La Quinta Hotel
La Quinta, CA 92253
(619) 564-5708**
GUILD Artist: John Kennedy, see
page 132.

THE LIMN COMPANY
457 Pacific St
San Francisco, CA 94133
(415) 986-3884

THE LOS ANGELES ART
EXCHANGE
2451 Broadway
Santa Monica, CA 90404
(213) 828-6866

THE MEADOWLARK GALLERY
**317 Corte Madera
Town Center
Corte Madera, CA 94925
(415) 924-2210**
GUILD Artists: Bob Brown and Judy
Dykstra-Brown, see page 154.

Gallery Resources

THE MUSEUM OF
CONTEMPORARY ART
250 S Grand Ave
Los Angeles, CA 90012
(213) 621-2766

THE PACIFIC GALLERY
228 Forest Ave
Laguna Beach, CA 92651
(714) 494-8732

THE PALUMBO GALLERY
Dolores St (at Sixth)
P.O. Box 5727
Carmel, CA 93921
(408) 625-5727

THE PANACHE GALLERY
45104 Main St
P.O. Box 57
Mendocino, CA 95460
(707) 937-1234

THE PERFECT GIFT GALLERY
250 Pine Creek Rd
Walnut Creek, CA 94598
(415) 930-6066

THE PLAZA GALLERY
746 Higuera St #8
San Luis Obispo, CA 93401
(805) 543-5681

THE PRINTWORKS GALLERY
5229 E Second St
Long Beach, CA 90803
(213) 434-5789

THE QUEST
777 Bridgeway
Sausalito, CA 94965
(415) 332-6832

THE RUBELL COLLECTION
11666 Goshen Ave #325
Los Angeles, CA 90049
(213) 473-2283

THE SCULPTURE GARDENS
GALLERY
1031 Abbott Kenny Blvd
Venice, CA 90291
(310) 396-5809

THE SOCO GALLERY
101 S Coombs St
Napa, CA 94559-4500
(707) 255-5954

THE TROVE GALLERY
73-700 El Paseo
Palm Desert, CA 92260
(619) 346-1999

THE VIEWPOINT GALLERY
224 Crossroads Blvd
Carmel, CA 93923
(408) 624-3369

THE WILD BLUE GALLERY
7220 Melrose Ave
Los Angeles, CA 90046
(213) 939-8434

THE YOUNTVILLE
MARKET, INC
6770 Washington St
Yountville, CA 95799
(707) 944-1393

THE ZOO GALLERY
9632 Santa Monica Blvd
Beverly Hills, CA 90210
(310) 278-3873
**GUILD Artist: Johanna Goodman,
see page 142.**

TOPS MALIBU GALLERY
23410 Civic Center Way
Malibu, CA 90265
(213) 456-8677
**GUILD Artist: Judy Stone, see
page 210.**

ULRICH CREATIVE ARTS
P.O. Box 684
Ventura, CA 93002
(805) 643-4160

VALERIE MILLER GALLERY
73-100 El Paseo
Palm Desert, CA 92260
(619) 773-4483
**GUILD Artist: John Kennedy, see
page 132.**

VARIOUS & SUNDRIES
411 San Anselmo Ave
San Anselmo, CA 94960
(415) 454-1442

VICTOR FISCHER GALLERIES
1525 Santanella Ter
Corona del Mar, CA 92625-1746
(714) 644-9655

VICTOR FISCHER GALLERIES
P.O. Box 192995
San Francisco, CA 94119
(415) 777-0717

VIEWPOINTS GALLERY
11315 Hwy 1
P.O. Box 670
Point Reyes Station, CA 94956
(415) 663-8861

VILLAGE ARTISTRY GALLERY
Dolores (between Ocean & 7th)
P.O. Box 5493
Carmel, CA 93921
(408) 624-7628
**GUILD Artists: Martha Chatelain,
see page 10. Susana England,
see page 12.**

VIRGINIA BREIER GALLERY
3091 Sacramento St
San Francisco, CA 94115
(415) 929-7173

VISUAL DIMENSIONS
GALLERY
302 Island Ave
San Diego, CA 92101
(619) 232-0396

WALLS ALIVE, INC
1754 Junction Ave
San Jose, CA 95112
(408) 436-8131
**GUILD Artist: Joan Schulze, see
page 51.**

WALTER WHITE FINE ARTS
107 Capitola Ave
Capitola, CA 95010-3202
(408) 476-7001

WHATEVER GALLERY
601 Laguna
San Francisco, CA 94102
(415) 864-2274

WITTENBORN &
HOLLINGSWORTH
8742A Melrose Ave
Los Angeles, CA 90069
(213) 659-7098

ZANTMAN ART GALLERIES
P.O. Box 5818
Carmel, CA 93921
(408) 624-8314

ZOSAKU FINE CRAFTS
GALLERY
2110 Vine St
Berkeley, CA 94709
(415) 549-3373

• Colorado

A SHOW OF HANDS GALLERY
2440 E Third Ave
Denver, CO 80206
(303) 920-3071

CAVIANO CONTEMPORARY
CRAFTS
5910 S University
Littleton, CO 80121
(303) 798-6696

COMMONWHEEL ARTIST
CO-OP
102 Canon Ave
Manitou Springs, CO 80829
(719) 685-1008

GOTTHELFF GALLERY
122 E Meadow
Vail, CO 81657
(303) 476-1777
**GUILD Artist: J.C. Homola, see
page 188.**

HEATHER GALLERY
555 E Durant
Aspen, CO 81611
(303) 925-6641

HIBBERD MCGRATH GALLERY
101 N Main St
P.O. Box 7638
Breckenridge, CO 80424
(303) 453-6391

J COTTER GALLERY
234 Wall St
P.O. Box 385
Vail, CO 81658
(303) 476-3131

JOAN ROBEY GALLERY
939 Broadway
Denver, CO 80203-2705
(303) 892-9600

MILL STREET GALLERY
112 S Mill St
Aspen, CO 81611
(303) 925-4988
**GUILD Artist: Sydney K.
Hamburger, see page 202.**

MUSEUMS OF THE WORLD
320 E. Hopkins Ave.
Aspen, CO 81611-1906
(303) 333-1631

NANCY LEE, LTD.
**Denver Merchandise Mart,
Suite 1508**
Denver, CO 80216
**GUILD Artist: Tiger Mountain
Woodworks, see page 127.**

OBJECTS, LTD
595 S Broadway #112E
Denver, CO 80209
(303) 777-6830
**GUILD Artist: Frank Colson, see
page 80.**

QUILTS UNLIMITED
308 S Hunter
Aspen, CO 81611
(303) 920-2893

SANDI ROACH GALLERIES
1142 13th St
Boulder, CO 80302
(303) 444-4968

SANDY CARSON GALLERY
1734 Wazee
Denver, CO 80202
(303) 297-8585

TAVELLI GALLERY
620 E Hyman Ave
Aspen, CO 81611
(303) 920-3071

TELLURIDE GALLERY
OF FINE ART
130 E Colorado
P.O. Box 1900
Telluride, CO 81435
(303) 728-3300

THE CLAY PIGEON
601 Ogden St
Denver, CO 80218
(303) 832-5538

THE PANACHE CRAFT
GALLERY
315 Columbine
Denver, CO 80206
(303) 321-8069

Gallery Resources

THE RACHAEL COLLECTION
433 E Cooper St
Aspen, CO 81611
(303) 920-1313
GUILD Artists: Michael K. Hansen and Nina Palidino, see page 187. Orient & Flume Art Glass, see page 193 Joan Irving, see page 144.

THE TWO MOON GALLERY
764 Main Ave
Durango, CO 81301
(303) 247-1488

THE UNIQUE GALLERY
11 E Bijou
Colorado Springs, CO 80903
(719) 473-9406

THE UPPEREDGE GALLERY
Snowmass Village - Upper Level
P.O. Box 5294
Snowmass Village, CO 81615
(303) 923-5373

THE WHITE HART GALLERY
843 Lincoln Ave
Steamboat Springs, CO 80477
(303) 879-1015

TOH-ATIN GALLERY
145 W Ninth St
Durango, CO 81301
(800) 525-384

• Connecticut

A TOUCH OF GLASS
P.O. Box 433
N Moodus Rd
Moodus, CT 06469
(203) 873-9709

AMERICAN HAND
125 Post Rd E
Westport, CT 06880
(203) 226-8883

ATELIER STUDIO GALLERY
27 East St
New Milford, CT 06776
(203) 354-7792

BROOKFIELD CRAFT CENTER
286 Whisconier Rd
Rt 25 Box 122
Brookfield, CT 06804
(203) 775-4526
GUILD Artist: Alexandra Friedman, see page 23.

BROOKFIELD SONO CRAFT CENTER
127 Washington St
Norwalk, CT 06854-3006
(203) 853-6155

BROWN GROTTA GALLERY
39 Grumman Hill Rd
Wilton, CT 06897-4541
(203) 834-0623

COMPANY OF CRAFTSMEN
43 W Main St
Mystic, CT 06355
(203) 536-4189

ENDLEMAN GALLERY
1014 Chapel St
New Haven, CT 06510
(203) 776-2517

EVERGREEN FINE CRAFTS
21 Boston St
Guilford, CT 06437
(203) 453-4324

FISHER GALLERY
25 Bunker Ln
Avon, CT 06001
(203) 678-1867

GALLERY/SHOP AT WESLEYAN
350 S Main St Rt 17
Middletown, CT 06457
(203) 344-0039

GUILFORD HANDCRAFTS, INC
411 Church St
Rt 77
Guilford, CT 06437
(203) 453-5947

HERON AMERICAN CRAFT GALLERY
Main St
Kent, CT 06757
(203) 927-4804
GUILD Artist: Helio Graphics, see page 167.

MENDELSON GALLERY
Titus Square
Washington Depot, CT 06794-1517
(203) 868-307
GUILD Artists: Elizabeth MacDonald, see pages 84 and 85. Ingemar Persson, see page 200. George Radeschi, see page 209.

NEW HORIZONS GALLERY
42 W Putnam Ave
Greenwich, CT 06830
(203) 622-6867

SILVERMINE GUILD ARTS CENTER
1037 Silvermine Rd
New Canaan, CT 06840
(203) 966-5617
GUILD Artist: Marjorie Tomchuk, see page 18.

STARSHINE GALLERY
319 Horse Hill Rd
Westbrook, CT 06498
(203) 399-5149

THE ELEMENTS
14 Liberty Way
Greenwich, CT 06830
(203) 661-0014

THE RED PEPPER GALLERY
41 Main St
Chester, CT 06412
(203) 526-4460

THE SILO GALLERY
44 Upland Rd
New Milford, CT 06776
(203) 355-0300

THE WOOL CONNECTION
Riverdale Farms
Rt 10 N
Avon, CT 06001
(203) 678-1710

VARIATIONS GALLERY
P.O. Box 246
Rt 20
Riverton, CT 06065
(203) 379-2964

WAYSIDE FURNITURE OF MILFORD
1650 Boston Post Rd
Milford, CT 06460
(203) 878-1781

WHITNEY MUSEUM OF ART
Fairfield County
One Champion Plaza
Stamford, CT 06921
(203) 358-7652

• Delaware

BLUE STREAK GALLERY
1723 Delaware Ave
Wilmington, DE 19806
(302) 429-0506

CRAFT COLLECTION
129D Rehoboth Ave
Rehoboth Beach, DE 19971
(302) 227-3640

THE STATION GALLERY
3922 Kennett Pike
Greenville, DE 19807
(302) 654-8638
GUILD Artist: Joan Kopchik, see page 16.

• District of Columbia

AMERICAN HAND PLUS
2906 M St NW
Washington, DC 20007
(202) 965-3273

ANNE O'BRIEN GALLERY
4829 Bending Ln NW
Washington, DC 20007-1527
(202) 265-9697

FARRELL COLLECTION
2633 Connecticut Ave NW
Washington, DC 20007-1522
(202) 483-8334
GUILD Artist: Claudia Hollister, see page 173.

FRANKLIN PARRASCH GALLERY
2114 R St NW
Washington, DC 20008
(202) 328-8222

GAZELLE GALLERY
5335 Wisconsin Ave NW
Washington, DC 20015
(202) 686-5656

INDIAN CRAFT SHOP
1050 Wisconsin Ave NW
Washington, DC 20007
(202) 342-3918

INDIAN CRAFT SHOP
Dept of the Interior
1849 C St NW #1023
Washington, DC 20240
(202) 737-4381

JACKIE CHALKLEY GALLERY
1455 Pennsylvania Ave NW
Washington, DC 20004
(202) 683-3060

JACKIE CHALKLEY GALLERY
3301 New Mexico Ave NW
Washington, DC 20016
(202) 686-8882

JACKIE CHALKLEY GALLERY
5301 Wisconsin Ave NW
Washington, DC 20015
(202) 537-6100

MAURINE LITTLETON GALLERY
1667 Wisconsin Ave NW
Washington, DC 20007
(202) 333-9307

MICHAEL STONE COLLECTION
1025 Thomas Jefferson St
Washington, DC 20007
(202) 333-5089

NATIONAL BUILDING MUSEUM
401 F St NW
Washington, DC 20001-2728
(202) 272-2448

OUTSIDE DESIGNS
5335 Wisconsin Ave
Washington, DC 20015
(800) 468-8743

SANSAR GALLERY
4200 Wisconsin Ave NW
Washington, DC 20016-2143
(202) 244-4448
GUILD Artists: Ronald C. Puckett, see page 123. Nick Strange, see page 113.

Gallery Resources

THE KELLOGG COLLECTION
3424 Wisconsin Ave NW
Washington, DC 20016
(202) 363-5089

THE TOUCHSTONE GALLERY
2009 R St NW
Washington, DC 20009
(202) 797-7278

UPTOWN ARTS
3236 P St NW
Washington, DC 20007
(202) 337-0600

• Florida

5G COLLECTION, ART PLUS
1000 Clintmoore Rd #109
Boca Raton, FL 33487
(407) 997-3300

A STEP ABOVE GALLERY
500 N. Tamiami Trail
Sarasota, FL 34236-4823
(813) 955-4477
GUILD Artist: Larry Raymond
Brown, see page 139.

AHAVA
Mizner Park
414 Plaza Real
Boca Raton, FL 33432
(407) 395-5001

ALBERTSON PETERSON
GALLERY
329 Park Ave S
Winter Park, FL 32789
(407) 628-1258

AMERICAN DETAILS
3107 Grand Ave
Coconut Grove, FL 33133
(305) 448-6163

ART BY THE PARK
2030D W First St
Ft Myers, FL 33901
(813) 337-7300

ART EXPRESSIONS
1006 E New Haven Ave
Melbourne, FL 32901
(407) 728-7053

ART GLASS
ENVIRONMENTS, INC
174 Glades Rd
Boca Raton, FL 33432
(407) 391-7310

ARTCETERA
3200 S Congress Ave #201
Boynton Beach, FL 33426
(407) 737-6953

CENTER STREET GALLERY
136 S Park Ave
Winter Park, FL 32789-4315
(407) 644-1545

CHRISTY TAYLOR ART
GALLERY
5050 Town Center Cir #243
Boca Raton, FL 33486
(407) 394-6387
GUILD Artist: Joan Irving, see
page 144.

CLAY SPACE GALLERY
924 Lincoln Rd
Miami Beach, FL 33139
(305) 534-3339

CLAYTON GALLERIES
4105 S MacDill Ave
Tampa, FL 33611
(813) 831-3753

COLLECTORS GALLERY
213 W Venice Ave
Venice, FL 34285
(813) 488-3029

COVE ART GALLERY
753 12th Ave S
Naples, FL 33940
(813) 263-244

DAKOTA GALLERY
5250 Town Center Cir #141
Boca Raton, FL 33486
(407) 394-9134

E.G. CODY GALLERY
80 NE 40th St
Miami, FL 33737
(305) 374-4777
GUILD Artists: Karen Adachi, see
page 9. Greg Sheres, see
page 143.

EXIT ART GALLERY
The Centre
5380 Gulf of Mexico Dr
Longboat Key, FL 34228
(813) 383-4099
GUILD Artists: Cathy Richardson,
see page 158. Ellen Zahorec, see
page 19.

FAST BUCK FREDDIES
500 Duval St
Key West, FL 33040
(305) 294-2007

FLORIDA CRAFTSMEN
GALLERY
237 Second Ave S
St Petersburg, FL 33701
(813) 821-7391

FLORIDA GLOBAL
GALLERY, INC
Tampa International Airport
Third Floor - Center
Tampa, FL 33607
(813) 276-3957

GALLERY CAMINO REAL
Gallery Center
608 Banyan Trail
Boca Raton, FL 33431-5605
(407) 241-1606

GALLERY FIVE
363 Tequesta Dr
Tequesta, FL 33469
(407) 747-5555

GALLERY ONE
1301 Third St S
Naples, FL 33940
(813) 263-835
GUILD Artist: Frank Colson, see
page 80.

GRAND CENTRAL GALLERY
442 Grand Central Ave #100
Tampa, FL 33606
(813) 254-4977
GUILD Artists: Alexandra
Friedman, see page 23. Betsy
Ross, see page 176.

GREAT SOUTHERN GALLERY
910 Duval Street
Key West, FL 33040
GUILD Artist: Anne Mayer Meier,
see page 206.

H.B. BRICKELL GALLERY
905 S Bayshore Dr
Miami, FL 33131
(305) 358-2088

HABITAT GALLERIES
Gallery Center
608 Banyan Trail
Boca Raton, FL 33431-5605
(407) 241-4544

HEARTWORKS
820 Lomax St
Jacksonville, FL 32204-3902
(904) 355-6210

HODGELL GALLERY
46 South Palm Avenue
Sarasota, FL 34236
(813) 366-1146
GUILD Artist: Patricia Weyer, see
page 196.

HOFFMAN GALLERY
2000 E Sunrise Blvd
Level 2
Ft Lauderdale, FL 33304
(305) 763-5371

IMAGE GALLERY
P.O. Box 3349
Sarasota, FL 34230
(813) 366-5097

IMAGES ART GALLERY
7400 N Tamiami Tr #101
Naples, FL 33963
(813) 598-3455

J. LAWRENCE GALLERY
1010 E New Haven Ave
Melbourne, FL 32901
(407) 728-7051

KOUCKY GALLERY
1246 Third Street S
Naples, FL 33940
(813) 261-8988

LEWIS CHARLES GALLERY
3105 Bay to Bay Blvd #1
Tampa, FL 33629
(813) 839-5320

LUCKY STREET GALLERY
919 Duval Street
Key West, FL 33040
(305) 294-3976
GUILD Artist: Helio Graphics, see
page 167.

LUVER GALLERY
19575 Biscayne Blvd
North Miami, FL 33180
(305) 935-3578

MARIE FERRER GALLERY
309 N Park Ave
Winter Park, FL 32789
(407) 647-7680

MASTERPIECE GALLERY
449 Plaza Real
Boca Taton, FL 33432
(407) 394-0070
GUILD Artist: Wendy Saxon-
Brown, see page 139.

NANCY KAYE GALLERY
201 E. Palmetto Park Road
Boca Raton, FL 33432
(407) 392-8220
GUILD Artist: Tom Neugebauer,
see page 174.

OEHLSCHLAEGER GALLERY II
28 South Blvd. of Presidents, Saint
Armand's Cir.
Sarasota, FL 34236
(813) 388-3312
GUILD Artist: Linda Bruce
Salomon, see page 177.

PLANTATION POTTERS
717 Duval St
Key West, FL 33040
(305) 294-3143

RALEIGH GALLERY
1855 Griffin Rd #B482
Danna, FL 33004
(305) 922-3330

RICK MOORE FINE ART
GALLERY
4230 Shore Blvd. N.
Naples, FL 33940
(813) 434-6464
GUILD Artist: Patricia Weyer, see
page 196.

RICK SANDERS GALLERIES
409-411-413 St Armands Cir
Sarasota, FL 34236
(813) 388-1000

ROBERT WINDSOR GALLERY
1855 Griffin Rd
Dania, FL 33004
(305) 923-9100
GUILD Artist: Martin Sturman, see
page 220.

Gallery Resources

SELDOM SEEN GALLERY
1515 SE 17th St
Ft Lauderdale, FL 33316
(305) 522-7556

SOUTHWINDS ART GALLERY
Mission Bay Plaza
10101 Glades Rd
Boca Raton, FL 33498
(407) 479-3535

SPANISH STREET WOOD ART
36 Spanish St
St Augustine, FL 32084
(904) 829-0913

SPECTRUM OF AMERICAN
ARTISTS
3101 PGA Blvd #B117
Palm Beach, FL 33410
(407) 622-2527

STELLERS, INC
4217 Baymeadows Rd
Jacksonville, FL 32217
(904) 739-0170

SUWANNEE TRIANGLE
GALLERY
P.O. Box 341
Cedar Key, FL 32625
(904) 543-5744

TEQUESTA GALLERIES, INC
361 Tequesta Dr
Tequesta, FL 33469
(407) 744-2534

THE PARK SHORE GALLERIES
3333 N Tamiami Trail
Naples, FL 33940
(813) 434-0833

THE RAIN BARREL
86700 Overseas Hwy
Islamorada, FL 33036
(305) 852-3084

THE RED LION GALLERY
545 Beachland Blvd
Vero Beach, FL 32963
(407) 231-1330
GUILD Artists: Charles Pearson and
Timothy Roeder, see page 175.

THE TURNBERRY ART
GALLERY
19707 Turnberry Way
Miami, FL 33180
(305) 931-5272

TIMOTHY'S GALLERY
232 Park Ave N
Winter Park, FL 32789
(407) 629-707
GUILD Artist: Anne Mayer Meier,
see page 206.

• Georgia

ARTSPACE
50 Hurt Plaza #150
Atlanta, GA 30303
(404) 577-1988

BY HAND SOUTH
W Ponce Place
308 W Ponce de Leon Ave #E
Decatur, GA 30030
(404) 378-0118

CONNELL GALLERY
333 Buckhead Ave
Atlanta, GA 30305-2305
(404) 261-1712
GUILD Artists: Joyce Marquess
Carey, see page 35. Gloria E.
Crouse, see page 36.

FAY GOLD GALLERY
247 Buckhead Ave
Atlanta, GA 30305
(404) 233-3843

GLASS ACT
10 Sylvan Dr #15
St Simons Island, GA 31522
(912) 634-1228

HEATH GALLERY, INC
416 E Paces Ferry Rd
Atlanta, GA 30305
(404) 262-6407

MARC WEINBERG GALLERY
2140 Peachtree Rd #225
Atlanta, GA 30309
(404) 351-0803
GUILD Artist: Ronald C. Puckett,
see page 123.

OUT OF THE WOODS
GALLERY
22B Bennett St NW
Atlanta, GA 30309
(404) 351-0446

SOUTHERN ACCESSORIES
TODAY
Atlanta Merchandise Mart,
Suite 12A2
Atlanta, GA 30303
(404) 581-0811
GUILD Artist: Tiger Mountain
Woodworks, see page 127.

THE BERMAN GALLERY
1131 Euclid Ave
Atlanta, GA 30307
(404) 525-2529

THE MAIN STREET GALLERY
Main St
Clayton, GA 30525
(404) 782-2440

THE MCINTOSH GALLERY
One Virginia Hill
587 Virginia Ave
Atlanta, GA 30306
(404) 892-4023
GUILD Artist: John P. Ashley, see
page 93.

THE RIVERWORKS CRAFT
GALLERY
105 E River St
Savannah, GA 31401
(912) 236-2012

THE SIGNATURE SHOP &
GALLERY
3267 Roswell Rd NW
Atlanta, GA 30305
(404) 237-4426
GUILD Artists: Joseph L.
Brandom, see page 214. Charles
Pearson and Timothy Roeder,
see page 175.

THE TULA GALLERIES
75 Bennet St #D1
Atlanta, GA 30309
(404) 351-6724

UP THE CREEK GALLERY
Hwys 115 & 105
Demorest, GA 30535
(404) 754-4130

VESPERMANN GLASS
GALLERY
2140 Peachtree Rd
Atlanta, GA 30309
(404) 350-9698

WINN/REGENCY GALLERY
2344 Lawrenceville Hwy
Atlanta, GA 30033
(404) 633-1789

• Hawaii

COAST GALLERY
P.O. Box 565
Hana, HI 96713
(808) 248-8636
GUILD Artist: Karen Davidson, see
page 11.

MADALINE MICHAELS
GALLERY
108 Lopaka Pl
Kula, HI 96790
(800) 635-9369

THE BIG ISLAND GALLERY
95 Waianuenue Ave
Hilo, HI 96720
(808) 969-3313

VILLAGE GALLERIES
120 Dickenson Street
Lahaina, HI 96741
(808) 248-8636
GUILD Artist: Karen Davidson, see
page 11.

• Idaho

ANNE REED GALLERY
620 Sun Valley Rd
P.O. Box 597
Ketchum, ID 83340
(208) 726-3036

GAIL SEVERN GALLERY
620 Sun Valley Rd
P.O. Box 1679
Ketchum, ID 83340
(208) 726-5079

RICHARD KAVESH GALLERY
P.O. Box 6080
Ketchum, ID 83340
(208) 726-2523

THE RIVER RUN GALLERY
291 First Ave
Ketchum, ID 83340
(208) 726-8878
GUILD Artist: Anne Mayer Meier,
see page 206.

• Illinois

A UNIQUE PRESENCE
2121 N Clybourn
Chicago, IL 60614
(312) 929-4292

ACCENT ART
166 Hilltop Court
Sleepyhollow, IL 60118
(708) 426-8842
GUILD Artist: Joseph Gallo, see
page 13.

ARC GALLERY
1040 West Huron Street
Chicago, IL 60622
(312) 733-2787

ART EFFECT
641 W Artmitage
Chicago, IL 60614
(312) 664-0997

ART INSTITUTE OF CHICAGO
Michigan Ave (at Adams St)
Chicago, IL 60603
(312) 443-3750

ART MECCA
3352 N Halsted
Chicago, IL 60657
(312) 935-3255

ARTISTS FRAME SERVICE
1915 N Clybourne
Chicago, IL 60614
(312) 525-3100

ARTSCAPE
1625 North Alpine Road
Rockford, IL 61107
(815) 397-1223
GUILD Artist: David M. Bowman,
see page 215.

Gallery Resources

BARRINGTON AREA ART
COUNCIL
104 W Main St
Barrington, IL 60011
(708) 382-5626

BETSY ROSENFIELD GALLERY
212 W Superior St
Chicago, IL 60610
(312) 787-8020

BILLY HORK GALLERY
272 E Gold Rd
Arlington Heights, IL 60005
GUILD Artist: Dave Kuhn, see
page 103.

CAREY GALLERY
1062 W Chicago Ave
Chicago, IL 60622
(312) 942-1884

CENTER FOR
CONTEMPORARY ART
325 Huron
Chicago, IL 60610
(312) 944-0094

CHIAROSCURO
700 N. Michigan Avenue
Chicago Place
Chicago, IL 60611
(312) 988-9253
GUILD Artists: Marsha Lega, see
page 133 and Christine E.
McEwan, see page 189.

CHICAGO STREET GALLERY
204 S Chicago St
Lincoln, IL 62656
(217) 732-5937

CITY WOODS
659 Central Ave
Highland Park, IL 60035
(708) 432-9393

CORPORATE ART SOURCE
900 N Franklin St
Chicago, IL 60610
(312) 751-1300
GUILD Artist: Victor Jacoby, see
page 25.

CORPORATE ARTWORKS
1300 Remington - Suite H
Schaumburg, IL 60173
(708) 843-3636
GUILD Artist: Irene De Gair, see
page 24.

CYRNA INTERNATIONAL, INC
12-101 Merchandise Mart
Chicago, IL 60654
(312) 329-0906

DOUGLAS DAWSON
GALLERY
814 N Franklin
Chicago, IL 60610
(312) 751-1961

DREAM FAST GALLERY
2035 W Wabansia
Chicago, IL 60647
(312) 235-4779

ELEMENTS GALLERY
738 N Wells St
Chicago, IL 60610
(312) 642-6574

FABRILE GALLERY
224 S. Michigan Ave
Chicago, IL 60604
(312) 427-1510
GUILD Artist: Christine E. McEwan,
see page 189.

FUMIE GALLERY
19 S LaSalle St
Chicago, IL 60603
(312) 726-0080

GALESBURG CIVIC ART
CENTER
114 E Main St
Galesburg, IL 61401
(309) 342-7415

GALLERIE STEPHANIE
2123 N Clark St
Chicago, IL 60614
(312) 880-0995

GIMCRACKS
1513 Sherman Ave
Evanston, IL 60201
(312) 475-0900

HOKIN KAUFMAN GALLERY
210 W Superior St
Chicago, IL 60610
(312) 266-1212

HOUSE OF ART
108 N Walnut St
Champaign, IL 61820
(217) 352-3604

ILLINOIS ARTISANS GALLERY
100 W Randolph St
Chicago, IL 60601
(312) 814-5321

JOY HORWICH GALLERY
226 E Ontario St
Chicago, IL 60611
(312) 787-0171
GUILD Artist: Marie-Laure Ilie, see
pages 42 and 43.

LILL STREET GALLERY
1021 W Lill St
Chicago, IL 60614
(312) 477-6185

LOVELY FINE ARTS, INC
18 W 10022nd St
Oakbrook Terrace, IL 60181
(708) 369-2999

LYMAN HEIZER ASSOCIATES
325 W Huron St #407
Chicago, IL 60610-3617
(312) 751-2985

MANDEL & CO.
1600 Mechandise Mart
Chicago, Il 60654
(312) 644-8242
GUILD Artist: Greg Sheres, see
page 143.

MARC MARKETING
1532 Chicago Merchandise Mart
Chicago, Il 60654
(312) 822-0630
GUILD Artist: Tiger Mountain
Woodworks, see page 127.

MARX GALLERY
208 W Kinzie St
Chicago, IL 60610
(312) 464-0400

MASTERWORKS GALLERY
1874 Sheridan Rd
Highland Park, IL 60035
(708) 432-2787
GUILD Artists: Barrett DeBusk, see
page 99. Marsha Lega, see
page 133.

MERRILL CHASE GALLERIES
1090 Johnson Dr
Buffalo Grove, IL 60089
(708) 215-4900
GUILD Artists: Vincent Tolpo and
Carolyn L. Tolpo, see page 108.

MINDSCAPE
1506 Sherman Ave
Evanston, IL 60201-4407
(708) 864-2660
GUILD Artists: Don Drumm, see
page 216. Michael K. Hansen
and Nina Palidino, see page 187.
Jonathan Winfisky, see page 197.

OBJECTS GALLERY
230 W Huron St
Chicago, IL 60610
(312) 664-6622

PAS DE CHAT GALLERY
3542 N Southport
Chicago, IL 60657
(312) 871-2818

PIECES
644 Central Ave
Highland Park, IL 60015
(312) 432-2131

SCHNEIDER BLUHM LOEB
GALLERY
230 W Superior St
Chicago, IL 60610
(312) 988-4033

STUDIO OF LONG GROVE
GALLERY
360 Old McHenry Rd
Long Grove, IL 60047
(708) 634-4244

SUNRISE ART GALLERY
227 S Third St
Geneva, IL 60134
(708) 232-0730

THE ARTISAN SHOP &
GALLERY
1515 Sheridan Rd
Plaza Del Lago
Wilmette, IL 60091
(312) 251-3775

THE PERIMETER GALLERY
750 N Orleans St
Chicago, IL 60610-3540
(312) 266-9473

THE PLUM LINE GALLERY
1511 Chicago Ave
Evanston, IL 60201
(708) 328-7586

TOM'S WOODSHOP
106 S Third St #4
Bloomingdale, IL 60108
(708) 894-6282
GUILD Artist: Robert Hargrave,
see page 203.

UNIQUE ACCENTS
3137 Dundee Rd
Northbrook, IL 60062
(708) 205-9400

WENTWORTH GALLERY
835 N Michigan Ave
Fifth Level
Chicago, IL 60611
(312) 944-0079

• Indiana

ARTIFACTS
6327 Guilford Ave
Indianapolis, IN 46220
(317) 255-1178

BY HAND GALLERY
104 E Kirkwood Ave
Bloomington, IN 47401
(812) 334-3255

CENTRE ART GALLERY
301B E Carmel Dr
Carmel, IN 46032
(317) 844-6421

CHESTERTON ART GALLERY
115 Fourth St
Chesterton, IN 46304
(219) 926-4711

CORNERSTONE GALLERY
176 W Main St
Greenwood, IN 46142
(317) 887-2778

FABLES GALLERY
317 Lincolnway E
Mishawaka, IN 46544
(219) 255-9191

Gallery Resources

**J M MALLON
GALLERIES/EDITIONS LIMITED**
2727 E. 86th Street
Indianapolis, IN 46240
GUILD Artist: Dave Kuhn, see
page 103.

KATHERINE TODD FINE ARTS
5356 Hillside Ave
Indianapolis, IN 46220
(317) 253-250

THE GALLERY
109 E Sixth St
Bloomington, IN 47408
(912) 336-564

• Iowa

ARTS CENTER
129 E Washington St
Iowa City, IA 52240
(319) 337-7447

BRUNNIER MUSEUM STORE
290 Scheman
Iowa State University
Ames, IA 50011
(515) 294-3342
GUILD Artist: Christine E. McEwan,
see page 189.

FROM GIFTED HANDS
400 Main (on the Park)
Ames, IA 50010
(515) 232-5656

OCTAGON CENTER FOR
THE ARTS
427 Douglas Ave
Ames, IA 50010
(515) 232-5331

THE LAGNIAPPE
114 Fifth St
West Des Moines, IA 50265
(515) 277-0047
GUILD Artist: Cathy Richardson,
see page 158.

THE PEPPERTREE STUDIOS
211 First Ave SE
Cedar Rapids, IA 52401
(319) 365-5178

• Kansas

GALLERY AT HAWTHORNE
4833 W 119th St
Overland Park, KS 66209-1560
(913) 469-8001

PRIVATE STOCK GALLERY
2400 Drury Ln
Shawnee Mission, KS 66208-1236
(913) 236-4182

THE SILVER WORKS & MORE
715 Massachusetts St
Lawrence, KS 66044
(913) 842-1460

• Kentucky

ARTIQUE GALLERY
410 W Vine St
First Level
Lexington, KY 40507
(606) 233-1774

BENCHMARK GALLERY
I-75 Interchange
Berea, KY 40403
(606) 986-9413

EDENSIDE GALLERY
1422 Bardstown Rd
Louisville, KY 40204
(502) 459-2787

KENTUCKY ART & CRAFT
609 W Main St
Louisville, KY 40202
(502) 589-0102

PROMENADE GALLERY
204 Center St
Berea, KY 40403
(606) 986-1609

THE LIBERTY GALLERY
416 W Jefferson Ave
Louisville, KY 40202
(502) 566-2081

THE ZEPHYR GALLERY
637 W Main St
Louisville, KY 40202
(502) 585-5646

• Louisiana

ARIODANTE:
CONTEMPORARY CRAFT
535 Julia St
New Orleans, LA 70130
(604) 524-3233
GUILD Artist: Steven Holman, see
page 121.

ARTISTS ALLIANCE
125 W Vermilion St
Lafayette, LA 70501-6915
(318) 233-7518

BATON ROUGE GALLERY
1442 City Park Ave
Baton Rouge, LA 70808
(504) 383-1470

CAFFERY STUDIO
4820 Government St
Baton Rouge, LA 70896
(504) 928-1945

GALLERIE I/O
1812 Magazine St
New Orleans, LA 70130
(800) 875-2113

INTERIORS & EXTRAS
324 Metairie Rd
Metairie, LA 70005
(504) 835-9902

MOREHEAD FINE ARTS
GALLERY
603 Julia St
New Orleans, LA 70130
(504) 568-5470

RICHARD RUSSELL GALLERY
639 Royal
New Orleans, LA 70130
(504) 523-0533
GUILD Artist: Barrett DeBusk, see
page 99.

STONER ARTS CENTER
614 Edwards Street
Shreveport, LA 71101-3641
(318) 222-1780

THE SIGNATURE COLLECTION
Jax Brewery
600 Decatur St #301
New Orleans, LA 70130
(504) 581-2063

• Maine

ABACUS HANDCRAFTERS
GALLERY
44 Exchange St
Portland, ME 04101
(207) 772-4880

ABACUS HANDCRAFTERS
GALLERY
8 McKown St
Boothbay Harbor, ME 04538
(207) 633-2166

BENSON'S FIBER &
WOOD, ETC
59 Mountain St
Camden, ME 04843
(207) 236-6564

EARTHLY DELIGHTS
81 Water St
Hallowell, ME 04347
(207) 622-9801

ELEMENTS GALLERY
19 Mason St
Brunswick, ME 04011
(207) 729-1108

FRICK GALLERY
139 High St
Belfast, ME 04915
(207) 338-3671

GREEN HEAD FORGE
Old Quarry Rd
Stonington, ME 04681
(207) 367-2632

MAINE COTTAGE FURNITURE
Lower Falls Landing
Yarmouth, ME 04046
(207) 846-602

NANCY MARGOLIS GALLERY
367 Fore St
Portland, ME 04101-5010
(207) 775-3822

PHILIP STEIN GALLERY
20 Milk St
Portland, ME 04101
(207) 772-9072

PLUM DANDY GALLERY
21 Dock Square
Kennebuckport, ME 04046
(207) 967-4013

THE BLUE HERON GALLERY
Church St
Deer Isle, ME 04627
(207) 348-6051

THE SHORE ROAD GALLERY
112 Shore Rd
Ogunquit, ME 03907
(207) 646-5046

THE VICTORIAN STABLE
GALLERY
Water St,
P.O. Box 728
Damariscotta, ME 04543
(207) 563-1991

• Maryland

ART INSTITUTE & GALLERY
Rte 50 & Lemmon Hill Ln
Salisbury, MD 21801
(301) 546-4748

ARTISANS COLLECTION, LTD
11216 Old Carriage Rd
Glen Arm, MD 21057
(301) 661-1118

AURORA GALLERY
67 Maryland Ave
Annapolis, MD 21401
(301) 263-9150

BARBARA FENDRICK
GALLERY
4104 Leland St
Bethesda, MD 20815-5033
(212) 226-3881

CATHY HART POTTERY
STUDIO
Mill Centre Studio #221
Balitmore, MD 21211
(301) 467-4911

Gallery Resources

CHESAPEAKE EAST
Ford's General Store
Upper Fairmount, MD 21867
(301) 543-8175

DISCOVERIES
Columbia Mall
Columbia, MD 21044
(410) 740-5800

GAZELLE GALLERY
5100 Falls Rd
Baltimore, MD 21210
(301) 433-3305

JURUS, LTD
5618 Newbury St
Baltimore, MD 21209
(410) 542-5227

MARGARET SMITH GALLERY
8090 Main St
Ellicott City, MD 21043
(410) 461-0870

MEREDITH GALLERY
805 N Charles St
Baltimore, MD 21201-5307
(301) 837-3575

PIECES OF OLDE
716 W 36th St
Baltimore, MD 21211
(301) 366-4949

RUBY BLAKENEY GALLERY
Savage Mill, 8600 Foundry Street
Savage, MD 20763
(410) 880-4935
GUILD Artists: Linda Dixon and
Drew Krouse, see page 170.

**THE BRASSWORKS
COMPANY, INC**
1641 Thames St
Baltimore, MD 21231
(301) 327-7280

THE GLASS GALLERY
4720 Hampden Ln
Bethesda, MD 20814
(301) 657-3478

THE KELLOGG COLLECTION
10300 Mill Run Circle #1116
Owings Mills, MD 21117
(301) 581-2297

THE PARTNERS GALLERY, LTD
6500 Rock Springs Dr
Bethesda, MD 20817
(301) 657-2781

**TOMLINSON CRAFT
COLLECTION**
711 W 40th St
Baltimore, MD 21211
(410) 338-1572

ZYZYX
1809 Reisterstown Rd #130
Baltimore, MD 21208
(410) 486-9785

• Massachusetts

**ALIANZA CONTEMPORARY
CRAFTS**
154 Newbury St
Boston, MA 02116
(617) 262-2385
GUILD Artist: Ruth Gowell, see
page 39.

ARTIQUE GALLERY
400 Cochituate Rd
Framingham, MA 01701
(508) 872-3373

**ARTISTS & CRAFTSMEN
GALLERY**
72 Main St
West Harwich, MA 02671
(508) 432-7604

BARACCA GALLERY
P.O. Box 85
North Hatfield, MA 01066
(413) 247-5262

BHADON GIFT GALLERY
1075 Pleasant St
Worcester, MA 01602
(508) 798-0432

**BLACKS HANDWEAVING
SHOP**
597 Main St
West Barnstable, MA 02668
(508) 362-3955

BOSTON CORPORATE ART
470 Atlantic Avenue
Boston, MA 02210
(617) 426-8880
GUILD Artist: Irene De Gair, see
page 24.

**BRAMHALL & DUNN
GALLERY**
16 Federal St
Nantucket, MA 02554
(508) 228-4688

CARRIAGE HOUSE STUDIO
1 Fitchburg St #C-207
Somerville, MA 02143
(617) 629-2337

CHOICES GALLERY
11 Pleasant St
Newburyport, MA 01950
(508) 462-5577

CHOUETTE CRAFT GALLERY
7 Old South St
Northampton, MA 01060
(413) 584-4336

CLARK GALLERY
P.O. Box 339
Lincoln Station
Lincoln, MA 01773
(617) 259-8303

CRAFTY YANKEE
1838 Massachusetts Ave
Lexington, MA 02173
(617) 863-1219

CROMA GALLERY
94 Central St
Wellesley, MA 02181
(617) 235-6230

DECOR INTERNATIONAL, INC
171 Newbury St
Boston, MA 02116
(617) 262-1529

**DIVINITY'S SPLENDOUR
GLOW**
8 Medford St
Arlington, MA 02174
(617) 648-7100

FERRIN GALLERY
Pinch Pottery
179 Main St
Northampton, MA 01060-3147
(413) 586-4509

FIBER DESIGNS
Main St
P.O. Box 614
Wellfleet, MA 02667
(508) 349-7434

FIRE OPAL
7 Pond St
Jamaica Plain, MA 02130
(617) 524-0262

**FULLER MUSUEM OF ART
MUSEUM SHOP**
455 Oak St
Brockton, MA 02401
(508) 588-6000

G.M. GALLERIES
Main St
West Stockbridge, MA 01266
(413) 232-8519

GALLERY NAGA
67 Newbury St
Boston, MA 02116
(617) 267-9060

GIFTED HAND GALLERY
32 Church St
Wellesley, MA 02181
(617) 235-7171

GORDON/HARTMAN
Boston Design Ctr
1 Design Center Place #329
Boston, MA 02210-2399
(617) 737-7573

HALF MOON HARRY
19 S Bearskin Neck
Rockport, MA 01966
(508) 546-6601

**HAND OF MAN CRAFT
GALLERY**
29 Wendell Ave
Pittsfield, MA 01201
(413) 443-6033

**HAND OF MAN CRAFT
GALLERY**
The Curtis Shops
Walker St
Lenox, MA 01240
(413) 637-0632

HOLSTEN GALLERIES
Elm St
Stockbridge, MA 01262
(413) 298-3044
GUILD Artists: Cohn-Stone
Studios, see page 185.
Elizabeth MacDonald, see
pages 84 and 85.

HOORN ASHBY GALLERY
10 Federal St
Nantucket, MA 02554
(508) 228-9314

IMPULSE
188 Commercial St
Provincetown, MA 02657
(508) 487-1154

JOHN LEWIS, INC
97 Newbury St
Boston, MA 02116
(617) 266-6665

JUBILATION
91 Union St
Picadilly Station
Newton Centre, MA 02159
(617) 965-0488

JUDITH N WOLOV GALLERY
1 Design Ctr
Boston Design #141
Boston, MA 02210
(617) 426-5511
GUILD Artist: Tom Neugebauer,
see page 174.

LIMITED EDITIONS, INC
1176 Walnut St
Newton Highlands, MA 02161
(617) 965-5474

MOBILIA GALLERY
358 Huron Ave
Cambridge, MA 02138
(617) 876-2109

**NEAL ROSENBLUM
GOLDSMITHS**
287 Park Ave
Worcester, MA 01609
(508) 755-4244

NEW ENGLAND SAMPLER
10 Huntington Ave
Westin Hotel
Boston, MA 02116
(617) 337-8391

Gallery Resources

NORTHSIDE CRAFT GALLERY
933 Main St
Yarmouthport, MA 02675
(508) 362-5291

ORIEL
17 College St
South Hadley, MA 01075
(413) 532-6469

PACCHETTO
831 Beacon St
Newton Centre, MA 02159
(617) 969-6627

RICE/POLAK
432 Commercial Street
Provincetown, MA 02657
(508) 487-1052
GUILD Artist: Larry Benjamin, see
page 137.

SALMON FALLS ARTISANS
SHOWROOM
P.O. Box 17
Ashfield Rd
Shelburne Falls, MA 01370
(413) 625-9833

SAWDUST, INC
192 Commercial St
Provincetown, MA 02657
(504) 487-4511

SERENDIPITY GALLERY
10 South Rd
Rockport, MA 01966
(508) 546-3731

SIGNATURE GALLERY
10 Steeple St
Mashpee, MA 02649
(508) 539-0029

SIGNATURE GALLERY
Dock Square
24 North St
Boston, MA 02109
(617) 227-4885

SIGNATURE GALLERY
The Mall at Chestnut Hill
Chestnut Hill, MA 02167
(617) 332-7749

SILVER & GOLD GALLERY
64 Main St
Vineyard Haven, MA 02568
(509) 693-0243

SILVER RIBBON GALLERY
15 Columbia Rd
Pembroke, MA 02359-1841
(617) 826-1525

SILVERSCAPE DESIGNS
264 N Pleasant St
Amherst, MA 01002
(413) 253-3324

SKERA GALLERY
221 Main St
Northampton, MA 01060
(413) 586-4563

SOCIETY OF ARTS & CRAFTS
175 Newbury St
Boston, MA 02116
(617) 266-1810

SPECTRUM OF AMERICAN
ARTISTS
369 Old Kings Hwy
Brewster, MA 02631
(508) 385-3322

TEN ARROW GALLERY
10 Arrow St
Cambridge, MA 02138
(617) 876-1117

THE ARTFUL HAND GALLERY
36 Copley Place
100 Huntington Ave
Boston, MA 02116
(617) 262-9601
GUILD Artist: Jonathan Winfisky,
see page 197.

THE BALCONY
P.O. Box 489
Vineyard Haven, MA 02568
(508) 693-5127

THE GLASS EYE
Main Street Mercantile, Rt. 6
N. Eastham, MA 02651
(508) 255-5044
GUILD Artist: Alan Steinberg, see
page 89.

WEAVERS FANCY GALLERY
69 Church St
Lenox, MA 01240
(413) 637-2013

WESLEY DESIGN CENTRE
9 Crest Rd
Wesley Square, MA 02181
(617) 237-2944

WHIPPOORWILL CRAFTS
GALLERY
126 S Market St
Faneuil Hall Market
Boston, MA 02109
(617) 523-5149

• Michigan

ANN ARBOR ART
ASSOCIATION
117 W Liberty St
Ann Arbor, MI 48104
(313) 994-8004

ANN ARBOR ARTIST CO-OP
617 E Huron St
Ann Arbor, MI 48104
(313) 668-6769

ARIANA GALLERY
386 E Maple Rd
Birmingham, MI 48009
(313) 647-6405

ARTFINDERS OF MICHIGAN
107 Washington Ave
Grand Haven, MI 49417
(616) 847-9150

BELL ROSS FINE ARTS
GALLERY
257 E Main St
Harbor Springs, MI 49740
(616) 526-9855

BOYER GLASSWORKS
207 N State St
Harbor Springs, MI 49740
(616) 526-6359

CAROL HOOBERMAN
GALLERY
124 S Woodward St #12
Birmingham, MI 48009
(313) 647-3666

CAROL JAMES GALLERY
301 S Main St
Royal Oak, MI 48067
(313) 541-6216

COURTYARD GALLERY
813 E Buffalo
New Buffalo, MI 49117
(616) 469-4110

DECO ART
815 First St
Menominee, MI 49858
(906) 863-3300

DETROIT GALLERY OF
CONTEMPORARY CRAFTS
104 Fisher Bldg
Detroit, MI 48202
(313) 873-7888

DONNA JACOBS
GALLERY, LTD
574 N Woodward Ave
Second Floor
Birmingham, MI 48009
(313) 540-1600

FRIENDS UNIQUE
FURNISHINGS & DESIGN
126 Main Centre
Northville, MI 48167
(313) 380-6930
GUILD Artist: Murray P. Gates, see
page 118.

GALLERIE 454
15105 Kercheval Ave
Grosse Pointe, MI 48230
(313) 822-4454

GALLERIE INTERNATIONAL
34665 Thornbrook Dr
Farmington Hills, MI 48335
(313) 476-1625

GALLERY FOUR FOURTEEN
414 Detroit St
Ann Arbor, MI 48104
(313) 747-7004

GALLERY ON THE ALLEY
611 Broad St
St Joseph, MI 49085
(616) 983-6161

GOOD GOODS
106 Mason St
Saugatuck, MI 49453
(616) 857-1557

HABITAT GALLERIES
Triatria Bldg #45
32255 Northwestern Hwy
Farmington Hills, MI 48334-1566
(313) 851-9090

HABITAT/SHAW GALLERY
Triatria Bldg #25
32255 Northwestern Hwy
Farmington Hills, MI 48334-1566
(313) 851-8767

HANDIWORKS, LTD
5260 Helena St
Alden, MI 49612
(616) 331-6787

HOOVER HOUSE GALLERY
340 State St
Harbor Springs, MI 49740
(616) 526-9819

HUZZA
136 Main St E
Harbor Springs, MI 49740
(616) 526-2128

ILONA GALLERY
31045 Orchard Lake Rd
Farmington Hills, MI 48018
(313) 855-4488

J WETSMAN
DECORATIVE ART
233 Oakland St
Birmingham, MI 48009
(313) 647-3666

JOYCE PETTER GALLERY
161 Bluestar Highway
Douglas/Saugatuck, MI 49406
GUILD Artist: Thomas Lollar, see
page 83.

JUDITH RACHT GALLERY, INC
13707 Prairie Rd
Harbert, MI 49115
(616) 469-1080

KOUCKY GALLERY
319 Bridge St
Charleuoix, MI 49720
(616) 547-2228

LINDA HAYMAN GALLERY
32500 Northwestern Hwy
Farmington Hills, MI 48336
(313) 932-0080

NICOL STUDIO & GALLERY
2531 Charlevoix Ave
Petoskey, MI 49770
(616) 347-0227

Gallery Resources

PEWABIC POTTERY
10125 E Jefferson Ave
Detroit, MI 48214-3196
(313) 822-0954

PRESTON BURKE GALLERY
240 E Grand River Ave
Detroit, MI 48226-2107
(313) 963-2350

PRIVATE COLLECTION
GALLERY
6736-A Orchard Lake Rd
West Bloomfield, MI 48322
(313) 737-4050

ROBERT KIDD GALLERY
107 Townsend St
Birmingham, MI 48009
(313) 642-3909

SANDRA COLLINS, INC
470 N Woodward Ave
Birmingham, MI 48009
(313) 642-4795
GUILD Artist: Jeffrey Cooper, see
page 98.

SELO SHEVEL GALLERY
301 S Main St
Ann Arbor, MI 48104
(313) 761-6263

SIGNATURE ARTS, INC
1700 Stutz St #106
West Bloomfield, MI 48084
(313) 643-4484

SUZIE VIGLAND GALLERY
1047 Michigan Ave
Benzonia, MI 49616
(616) 882-7203

SYBARIS GALLERY
301 W Fourth St
Royal Oak, MI 48067
(313) 544-3388

T'MARRA GALLERY
111 N First St
Ann Arbor, MI 48104
(313) 769-3223

T.R.A. ART
799 Industrial Court
Bloomfield Hills, MI 48013
(313) 332-7607
GUILD Artist: Joesph Gallo, see
page 13.

TAMARACK CRAFTSMEN
5039 NW Bay Shore Dr
Omena, MI 49674
(616) 386-5529

THE PENNIMAN SHOWCASE
827 Penniman Ave
Plymouth, MI 48170
(313) 455-5531

THE PINE TREE GALLERY
824 E Cloverland
US Hwy 2
Ironwood, MI 49938
(906) 932-5120

THE POSNER GALLERY
32407 N Western Hwy
Farmington Hills, MI 48332
(313) 626-6450

THE SAJON-MAY GALLERY
1410 Fairoaks Ct
E Lansing, MI 48823
(517) 347-0600

THE YAW GALLERY
550 N Woodward Ave
Birmingham, MI 48009
(313) 747-5470

TOUCH OF LIGHT GALLERY
23426 Woodward Ave
Ferndale, MI 48220
(313) 543-1868

• Minnesota

ATAZ
The Galleria
3480 W 70th St
Edina, MN 55435
(612) 925-4883

ANDERSON & ANDERSON
GALLERY
414 First Ave N
Minneapolis, MN 55401
(612) 332-4889

ART LENDING GALLERY
25 Groveland Ter
Minneapolis, MN 55403
(612) 377-7800

ART RESOURCES GALLERY
494 Jackson St
St Paul, MN 55101
(612) 222-4431

BOIS FORT GALLERY
130 E Sheridan St
Ely, MN 55731
(218) 365-5066

BROKKEN ARTS
121 Main St N
P.O. Box 475
Harmony, MN 55939
GUILD Artist: J.C. Homola, see
page 188.

ELAYNE GALLERIES
6111 Exelsior Blvd
Minneapolis, MN 55416
(612) 926-1511
GUILD Artist: Marjorie Tomchuk,
see page 18.

FORUM GALLERY
1235 Yale Pl #1308
Minneapolis, MN 55403-1947
(612) 333-1825

GEOMETRIE GALLERY
122 N Fourth St
Minneapolis, MN 55401
(612) 340-1635

GLASSPECTACLE
402 N Main St
Stillwater, MN 55082
(612) 439-0757

GOLDSTEIN GALLERY
250 McNeal Hall
1985 Buford Ave
St Paul, MN 55108
(612) 624-7434

GRAND AVENUE FRAME &
GALLERY
964 Grand Ave
St Paul, MN 55105
(612) 224-9716

JAVIER PUIG
DECORATIVE ARTS
118 N Fourth St
Minneapolis, MN 55401
(612) 332-6001

M.C. GALLERY
400 First Ave N #336, Third Floor
Minneapolis, MN 55401
(612) 339-1480

M.J.L. IMPRESSIONS
International Market Square
275 Market St #162
Minneapolis, MN 55405
(800) 342-0989
GUILD Artist: William C. Richards,
see page 89.

MADE IN THE SHADE
GALLERY
600 E Superior St
Duluth, MN 55802
(218) 722-1929

MIDDLEMARCH
BOOKS & ART
4824 Penn Ave
Minneapolis, MN 55409
(612) 378-2755

NORTHERN CLAY CENTER
2375 University Ave W
St Paul, MN 55114
(612) 642-1735

PERSPECTIVES CRAFTS
GALLERY
81 S Ninth St #220
Minneapolis, MN 55402
(612) 339-6076

PETER M DAVID GALLERY
3351 St Louis Ave
Minneapolis, MN 55416-4394
(612) 339-1825

RAYMOND AVENUE
GALLERY
761 Raymond Ave
St Paul, MN 55114
(612) 644-9200

ROURKE'S GALLERY
523 S Fourth St
Moorehead, MN 56560
(218) 236-8861

SAYER STRAND GALLERY
275 Market St #222
Minneapolis, MN 55405-1604
(612) 375-0838

SONIA'S GALLERY, INC
400 First Avenue N #318
Minneapolis, MN 55404
(612) 338-0350

SUPERIOR LAKE - N
AMERICA, INC
716 E Superior St
Duluth, MN 55802
(218) 722-6998

SUZANNE KOHN GALLERY
1690 Grand Ave
St Paul, MN 55105
(612) 699-0417

TECHNIC GALLERY
1055 Grand Ave
St Paul, MN 55105
(612) 222-0188

TEXTILE ARTS
INTERNATIONAL, INC
400 First Ave N #340
Minneapolis, MN 55401
(612) 338-6776

THE ROOMERS GALLERY
3001 S Hennepin Ave
Minneapolis, MN 55408
(612) 822-9490

THE WHITE OAK GALLERY
3939 W 50th St
Edina, MN 55424
(614) 927-3575

THREE ROOMS UP GALLERY
The Galleria
3515 W 69th St
Edina, MN 55435
(612) 926-1774

• Mississippi

BAY CRAFTERS
107 N Beach St
Bay St Louis, MS 39520
(601) 466-2501

BRYANT GALLERIES
2845 Lakeland Dr
Jackson, MS 39208
(601) 932-1993
GUILD Artist: George Radeschi,
see page 209.

CHIMNEYVILLE CRAFTS
1150 Lakeland Dr
Jackson, MS 39216
(601) 988-9253

Gallery Resources

HILLYER HEALTH, INC
207 E Scenic Dr
Pass Christian, MS 39571
(601) 452-4810

MISSISSIPPI CRAFTS CENTER
Natchez Trace Pkwy
Ridgeland, MS 39158
(601) 856-7546

THE OLD TRACE
GALLERY, LTD
120 E Jefferson
P.O. Box 307
Kosciusko, MS 39090
(601) 289-9170

• Missouri

ART ATTACK GALLERY
420 W Seventh St
Kansas City, MO 64105-1407
(816) 474-7482

BARUCCI GALLERY
8407 Olive Blvd
St Louis, MO 63132
(314) 993-4317
GUILD Artist: Tom Neugebauer,
see page 174.

BLUESTEM MISSOURI CRAFTS
13 S Ninth St
Columbia, MO 65201
(314) 442-0211

CORPORATE ART SERVICES
2105 Burlington
North Kansas City, MO 64116
(816) 421-4848
GUILD Artist: J.C. Homola, see
page 188.

CRAFT PLACE
506 S Main St
St Charles, MO 63301
(314) 723-9398

GALLERY 525
100 S Brentwood
St Louis, MO 63105
(314) 727-7770
GUILD Artist: David M. Bowman,
see page 215.

GLYNN BROWN DESIGN
GALLERY
420 W Seventh St
Kansas City, MO 64105
(816) 842-2115

GRIFFIN GALLERY
10411 Clayton Rd #311
St Louis, MO 63131
(314) 993-5200

INTERWOVEN DESIGNS
4400 Luclede Ave
St Louis, MO 63108
(314) 531-6200

LEEDY VOULKOS GALLERY
1919 Wyandotte St
Kansas City, MO 64108-1950
(816) 474-1919

MID AMERICAN ART
BROKERS
8 Sona Lane
Saint Louis, MO 63141
(314) 991-2291
GUILD Artist: Joesph Gallo, see
page 13.

NEW ACCENTS GALLERY
506 S Main St
St Charles, MO 63301
(314) 723-9398

PORTFOLIO GALLERY
3514 Delmar
St Louis, MO 63106
(314) 533-3323

PRO-ART GALLERY
1214 Washington Ave
St Louis, MO 63103
(314) 231-5848

RANDALL GALLERY
999 N 13th St
St Louis, MO 63106
(314) 231-4808

SOURCE FINE ARTS
208 Delaware
Kansas City, MO 64105
(816) 842-6466

THE CRAFT ALLIANCE
GALLERY
6640 Delmar
St Louis, MO 63130
(214) 725-1151

THE MORGAN GALLERY
412 Delaware St #A
Kansas City, MO 64105
(816) 842-8755

UNION HILL ARTS GALLERY
3013 Main St
Kansas City, MO 64108
(816) 561-3020
GUILD Artists: Vincent Tolpo and
Carolyn L. Tolpo, see page 108.

• Montana

ARTISTIC TOUCH
209 Central Ave
Whitefish, MT 59937
(406) 862-4813

CHANDLER GALLERY
Front St
Missoula, MT 59802
(406) 721-5555

FURNITURE, ETC.
17 Main St
Kallispell, MT 59901
(406) 756-8555
GUILD Artist: J. Dubs, see
page 217.

• Nebraska

ADAM WHITNEY GALLERY
8725 Shamrock Rd
Omaha, NE 68114
(402) 393-1051
GUILD Artist: Edith A. Ehrlich, see
page 171.

ANDERSON/O'BRIEN
GALLERY
8724 Pacific St
Omaha, NE 68114
(402) 390-0717
GUILD Artist: Susan J. Brasch, see
page 148.

HAYMARKET GALLERY
119 S Ninth St
Lincoln, NE 68508
(402) 475-1061
GUILD Artist: Susan J. Brasch, see
page 148.

LEWIS ART GALLERY
8025 W Dodge Rd
Omaha, NE 68114-3413
(402) 391-7733

UNIVERSITY PLACE ART
CENTER
2601 N 48th St
Lincoln, NE 68504
(402) 466-8692
GUILD Artist: Susan J. Brasch, see
page 148.

• Nevada

MARK MASUOKA GALLERY
1149 S Maryland Pkwy
Las Vegas, NV 89104-1738
(702) 366-0377

MINOTAUR FINE ARTS
3500 Las Vegas Blvd
Las Vegas, NV 89109
(702) 737-1400
GUILD Artist: Orient & Flume Art
Glass, see page 193.

MOONSTRUCK GALLERY
6368 W Sahara Ave
Las Vegas, NV 89102
(702) 364-0531

SIERRA CRYSTAL MINES
GALLERY
160A E Plumb Lane
Reno, NV 89502
(702) 829-7727

• New Hampshire

AVA GALLERY
4 Bank St
Lebanon, NH 03766
(603) 448-3117
GUILD Artist: S.M. Warren, see
page 211.

AYOTTES DESIGNERY
P.O. Box 287
Maple St
Center Sandwich, NH 03227
(603) 284-6915

GALLERY THIRTY THREE
111 Market St
Portsmouth, NH 03801
(603) 431-7403

LEAGUE OF NEW
HAMPSHIRE CRAFT CENTER
205 N. Main Street
Concord, NH 03301
(603) 228-8171
GUILD Artist: Jeffrey Cooper, see
page 98.

LEAGUE OF NEW
HAMPSHIRE CRAFTS CENTER
13 Lebanon St
Hanover, NH 03755
(603) 643-5050

MCGOWAN FINE ART, INC
10 Hills Ave
Concord, NH 03301
(603) 225-2515

MOLLY GRANT DESIGNS
112 State St
Portsmouth, NH 03801
(603) 436-7077

SHARON ARTS CENTER
Rte 123
Sharon, NH 03458
(603) 924-7256

THE ARTISANS GROUP
Box 1039 Main Street
Dublin, NH 03444
(603) 563-8782
GUILD Artist: Steven Holman, see
page 121.

THE SHOP AT THE INSTITUTE
148 Concord St
Manchester, NH 03104
(603) 623-0313

• New Jersey

ALICE WHITE GALLERY
105 Pulis Ave
Franklin Lakes, NJ 07417
(201) 848-1855

ART DIRECTIONS
60 Baldwin Rd
Parsippany, NJ 07054
(201) 263-1420

ARTFORMS
16 Monmouth St
Red Bank, NJ 07701
(908) 530-4330

BY HAND FINE CRAFT GALLERY
142 Kings Hwy E
Haddonfield, NJ 08033
(609) 429-2550

CONTRASTS
49 Broad St
Red Bank, NJ 07701
(908) 741-9177

CREATIVE GLASS CENTER OF AMERICA
P.O. Box 646
Millville, NJ 08332
(609) 825-6800

DEXTERITY, LTD
26 Church St
Montclair, NJ 07042
(201) 746-5370

ELVID GALLERY
41 E Palisade Ave
Englewood, NJ 07631
(201) 871-8747

GOLDSMITHS
26 N Union St
Lambertville, NJ 08530
(609) 398-4590

KIMBERLY DESIGNS
1111 Park Ave
Plainfield, NJ 07060
(201) 561-5344

KORNBLUTH GALLERY
7-21 Fairlawn Ave
Fair Lawn, NJ 07410
(201) 791-3374

LA GALLERIE DU VITRAIL
70 Tanner St #2
Haddonfield, NJ 08033-2417
(609) 428-6712

LIMITED EDITIONS, INC
2200 Long Beach Blvd
Surf City, NJ 08008
(609) 494-0527

MARGARET'S CRAFT SHOP
413 Raritan Ave
Highland Park, NJ 08904
(908) 247-2210

MELME GALLERY
Bridgewater Commons
400 Commons Way, Suite 256
Bridgewater, NJ 08807
GUILD Artist: Alan Steinberg, see page 89.

N K THAINE GALLERY
150 Kings Hwy E
Haddonfield, NJ 08033
(609) 428-6961

NATHANS GALLERY
1205 McBride Ave
West Paterson, NJ 07424
(201) 785-9119

PETERS VALLEY CRAFT GALLERY
Rt 615
Layton, NJ 07851
(201) 948-5202

SCHERER GALLERY
93 School Rd W
Marlboro, NJ 07746
(201) 536-9456

SHEILA NUSSBAUM GALLERY
341 Millburn Ave
Millburn, NJ 07041
(201) 467-1720
GUILD Artists: Michael K. Hansen and Nina Palidino, see page 187. Robert Hargrave, see page 203. Claudia Hollister, see page 173.

SIGNATURE DESIGNS
5 W Main St
Moorestown, NJ 08057
(609) 778-8657

STREICHLER GALLERY
46 N Dean St
Englewood, NJ 07631
(201) 567-8120

THE QUEST
38 Main St
Chester, NJ 07930
(908) 879-8144

• New Mexico

ANDREWS PUEBLO GALLERY
400 San Felipe NW
Albequerque, NM 87104
(505) 243-0414

BELLAS ARTES
653 Canyon Rd
Santa Fe, NM 87501
(212) 274-1115

CLAY & FIBER GALLERY
126 W Plaza Dr
Taos, NM 87571
(505) 758-8093

EL PRADO GALLERIES, INC
112 E San Francisco St
Santa Fe, NM 87501
(505) 988-2906

FORM & FUNCTION
328 Guadalupe St
Santa Fe, NM 87501
(505) 984-8226

GARLAND GALLERY
125 Lincoln Ave #113
Santa Fe, NM 87501
(505) 984-1555

GERALD PETERS GALLERY
P.O. Box 908
Santa Fe, NM 87504
(505) 988-8961

HANDCRAFTERS GALLERY
227 Galisteo St
Santa Fe, NM 87501
(505) 982-4880

HANDSEL GALLERY
155 E Palace Ave #29
Santa Fe, NM 87501
(505) 988-4030
GUILD Artist: George Alexander, see page 79.

HANDWOVEN ORIGINALS
211 Old Santa Fe Tr
Santa Fe, NM 87501
(505) 982-4118

INTERIOR DESIGN CENTERS, INC
4730 Pan American Frwy
Albuquerque, NM 87109
(505) 881-7517

JOHNSON-BENKERT
128 W Water St
Santa Fe, NM 87501
GUILD Artist: Christopher Thomson, see page 155.

JUNE KENT GALLERIES
130 Lincoln St
Santa Fe, NM 87501
(505) 988-1001
GUILD Artist: Rebecca Bluestone, see page 21.

LA MESA OF SANTA FE
225 Canyon Rd
Santa Fe, NM 87501
(505) 984-1608
GUILD Artist: Christopher Thomson, see page 155.

LAURA CARPENTER FINE ART
309 Read St
Santa Fe, NM 87501
(505) 986-9090

MABEL'S WEST
201 Canyon Rd
Sante Fe, NM 87501
(505) 986-9105

MADE IN THE USA GALLERY
110 W San Francisco St
Santa Fe, NM 87501
(505) 982-3232

MARIPOSA GALLERY
225 Canyon Rd
Sante Fe, NM 87501
(505) 982-3032

MICHAEL WIGLEY GALLERIES, LTD
1111 Paseo de Peralta
Santa Fe, NM 87501-2737
(505) 984-8986

NEDRA MATTEUCCI FINE ART
300 Garcia at Canyon Rd
Santa Fe, NM 87501
(505) 983-2731

NEW TRENDS GALLERY
225 Canyon Rd
Santa Fe, NM 87501
GUILD Artists: Doug Weigel, see pages 135 and 222. Nancy J. Young and Allen Young, see page 212.

OFF THE WALL GALLERY
616 Canyon Rd
Santa Fe, NM 87501
(505) 983-8337

OKUN GALLERY
301 N Guadalupe
Santa Fe, NM 87501
(505) 989-4300

PHILLIP BAREISS CONTEMPORARY ART
P.O. Box 2739
Taos, NM 87571-2739
(505) 776-2284
GUILD Artist: Sydney K. Hamburger, see page 202.

QUILTS, LTD
625 Canyon Rd
Santa Fe, NM 87501
(505) 988-5888

SHIDONI CONTEMPORARY GALLERY
Bishop Lodge Rd
P.O. Box 250
Tesuque, NM 87574-0250
(505) 988-8001

THE LIGHTSIDE GALLERY
225 Canyon Rd
Santa Fe, NM 87501-2714
(505) 982-5501
GUILD Artist: Susana England, see page 12.

THE RUNNING RIDGE GALLERY
640 Canyon Rd
Santa Fe, NM 87501
(505) 988-2515

Gallery Resources

THE WINDMILL GALLERY
10415 N Scottsdale Rd
Scottsdale, NM 85253
(602) 948-7337

**WEAVING SOUTHWEST
GALLERY**
216B Paseo Del Pueblo N
Taos, NM 87571
(505) 758-0433
**GUILD Artist: Rebecca Bluestone,
see page 21.**

WEEMS GALLERY
2801 Eubank NE
Albuquerque, NM 87112
**GUILD Artists: Nancy J. Young
and Allen Young, see page 212.**

WEYRICH GALLERY
2935D Louisiana NE
Albuquerque, NM 87110
(505) 883-7410

WORTH GALLERY
112A Camino de la Placita
Taos, NM 87571
(505) 751-0816

• New York

CENTER ITHACA
171 E State St
Ithaca, NY 14850
(607) 272-4902

AARON FABER GALLERY
666 Fifth Ave
New York, NY 10019
(212) 586-8411

ADRIEN LINFORD
1320 Madison Ave
New York, NY 10128
(212) 289-4427

AFTER THE RAIN
149 Mercer St
New York, NY 10012
(212) 431-1044

AMERICA HOUSE
466 Piermont Ave
Piermont on Hudson, NY 10968
(914) 359-0106

AMERICAN BIRD &
CRAFT STUDIO
1 Main St
Essex, NY 12936
(518) 963-7121

AMERICAN CRAFT MUSEUM
GIFTSHOP
40 W 53rd St
New York, NY 10019
(212) 956-3535

ARCHETYPE GALLERY
137 Spring St
New York, NY 10012-3802
(212) 334-0100

ARTISANS INTERNATIONAL
89 Main St
Westhampton Beach, NY 11978
(516) 288-2222

ASHLEY COLLECTION
322 W 57th St #19S
New York, NY 10019
(212) 247-7294

AUSTIN HARVARD GALLERY
Northfield Common
50 State St
Pittsford, NY 14534
(716) 383-1472

BABCOCK GALLERIES
724 Fifth Ave
New York, NY 10019
(212) 767-1852

BART DANIELS GALLERY
24 Whitney Place
Buffalo, NY 14201
**GUILD Artist: George Alexander,
see page 79.**

BELLWIDO, LTD
100 Christopher St
New York, NY 10014
(212) 675-2668

BEN JANE ARTS
P.O. Box 298
West Hempsted, NY 11552
(516) 483-1330

BERNICE STEINBAUM
GALLERY
132 Greene St
New York, NY 10012
(212) 431-4224

CERAMICS & MORE
197 Hawkins St
City Island, NY 10464
(212) 885-0319

CERES GALLERY
91 Franklin St
New York, NY 10013
(212) 226-4725

CHARLES COWLES GALLERY
420 W Broadway
New York, NY 10012
(212) 925-3500

CIVILISATION
78 Second Ave
New York, NY 10003
(212) 254-3788

CLOUDS GALLERY
1 Mill Hill Rd
Woodstock, NY 12498
(914) 679-8155

COE KERR GALLERY
49 E 82nd St
New York, NY 10028
(212) 628-1340

CONTEMPORARY
PORCELAIN GALLERY
105 Sullivan St
New York, NY 10012
(212) 219-2172

COUNTRY GEAR, LTD
Main St
Bridgehampton, NY 11932
(516) 537-1032

CRAFT ART COLLECTIONS
941 Park Ave
New York, NY 10028
(212) 628-1360

CRAFT COMPANY #6
785 University Ave
Rochester, NY 14607
(716) 473-3413

CRAFTSMAN'S GALLERY, LTD
16 Chase Rd
Scarsdale, NY 10583
(914) 725-4644

CROSS HARRIS FINE CRAFTS
D & D Building
979 Third Ave
New York, NY 10022-1234
(212) 888-7878
**GUILD Artist: Claudia Hollister,
see page 173. Tom Neugebauer,
see page 174. Betsy Ross, see
page 176.**

DAWSON GALLERY
349 East Ave
Rochester, NY 14604-2617
(716) 454-6966

DENNIS MILLER ASSOCIATES
19 W 21st St
New York, NY 10010
(212) 242-7842

DESIGNER ACCENTS
212 Jericho Turnpike
Syosset, NY 11791
(516) 921-2721
**GUILD Artist: Larry Benjamin, see
page 137.**

DESIGNERS' STUDIO
492 Broadway
Saratoga Springs, NY 12866
(518) 584-0987

DESIGNERS, TOO
8037 Jericho Tnpk
Woodbury, NY 11797
(516) 921-8080

DIRECTIONAL FURNITURE
200 Lexington Avenue
New York, NY 10016
(212) 696-1088
**GUILD Artist: Larry Benjamin, see
page 137.**

DISTANT ORIGIN GALLERY
150 Mercer St
New York, NY 10012
(212) 941-0024

ELDER CRAFTSMEN, INC
846 Lexington Ave
New York, NY 10021
(212) 861-3294

ENCHANTED FOREST
85 Mercer St
New York, NY 10012
(212) 925-6677

ENGEL GALLERY
51 Main St
East Hampton, NY 11937
(516) 324-6462

ERIC ZETTERQUIST GALLERY
24 E 81st St #5C
New York, NY 10028
(212) 988-3399

EXPO DESIGN
7 Northern Blvd
Greenvale, NY 11548
(516) 484-9020

FABULOUS FURNITURE, INC
Rte 28
Boiceville, NY 12412
(914) 657-6317

FAST FORWARD GALLERY
580 Fifth Ave
Penthouse
New York, NY 10036
(212) 302-5518

FINISHED ROOM GALLERY
1234 Madison Ave
New York, NY 10128
(212) 996-9610

FIRSTHAND GALLERY
Main St
Sag Harbor, NY 11963
(516) 725-3648

FRANKLIN PARRASCH
GALLERY
584 Broadway
New York, NY 10012-3254
(212) 925-7090

GALLERY 514, LTD
98 Wheatley Rd
Old Westbury, NY 11568
(516) 626-0387

GALLERY AT THE
COURTYARD
223 Katonah Ave
Katonah, NY 10536
(914) 232-9511

GALLERY AUTHENTIQUE
1499 Old Northern Blvd
Roslyn, NY 11576
(516) 484-7238

GALLERY NINETY ONE
91 Grand St
New York, NY 10013
(212) 966-3722

Gallery Resources

GALLERY TEN
7 Greenwich Ave
New York, NY 10014
(212) 206-1058

GALLERY ZERO
11 Rockefeller Plaza
New York, NY 10020
(212) 397-2800

GARGOYLES, LTD
138 W 25th St
New York, NY 10001
(212) 255-0135
GUILD Artist: Myron Wasserman,
see page 221.

GARTH CLARK GALLERY
24 W 57th St
New York, NY 10019
(212) 246-2205

GAYLE WILLSON GALLERY
16 Job's Lane
Southampton, NY 11968
(516) 283-7430
GUILD Artist: Nancy Moore Bess,
see page 199.

GIMPEL WEITZENHOFFER
GALLERY
415 W Broadway
New York, NY 10012
(212) 925-9060

GRAHAM GALLERY
1014 Madison Ave
Main Floor
New York, NY 10021
(212) 535-5767

GREENHUT GALLERIES
Stuyvesant Plaza
Albany, NY 12203
(518) 482-1984

HAMPTON POTTERS
Newton Lane #53
Easthampton, NY 11937
(516) 324-6383

HAND OF THE CRAFTMAN 2
5 S Broadway
Nyack, NY 10960
(914) 358-3366

HAND OF THE CRAFTSMAN
58 S Broadway
Nyack, NY 10960
(914) 358-6622

HELEN DRUTT GALLERY
724 Fifth Ave
Ninth Floor
New York, NY 10019
(212) 974-7700

HELLER GALLERY
71 Greene St
New York, NY 10012-4338
(212) 966-5948

HENOCH GALLERY
80 Wooster St
New York, NY 10012
(212) 966-0303

HOLTHOUSE FIBER ART
GALLERY
7 Irma Ave
Port Washington, NY 11050
(506) 883-8620

HUDSON RIVER GALLERY
217 Main St
Ossining, NY 10562
(914) 762-5300

HUDSON RIVER MUSEUM
GIFT SHOP
511 Warburton Ave
Yonkers, NY 10701
(914) 963-4550

HUMMINGBIRD DESIGNS
29 Third St
Troy, NY 12180
(518) 272-1807

HUMMINGBIRD JEWELERS
14 E Market St
Rhinebeck, NY 12572
(914) 876-4585

IMAGES ART GALLERY
1157 Pleasantvile Rd
Briarcliff Manor, NY 10510
(914) 762-3000

IMPORTANT AMERICAN
CRAFT
70 Riverside Dr
New York, NY 10024
(212) 496-1804

IMPRESSIVE INTERIOR
GALLERY
14 Old Indian Tr
Milton, NY 12547
(914) 795-5101

JARO ART GALLERIES
955 Madison Ave
New York, NY 10021
(212) 734-5475

JOEL SCHWALB GALLERY
12 S Broadway
Nyack, NY 10960
(914) 358-1701

JOHN CHRISTOPHER
GALLERY
131 Main St
Stony Brook, NY 11790
(516) 689-1601

JOHN CHRISTOPHER
GALLERY
43 Main St
Cold Spring Harbor, NY 11724
(516) 367-3978

JULIE ARTISANS GALLERY
687 Madison Ave
New York, NY 10021
(212) 688-2345

KELMSCOTT GALLERY
131 Main St.
Cold Spring, NY 10516
(914) 265-2379
GUILD Artist: Edith A. Ehrlich, see
page 171.

LEATHER ARTISANS
Rt 3
Childwold, NY 12922
(518) 359-3102

LEE GALLERY
83 Main St
Southampton, NY 11968
(516) 287-2361

LEO KAPLAN MODERN
969 Madison Ave
New York, NY 10021
(212) 535-2407

LEWIS DOLIN GALLERY, INC
P.O. Box 239
Katonah, NY 10536-0239
(212) 941-8130

LIMESTONE GALLERY
205 Thompson St
Fayetteville, NY 13066
(315) 637-0460

MABEL'S
849 Madison Ave
New York, NY 10021
(212) 734-3263

MARI GALLERIES OF
WESTCHESTER
133 E Prospect Ave
Mamaroneck, NY 10543
(914) 698-0008

MARK MILLIKEN GALLERY
1200 Madison Ave
New York, NY 10128-0507
(212) 534-8802

MAX PROTECH GALLERY
560 Broadway
New York, NY 10012
(212) 966-5454

MEISNER SOHO GALLERY
96 Greene St
New York, NY 10012
(212) 431-9589

MELE GALLERY
40 Central Park South
New York, NY 10019
(212) 486-8304
GUILD Artist: Thomas Lollar, see
page 83.

MICHAEL INGBAR GALLERY
OF ART
568 Broadway
New York, NY 10012
(212) 334-1100

MILLER GALLERY
560 Broadway (At Prince St)
Fourth Floor
New York, NY 10012
(212) 226-0702

MODERN STONE AGE, LTD
111 Greene St
New York, NY 10012
(212) 966-2570

NAN MILLER GALLERY
3450 Winton Pl
Rochester, NY 14623
(716) 292-1430

NANCY MARGOLIS GALLERY
251 W 21st St
New York, NY 10011
(212) 255-0386

NEW GLASS GALLERY
345 W Broadway
New York, NY 10013
(212) 431-0050
GUILD Artist: Mesolini Glass
Studio, see page 192.

OBJECTS OF BRIGHT PRIDE
455A Columbus Ave
New York, NY 10024
(212) 721-4579

OF CABBAGES & KINGS
587 E Boston Post Rd
Mamaroneck, NY 10543
(914) 698-0445

ONE OF A KIND, LTD
978 Broadway
Thornwood, NY 10594
(914) 769-5777

OPUS II
979 Third Ave
Eighth Floor
New York, NY 10022-1234
(212) 980-1990

PETER JOSEPH GALLERY
745 Fifth Ave
New York, NY 10151-0407
(212) 751-5500

PRITAM & EAMES GALLERY
29 Race Lane
East Hampton, NY 11937-2445
(516) 324-7111
GUILD Artist: Ronald C. Puckett,
see page 123.

PRODIGY
126 W Main St
Eudicott, NY 13760
(607) 748-0190

Gallery Resources

ROCHESTER MEMORIAL
GALLERY
500 University Ave
Rochester, NY 14607
(716) 473-7720

RUTH RAIBLE GALLERY
41 Forest Ave
Hastings-on-Hudson, NY 10706
(914) 478-0585

RUTH SIEGEL GALLERY
24 W 57th St
New York, NY 10019
(212) 586-0605

SCOTT JORDAN FURNITURE
137 Varick At Spring
New York, NY 10013
(212) 620-4682

SHOWCASE GALLERY
169 Main St
Cold Spring Harbor, NY 11724
(516) 367-3037

SILVER FOX GIFT GALLERY
7935 Boston State Rd
Hamburg, NY 14075
(716) 649-0300

SOUTHWEST STUDIO
CONNECTION
65 Main St
Southampton, NY 11968
(516) 283-9649

STEINHARDT GALLERY
370 New York Ave
Huntington, NY 11743
(516) 549-4430

STUDIO GALLERY
133 S Salina St
Syracuse, NY 13202
(315) 472-0805

SYMMETRY GALLERY
348 Broadway
Saratoga Springs, NY 12866
(518) 584-5090

TERRCOTTA GALLERY
259 W Fourth St
New York, NY 10014
(212) 243-1952

THE CLAY POT
162 Seventh Ave
Brooklyn, NY 11215-2243
(718) 788-6564

THE DAVID COLLECTION
161 W 15th St
New York, NY 10011
(212) 929-4602

THE INTERART CENTER
167 Spring St
Second Floor
New York, NY 10012
(212) 431-7500
GUILD Artist: Alexandra
Friedman, see page 23.

THE LANDING GALLERY
7956 Jericho Turnpike
Woodbury, NY 11797
(516) 364-2787

THE POTTER'S GALLERY
168 Thompson St
New York, NY 10012
(212) 995-3736

THE RICE GALLERY
135 Washington Ave
Albany, NY 12210
(518) 463-4478

THE UNIQUE GALLERY
5701 Transit Rd
East Amherst, NY 14051
(716) 689-2160

THE WEST END GALLERY
87 W Market St
Corning, NY 14830
(607) 962-8692

THE WHITE BUFFALO GALLERY
13 Mill Rd
Woodstock, NY 12498
(800) 724-2113

THE WHITE TREE GALLERY
140 King St
Chappaqua, NY 10514
(914) 238-4601

TONY SHAFRAZI GALLERY
130 Prince St
New York, NY 10012
(212) 274-9300

WBAI HOLIDAY CRAFTS FAIR
P.O. Box 889
Times Square Station
New York, NY 10018
(212) 695-4465

WARD MASSE GALLERY
178 Prince St
New York, NY 10012
(212) 925-6951

WHEELER SEIDEL GALLERY
129 Prince St
New York, NY 10012-3111
(212) 533-0545

WILLIAM BARTHMAN
GALLERY
174 Broadway
New York, NY 10038
(212) 227-3524
GUILD Artist: Orient & Flume Art
Glass, see page 193.

WINSTON & COMPANY
97A Seventh Ave
Brooklyn, NY 11215
(718) 638-7942

WOODSTOCK GUILD
CRAFT SHOP
34 Tinker St
Woodstock, NY 12498
(914) 679-2688

• North Carolina

ACCIPITER
107 Edinburg St #123
Cary, NC 27511
(919) 460-9309
GUILD Artist: Nick Strange, see
page 113.

AMERICAN CRAFT
SHOWROOM
Design Cntr D-408
International Home Furniture
High Point, NC 27260
(301) 889-2933

ARTEFINO
119 E Seventh St
Charlotte, NC 28202-2125
(704) 372-3903

BLUE SPIRAL I
38 Biltmore Ave
Asheville, NC 28801
(704) 251-9854
GUILD Artist: Ellen Zahorec, see
page 19.

BROWNING ARTWORK
P.O. Box 275
Hwy 12
Frisco, NC 27936
(919) 995-5538
GUILD Artists: Linda Dixon and
Drew Krouse, see page 170.

CITY ART WORKS
2908 Selwyn Ave
Charlotte, NC 28209
(704) 358-1810

COMPTON ART GALLERY
409 W Fisher Ave
Greensboro, NC 27401
GUILD Artist: Trena McNabb, see
page 105.

CONTINUITY, INC
P.O. Box 999
US HWY 19
Maggie Valley, NC 28751
(704) 926-0333

FINE LINE
304 S Stratford Rd
Winston-Salem, NC 27103
(919) 723-8066

FOLK ART CENTER
Milepost 382
Blue Ridge Pkwy
Asheville, NC 28805
(704) 298-7928

GALLERY C
432 Daniels St
Raleigh, NC 27605
(919) 828-3165

GALLERY OF THE MOUNTAINS
290 Macon Ave
Asheville, NC 28814
(714) 254-2068

HAYDEN CRANE GALLERY
7 S Main St
Burnsville, NC 28714
(704) 682-2010

HODGES TAYLOR GALLERY
227 N Tryon St
Charlotte, NC 28202
(704) 334-3799

HORIZON GALLERY
905 W Main St
Durham, NC 27701
(919) 688-0313

ISLAND ART GALLERY
P.O. Box 265
Hwy 64
Manteo, NC 27954
(919) 473-2838

JULIA RUSH GALLERY
216 Union Square
Hickory, NC 28601
(704) 324-0409

LICK LOG MILL STORE
Dillard Rd
Highlands, NC 28741
(704) 526-3934

LITTLE ART GALLERY
North Hills Mall
Raleigh, NC 27609
(919) 787-6317

LITTLE MOUNTAIN POTTERY
Peniel Rd
Tryon, NC 28782
(704) 894-8091

MASTER WORKS GALLERY
Wright Square
Main St
Highlands, NC 28741
(704) 526-2633

MOUNTAIN POTTERY
15 Church St
Dillsboro, NC 28725
(704) 586-9183

NEW ELEMENTS GALLERY
216 N Front St
Wilmington, NC 28401
(919) 343-8997

NEW MORNING GALLERY
7 Boston Way
Asheville, NC 28803
(704) 274-2831
GUILD Artist: David Westmeier,
see pages 90 and 181.

PEDEN GALLERY II
132 E Hargett St
Raleigh, NC 27601-1440
(919) 834-9800

PIEDMONT CRAFTSMEN, INC
1204 Reynolda Rd
Winston-Salem, NC 27104
(919) 725-1516
GUILD Artist: Joseph L. Brandom,
see page 214.

RALEIGH CONTEMPORARY
GALLERY
134 E Harget St
Raleigh, NC 27601
(919) 828-6500

SKILLBECK GALLERY
238 S Sharon Amity
Charlotte, NC 28211
(704) 366-9613

SOMERHILL GALLERY
3 Eastgate Shopping Center
E Franklin St
Chapel Hill, NC 27514-5816
(919) 967-1879
GUILD Artists: George Alexander,
see page 79. Trena McNabb, see
page 105. Ellen Zahorec, see
page 19.

SOUTHERN EXPRESSIONS
GALLERY
2157 New Hendersonville Hwy
Pisgah Forest, NC 28768
(704) 884-6242

THE MORNING STAR
GALLERY
Rt 1 Box 292-10
Banner Elk, NC 28604
(704) 963-6902

THE PICTURE HOUSE, INC
1520 E Fourth St
Charlotte, NC 28204
(704) 333-8235

URBAN ARTIFACTS GALLERY
Forum IV
3200 Northline Ave
Greensboro, NC 27408-7611
(919) 855-0557

• North Dakota

BROWNING ARTS
22 N Fourth St
Grand Forks, ND 58201
(701) 746-5090

• Ohio

ALAN GALLERY
61 W Bridge St
Berea, OH 44017
(216) 243-7794

AMERICAN CRAFTS GALLERY
13010 Larchmere Blvd.
Cleveland, OH 44120
(216) 231-2008
GUILD Artists: John Blazy, see
page 138. Joan Stubbins, see
page 54. Don Drumm, see
page 216.

ART AT THE POWERHOUSE
2000 Sycamore
Nautica Complex
Cleveland, OH 44113
(216) 696-1942

ART EXCHANGE
539 E Town St
Columbus, OH 43215
(614) 464-4611

ARTISANS ALL
111 Pearl Rd
Brunswick, OH 44212
(216) 225-1118

ARTSPACE
Center for Contemporary Art
8501 Carnegie Ave
Cleveland, OH 44106
(216) 421-8671

AVANTE GALLERY
2094 Murray Hill Rd
Cleveland, OH 44106-2359
(216) 791-1622
GUILD Artist: Anne Mayer Meier,
see page 206.

BENCHWORKS
2563 N High St
Columbus, OH 43202
(614) 263-2111

BONFOEY COMPANY
1710 Euclid Ave
Cleveland, OH 44115
(216) 621-0178

CARGO NET, INC
258 Delaware Ave
P.O. Box 369
Put-In-Bay, OH 43456
(419) 285-4231

CHELSEA GALLERIES
23225 Merchantile Rd
Beachwood, OH 44122
(216) 591-1066

DAYTON ART INSTITUTE
P.O. Box 941
Dayton, OH 45401
(513) 223-5277

DESIGNS OF ALL TIMES
28001 Chagrin Blvd
Cleveland, OH 44122
(216) 831-3010

DRUMM STUDIOS & GALLERY
437 Crouse St
Akron, OH 44311
(216) 253-6268
GUILD Artist: Don Drumm, see
page 216.

EAST SIDE WEST SIDE GALLERY
11427 Bellflower Rd
Cleveland, OH 44106
(216) 231-1616

FIORI GALLERY
2072 Murray Hill Rd
Cleveland, OH 44106
(216) 721-5319

GALLERY 400
4659 Dressler Rd NW
Canton, OH 44718
(216) 492-2600

HELEN WINNEMORE GALLERY
150 E Kosutch St
Columbus, OH 43206
(614) 444-5850

HELIOTROPE ART GALLERY
3001 Caltalpa Dr
Dayton, OH 45405
(513) 275-1071

MILLER GALLERY
2815 Erie Avenue
Cincinatti, OH 45208
(513) 871-4420
GUILD Artist: David Westmeier,
see pages 90 and 181.

MURIEL MERAY STUDIO SHOP
537 E Maple St
North Canton, OH 44720
(216) 494-3736

MURRAY HILL MARKET
2181 Murray Hill Rd
Cleveland, OH 44106
(216) 791-9679

OHIO DESIGNER
CRAFTSMEN GALLERY
2164 Riverside Dr
Columbus, OH 43221
(614) 486-7119

OSHER OSHER GALLERY
5662 Mayfield Rd
Lindhurst, OH 44124
(216) 397-1266

PRIVATE COLLECTION
GALLERY
21 E Fifth St
Cincinnati, OH 45202
(513) 381-1667

RILEY HAWK GLASS GALLERY
2026 Murray Hill Rd #103
Cleveland, OH 44106-2337
(216) 421-1445

RILEY HAWK GLASS GALLERY
642 N High St
Columbus, OH 43215-2010
(614) 228-6554

RUTLEDGE ART GALLERY
1964 N Main St
Dayton, OH 45406
(513) 278-4900

SANDUSKY CULTURAL
CENTER
2130 Hayes Ave
Sandusky, OH 44870
(419) 625-8097

SANTA CLARA GALLERY
1942 N Main St
Dayton, OH 45406
(513) 279-9100

SOMETHING DIFFERENT
3427 Memphis Ave
Cleveland, OH 44109
(216) 398-0472
GUILD Artist: Joan Stubbins, see
page 54.

STANLEY KAUFMAN GALLERY
4752 Rt 39
Berlin, OH 44610
(216) 893-2842

THE ART BANK GALLERY
317 W Fourth St
Cincinnati, OH 45202
(513) 621-7779

THE GILDAY GALLERY
13860 Ravenna Road
Newbury, OH 44065
GUILD Artist: John Blazy, see
page 138.

THE MALTON GALLERY
2709 Observatory Dr
Cincinnati, OH 45208-2107
(513) 321-8014

THE OMNI GALLERY
The Arcade
401 Euclid Ave #46
Cleveland, OH 44114
(216) 781-3444

THE PUMP HOUSE ART
GALLERY
Enderlin Circle
P.O. Box 1613
Chillicothe, OH 45601
(614) 772-5783

THE SCULPTURE CENTER
12206 Euclid Ave
Cleveland, OH 44115
(216) 229-6527

THE TURTLE CREEK GALLERY
6 S Broadway
Lebanon, OH 45036
(513) 932-2296

TONI BIRCKHEAD GALLERY
342 W Fourth St
Cincinnati, OH 45202
(513) 241-0212

VILLAGE ARTISANS
COOPERATIVE
220 Xenia Ave
Yellow Springs, OH 45387
(513) 767-1209

Gallery Resources

• Oklahoma

CRAIN WOLOV GALLERY
209 N Main St
Tulsa, OK 74103-2005
(918) 299-2299

DORAN GALLERY
3509 S Peoria St
Tulsa, OK 74105
(918) 748-8700

• Oregon

A BIZZILLION BEAUTIFUL THINGS
844 Pearl St
Eugene, OR 97401
(503) 485-1570

ALDER GALLERY & ART SERVICE
160 E Broadway
Eugene, OR 97401-3128
(503) 342-6411

ART DECOR GALLERY
136 High St SE
Salem, OR 97301
(503) 378-0876
GUILD Artist: Loraine A. Fischer, see page 82.

CONTEMPORARY CRAFTS GALLERY
3934 SW Corbett Ave
Portland, OR 97201-6498
(503) 223-2654
GUILD Artist: Sharon Marcus, see page 28.

EARTHWORKS GALLERY
2222 Hwy 101 N
Yachats, OR 97498
(503) 547-4300

GANGO GALLERY
205 SW First St
Portland, OR 97204
(503) 222-3850
GUILD Artist: William C. Richards, see page 89.

MAVEETY GALLERY
P.O. Box 148
Glen Eden Beach, OR 97388
(503) 764-2318

PORTLAND ART MUSEUM RENTAL AND SALES GALLERY
1219 SW Park
Portland, OR 97205
(503) 226-2911
GUILD Artist: Loraine A. Fischer, see page 82.

SAXON'S
3138 N Hwy 97
Bend, OR 97701
(503) 389-6655
GUILD Artist: Andrew Moritz, see page 219.

SKYLARK GALLERY
130 Spaulding Ave
Brownsville, OR 97327
(503) 466-5221
GUILD Artist: Andrew Moritz, see page 219.

THE INDIGO GALLERY
311 Ave B #B
Lake Oswego, OR 97034
(503) 636-3454
GUILD Artist: Loraine A. Fischer, see page 82.

THE REAL MOTHER GOOSE GALLERY
901 SW Yamhill
Portland, OR 97205
(503) 223-9510

THE WHITE BIRD GALLERY
N Hemlock Rd
P.O. Box 502
Cannon Beach, OR 97110
(503) 436-2681

• Pennsylvania

479 GALLERY
55 N Second St
Philadelphia, PA 19106
(215) 922-1444
GUILD Artist: Johanna Goodman, see page 142.

AART VARK GALLERY
17th At Locust
Philadelphia, PA 19103
(215) 735-5600

ABINGTON ART CENTER
515 Meetinghouse Rd
Jenkintown, PA 19046
(215) 887-4882

AHAVA
4371 Main St
Philadelphia, PA 19127
(215) 482-8863

ART AC'CENTS
350 Montgomery Ave
Merion, PA 19066
(215) 664-4444

ARTISANS GALLERY
Peddlers Village
P.O. Box 133
Lahaska, PA 18931
(215) 794-3112
GUILD Artist: Robert Hargrave, see page 203.

ARTISANS THREE
The Village Center
Spring House, PA 19477
(215) 643-4504

BEST FRIENDS
4329 Main St
Philadelphia, PA 19127
(215) 487-1250

CALICO CAT GALLERY
36 W King St
Lancaster, PA 17603
(717) 397-6372

CAT'S PAW GALLERY
31 Race St
Jim Thorpe, PA 18229
(717) 325-4041

CATHERINE STARR GALLERY
4235 Main St
Philadelphia, PA 19127-1602
(215) 482-7755

CHADDS FORD GALLERY
US Hwy 1 & 100
P.O. Box 179
Chadds Ford, PA 19317
(215) 459-5510

CLAY SPACE GALLERY
Mineo Bldg
5416 Walnut St
Pittsburg, PA 15232
(412) 682-3737

COUNTRY STUDIO
Rt 1 Box 1124
Hadley, PA 16130
(412) 253-2493

CRAFTSMEN'S GALLERY
Rt 6, East of Hawley
Hawley, PA 18428
(717) 226-4111

CREATIVE HANDS
Peddlers Village
Lahaska, PA 18931
(215) 794-7012

DESIGN ARTS GALLERY
Nesbitt College of Design Arts
33rd & Market Sts
Philadelphia, PA 19104
(215) 895-2386

DESIGN ELEMENTS
Rt 6 NW
Edinboro, PA 16412
(814) 734-5105

DINA PORTER GALLERY
3900 Hamilton Blvd
Allentown, PA 18103
(215) 434-7363

DISCOVERIES
P.O. Box 1552
Reading, PA 19603
(215) 372-2595

EARTHWORKS GALLERY
227 Haverford Ave
Narberth, PA 19072
(215) 667-1143

F.A.N GALLERY
311 Cherry St
Philadelphia, PA 19106
(215) 922-5155

GALERIE ATELIER
65 N Second St
Philadelphia, PA 19106
(215) 627-3624

GALLERIA TRICIA
102 Harrison Dr
New Cumberland, PA 17070
(717) 691-0263

GALLERIE NADEAU
118 N Third St
Philadelphia, PA 19106
(215) 574-0202

GALLERY "G"
211 Ninth Street
Pittsburgh, PA 15222
(412) 562-0912
GUILD Artists: Linda Dixon and Drew Krouse, see page 170.

GALLERY 500
Old York and Church Roads
Elkins Park, PA 19177
(215) 572-1203
GUILD Artist: George Radeschi, see page 209.

GALLERY RIGGIONE
Mallard Circle Village
130 Almshouse Rd
Richboro, PA 18954
(215) 322-5035

GLASS GROWERS GALLERY
701 Holland St
Erie, PA 16501
(814) 453-3758

GREENE & GREENE GALLERY
88 S Main St
New Hope, PA 18938
(215) 862-9620

HAHN GALLERY
8439 Germantown Ave
Philadelphia, PA 19188
(215) 247-8439

HELEN DRUTT GALLERY
1721 Walnut St
Philadelphia, PA 19103
(215) 735-1625

HONEY BROOK WOODS
102 Telegraph Rd
Honey Brook, PA 19344
(215) 273-2680

IMAGINE GALLERY & GIFTS
3330 W 26th St
Erie, PA 16506
(814) 858-8077

JESSICA BERWIND GALLERY
301 Cherry St
Philadelphia, PA 19106
(215) 574-1645

JOHN BIERS STUDIO
225 Race St
Philadelphia, PA 19106
(215) 923-8122

JOY BERMAN GALLERIES
2201 Pennsylvania Ave
Philadelphia, PA 19130
(215) 854-8166
GUILD Artist: Myron Wasserman,
see page 221.

JUN GALLERY
114 Market St
Philadelphia, PA 19106
(215) 627-5020

KAISER NEWMAN GALLERY
134 N Third St
Philadelphia, PA 19106
(215) 923-7438

LANGMAN GALLERY
Willow Grove Park
2500 Moreland Rd
Willow Grove, PA 19090
(215) 657-8333

LANNON'S
1007 Lancaster Ave
Bryn Mawr, PA 19132
(215) 525-4526

LARIMORE FURNITURE
160 N Third St
Philadelphia, PA 19106
(215) 440-7136

LATITUDES GALLERY
4325 Main St
Philadelphia, PA 19127
(215) 482-0417

LOCKS GALLERY
600 Washington Square S
Philadephia, PA 19106
(215) 629-1000

LUCKENBACH MILL GALLERY
1825 Watkins St
Bethlehem, PA 18017
(215) 691-0603

MADE BY HAND GALLERY
303 S Craig St
Pittsburgh, PA 15213
(412) 681-8346

MATERIA GALLERY
86 W State St
Doylestown, PA 18901-4222
(215) 348-7280

MOSER SHOWROOM &
GALLERY
210 W Washington Square
Philadelphia, PA 19106
(215) 922-6440

NEXUS/FOUNDATION FOR
TODAY'S ART
137 North 2nd Street
Philadelphia, PA 19106
(215) 629-1103
GUILD Artist: Loretta Mossman,
see page 29.

OLC GALLERY
152-154 N Third St
Philadelphia, PA 19106
(215) 923-6085

OWEN PATRICK GALLERY
4345 Main St
Philadelphia, PA 19127
(215) 482-9395

PITTSBURGH CENTER FOR
THE ARTS
6300 Fifth Ave
Pittsburgh, PA 15232
(412) 361-0873

REISBORD GALLERY
4313-17 Main St
Manayunk, PA 19127
(215) 483-3232
GUILD Artist: Loretta Mossman,
see page 29.

RICK SNYDERMAN GALLERY
303 Cherry Street
Philadelphia, PA
(215) 238-9576
GUILD Artist: George Radeschi,
see page 209.

ROCHE BOBOIS
Marketplace Design Center
2400 Market Street
Philadelphia, PA 19103-3041
GUILD Artist: Ervin Somogyi, see
page 106.

RODGER LAPELLE GALLERY
122 N Third St
Philadelphia, PA 19106
(215) 592-0232

RUTH ZAFIR GALLERY
13 S Second St
Philadelphia, PA 19106
(215) 627-7098

SANDE WEBSTER GALLERY
2018 Locust St
Philadelphia, PA 19103
(215) 732-8850
GUILD Artist: Myron Wasserman,
see page 221.

SAVOIR-FAIRE
837 W Rolling Rd
Springfield, PA 19064
(215) 544-8998

SIMCOE GALLERY
1925 Main St
Northampton, PA 18067
(215) 262-8154

SNYDERMAN GALLERY
303 Cherry St
Philadelphia, PA 19106-1803
(215) 238-9576

SOCIETY FOR ART IN CRAFTS
2100 Smallman Street
Pittsburgh, PA 15222
(412) 261-7003
GUILD Artist: Rebecca Bluestone,
see page 21.

SOCIETY FOR
CONTEMPORARY CRAFT
2100 Smallman St
Pittsburgh, PA 15222
(412) 261-7003

SOMETHING SPECIAL
153 Main St
Bradford, PA 16701
(814) 368-6011

STARR POTTERY
754 Abbottstown Pike
Hanover, PA 17331
(717) 632-0027

STRAWBERRY & COMPANY
7-9 W King St
Lancaster, PA 17603
(717) 392-5345

STUDIO IN SWARTHMORE
GALLERY
14 Park Ave
Swarthmore, PA 19081
(215) 543-5779

STYLE & SUBSTANCE GALLERY
Greengate Mall
Greensburg, PA 15601
(412) 834-9299

THE CLAY PLACE
5416 Walnut Street
Pittsburgh, PA 15232
(412) 682-3737

THE CLAY STUDIO
139 N Second St
Philadelphia, PA 19106
(215) 925-3453

THE FABRIC WORKSHOP
1100 Vine St
Thirteenth Floor
Philadelphia, PA 19107
(215) 922-7303

THE OTTER CREEK STORE
106 S Diamond St
Mercer, PA 16137
(412) 662-2830

THE PAINTED BRIDE GALLERY
230 Vine St
Philadelphia, PA 19106
(215) 925-9914

THE WORKS GALLERY
319 South St
Philadelphia, PA 19147
(215) 922-7775

• Rhode Island

RAMSON HOUSE ANTIQUES
36 Franklin St
Newport, RI 02840
(401) 847-0555

SPECTRUM OF AMERICAN
ARTISTS
306 Thames St
Newport, RI 02840
(401) 847-4477

VIRGINIA LYNCH GALLERY
Four Corners
3883 Main Rd
Riverton, RI 02878
(401) 624-3392

• South Carolina

BOHEMIAN
2112 Devine St
Columbia, SC 29205
(803) 256-0629

CAROL SAUNDERS GALLERY
922 Gervais St
Columbia, SC 29201
(803) 256-3046

CHECKERED MOON
GALLERY
208 West St
Beaufort, SC 29902
(802) 522-3466

CRAFTSELLER GALLERY
216 West St
Beaufort, SC 29902
(803) 525-6104

DUKE STREET GALLERY
109 Duke St
Pendleton, SC 29670
(803) 646-3469

EAST BAY GALLERY
264 King St
Charleston, SC 29401
(803) 723-5567

EAST BAY GALLERY
636 Coleman Blvd
Mt Pleasant, SC 29464
(803) 723-5567

GALLERY BY THE PARK
402 SE Main St
Simpsonville, SC 29681
(803) 963-4893

NINA LIU & FRIENDS
24 State St
Charleston, SC 29401
(803) 722-2724

SMITH GALLERIES OF
FINE CRAFTS
The Village at Wexford #J-11
Hilton Head Island, SC 29928
(803) 842-2280

Gallery Resources

• Tennessee

AMERICAN ARTISAN, INC
4231 Harding Rd
Nashville, TN 37205
(615) 298-4691

ARTIFACTS GALLERY
1007 Oakhaven Rd
Memphis, TN 38119
(901) 767-5236
GUILD Artist: Don Drumm, see
page 216.

BELL GALLERY OF FINE ART
6150 Poplar Avenue
Suite 118
Memphis, TN 38119
(901) 682-2189
GUILD Artists: Charles Pearson and
Timothy Roeder, see page 175.

**BELL ROSS FINE ARTS
GALLERY**
1080 Brookfield Rd
Memphis, TN 38119
(901) 682-2189

**BOONES CREEK POTTER'S
GALLERY**
4903 Kingsport Hwy 36
Johnson City, TN 37615
(615) 282-2801

CUMBERLAND GALLERY
4107 Hillsboro Cir
Nashville, TN 37215
(615) 297-0296

HANSON ARTSOURCE
5607 Kingston Pike
Knoxville, TN 37919
(615) 584-6097

HOVANEC GALLERY
408 Tenth St
Knoxville, TN 37916
(615) 624-5312

KURTS BINGHAM GALLERY
766 S White Station Rd
Memphis, TN 38117
(901) 683-6200
GUILD Artist: John P. Ashley, see
page 93.

THE BROWSERY
2794 Wilma Rudolph Blvd
Clarksville, TN 37040
(615) 552-2733

THE RIVER GALLERY
400 E Second St
Chatanooga, TN 37403
(615) 267-7353
GUILD Artist: Ruth Gowell, see
page 39.

**THE WINDOW ON
MAIN STREET**
348 Main St
Franklin, TN 37064
(615) 790-3480

• Texas

APPLE CORPS
23-24 University
Houston, TX 77005
(713) 524-2221

ART GROUP
1119 N Windomere
Dallas, TX 75208
(214) 942-0258

ART, INCORPORATED
9401 San Pedro
San Antonio, TX 78216
(210) 240-1091
GUILD Artist: Susan M. Oaks, see
page 207.

**ARTISANS FINE CRAFTS
GALLERY**
10000 Research Blvd
Austin, TX 78759
(512) 345-3001

BANKS FINE ART
3316 Royal Lane
Dallas, TX 75229
(214) 352-1811

BEVERLY GORDON GALLERY
2404 Cedar Springs Rd #100
Dallas, TX 75201
(214) 880-9600

BLAIRE CARNAHAN FINE ART
418 Villita Street
San Antonio, TX 78205
(210) 227-6313
GUILD Artist: Susan M. Oaks, see
page 207.

CARLYN GALLERY I
Olla Podrida Art Ctr
12215 Coit Rd
Dallas, TX 75251
(214) 702-0824

CARSON ART
1444 Oak Lawn - Suite 610
Dallas, TX 75207
(214) 747-3055
GUILD Artist: Irene De Gair, see
page 24.

CLARKSVILLE POTTERY
1013 W Lynn St
Austin, TX 78703
(512) 478-9079
GUILD Artist: Michael Saul, see
page 179.

CLARKSVILLE POTTERY 2
Arboretum Market
9722 Great Hills
Austin, TX 78759
(512) 794-8580

CONRAD'S GALLERY
217 Tremont
Galveston, TX 77550
(409) 762-3737

CREATIVE ARTS GALLERY
836 North Star Mall
San Antonio, TX 78216
(512) 342-8659
GUILD Artists: David Westmeier,
see pages 90 and 181. Michael
Saul, see page 179.

CULLER CONCEPTS
1347 Cedar Hill Ave
Dallas, TX 75208
(214) 942-1646

EVE FRANCE GALLERY
2039 W Gray St
Houston, TX 77109
(713) 526-9991

FOLK ART SHOP
1004 Milam St
Columbus, TX 78934
(409) 732-3864

FOSSIL RIM WILDLIFE CENTER
Rt 1 Box 210
Glen Rose, TX 76043
(817) 897-2960

FREE FLIGHT GALLERY
603 Monger Ave. #309
Dallas, TX 75202
(214) 720-9147
GUILD Artist: Alan Steinberg, see
page 89.

GOLDEN EYE GALLERY
20035 Katy Frwy
Katy, TX 77450
(713) 678-2820

HANSON GALLERIES
800 W Sam Houston Pkwy N
Houston, TX 77024
(713) 984-1242
GUILD Artists: Don Drumm, see
page 216. Tom Neugebauer, see
page 174.

HEARTLAND GALLERY
4006 S Lamar St #950
Austin, TX 78704
(512) 447-1171

JACK MEIER GALLERY
2310 Bissonnet
Houston, TX 77005
(713) 526-2983

JAMES GALLERY
5616 Royalton
Houston, TX 77081
(713) 661-8003

JANICE RUDY GALLERY
Pavillion
1800 Post Oak Blvd
Houston, TX 77056
(713) 960-1073

JUDY YOUENS GALLERY
2631 Colquitt St
Houston, TX 77098-2117
(713) 527-0303

LA DEAN GALLERY
5308 Birchman
Ft Worth, TX 76107
(817) 731-3593

MIXED EMOTIONS GALLERY
7026 Old Katy Rd #162
Houston, TX 77024
GUILD Artists: Karen Adachi, see
page 9. William C. Richards, see
page 89.

**MORGAN FITZGERALD
GALLERIES**
601 Hensel St
Bryan, TX 77801
(409) 846-1369

SOL DEL RIO ART GALLERY
1020 Townsend
San Antonio, TX 78209
GUILD Artist: Michael Saul, see
page 179.

SOUTHWEST CRAFT CENTER
300 Augusta
San Antonio, TX 78205
(512) 224-1848

THE ARRANGEMENT GALLERY
2605 Elm St
Dallas, TX 75226
(214) 748-4540
GUILD Artist: Christopher Thomson,
see page 155.

THE GALLERY AT LOS PATIOS
2015 N.E. Loop 410
San Antonio, TX 78217
(215) 655-0538
GUILD Artist: Susan M. Oaks, see
page 207.

THE NEW GALLERY
2639 Colquit
Houston, TX 77098
(713) 520-1753

THE ROCK HOUSE GALLERY
1311 W Abram
Arlington, TX 76013
(817) 265-5874

THE SPICEWOOD GALLERY
1206 W 38th St
Austin, TX 78705
(512) 458-6575

THE TWO FRIENDS GALLERY
2301 Strand
Galveston, TX 77550
(409) 765-7477

THE URSULINE GALLERY
300 Augusta Ave
San Antonio, TX 78205
(512) 224-1848

THE VILLAGE WEAVERS
418 Villita
San Antonio, TX 78205
(512) 222-0776

WM CAMPBELL
CONTEMPORARY ART
4935 Byers Ave
Ft Worth, TX 76107
(817) 737-9566

• Utah

UTAH DESIGNER CRAFTS
GALLERY
38W 200S
Salt Lake City, UT 84101
(801) 359-2770

• Vermont

CRAFT HAUS
Top of the Hill Rd
Wilmington, VT 05363
(802) 464-2164

HAWKINS HOUSE
262 North St
Bennington, VT 05201
(802) 447-1171

NORTH WIND ARTISAN
GALLERY
81 Central St
Woodstock, VT 05091
(802) 457-4587

SIMON PEARCE GLASS
The Mill
Quechee, VT 05059
(802) 295-2711

STOWE POTTERY & CRAFT
GALLERY
P.O. Box 262
Rte 108
Stowe, VT 05672
(802) 253-4693

THE SPIRAL GALLERY
P.O. Box 29
Marlboro, VT 05344
(802) 257-5696
GUILD Artist: Anne Shutan, see
page 125.

VERMONT ARTISAN DESIGNS
115 Main St
Brattleboro, VT 05301
(802) 257-7044

VERMONT STATE CRAFT
CENTER
Main Street
P.O. Box 1777
Windsor, VT 05089
(802) 674-6729

VERMONT STATE CRAFT
CENTER
Mill Street
Middlebury, VT 05753
(802) 388-3177
GUILD Artist: Steven Holman, see
page 121.

WINDHAM ART GALLERY
69 Main Street
Brattleboro, VT 05345
(802) 257-1881
GUILD Artists: Anne Shutan, see
page 125. S.M. Warren, see
page 211.

WOODSTOCK GALLERY
OF ART
Gallery Place
Rt 4 East
Woodstock, VT 05091
(802) 457-1900

• Virginia

A TOUCH OF EARTH
6580 Richmond Rd
Lighfoot, VA 23090
(804) 565-0425

AMERICAN ARTISAN INC
201 King St
Alexandria, VA 22314-3209
(703) 548-3431

BLUE SKIES GALLERY
120 W Queens Way #201
Hampton, VA 23669
(804) 727-0028

BREIT FUNCTIONAL CRAFTS
1701 Colley Ave
Norfolk, VA 23517
(804) 640-1012

BROADWAY GALLERY
11213-J Lee Highway
Fairfax, VA 22030
(703) 273-2388
GUILD Artist: Irene De Gair, see
page 24.

CAVE HOUSE CRAFT SHOP
279 E Main St
Abingdon, VA 24210
(703) 628-7721

COUNTRY HERITAGE
ANTIQUES & CRAFTS
P.O. Box 148
Washington, VA 22747
(703) 675-3738

CRAFTERS' GALLERY
Rt 12 Box 97
Charlottesville, VA 22901
(804) 295-7006

CUDAHY'S GALLERY
1314 E Cary St
Richmond, VA 23219
(804) 782-1776

D'ART CENTER
125 College Place
Norfolk, VA 23510
(804) 625-4211

EBASHAE GALLERY
309 Mill St
Occoquan, VA 22125
(703) 491-5984

ELECTRIC GLASS GALLERY
823 W Pembroke Ave
Hampton, VA 23669
(804) 722-6300

FIBER WORKS
105 N Union St
Alexandria, VA 22314
(703) 836-5807

GALLERY OF MOUNTAIN
SECRETS
Rt 250
Main St
Monterey, VA 24465
(703) 468-2020

GALLERY ONE
One Columbus Center #106
Virginia Beach, VA 23462
(804) 497-0300

GALLERY THREE
213 Market St
Roanoke, VA 24011
(703) 343-9698

GEM DECK
701 Lynchaven Pkwy
Virginia Beach, VA 23452
(804) 340-5365

JULIE'S DIXIE PIG
102 Fifth St Mall
Charlottesville, VA 22901
(804) 979-2478

LA DIFFERENCE
200 Zan Rd
Charlottesville, VA 22901
(804) 973-3122

MARINA SHORES GALLERY
2100 Marina Shores Dr
Virginia Beach, VA 23451
(804) 496-7000

MCMANN MCDADE
FINE ART
364 Walnut Ave SW
Roanoke, VA 24016
(703) 345-5123

METALLUM
105 N Union St
Alexandria, VA 22314
(703) 548-4600

ON THE HILL CREATIVE
ARTS CENTER
121 Alexander Hamilton
P.O. Box 222
Yorktown, VA 23690
(804) 898-3076

PALMER RAE GALLERY, INC
112 Granby St.
Norfolk, VA 23510
(804) 627-0081

PAULA LEWIS GALLERY
Court Square
216 Fourth St NE
Charlottesville, VA 22901
(804) 295-6244

PENINSULA FINE ARTS
CENTER
101 Museum Dr
P.O. Box 6438
Newport News, VA 23606
(804) 596-8175

PRIMAVERA GALLERY
4216 Virginia Beach Blvd
Virginia Beach, VA 23452
(804) 431-9393

QUILTS UNLIMITED
440-A Duke of Gloucester St
Williamsburg, VA 23185
(804) 253-8700

QUILTS UNLIMITED
The Homestead Resort
Hot Springs, VA 24445
(708) 839-5955

SIGNET GALLERY
212 Fifth St NE
P.O. Box 753
Charlottesville, VA 22902
(804) 296-6463
GUILD Artist: J. Dubs, see
page 217.

TACTILE
105 N Union St
Alexandria, VA 22314
(703) 549-8490

THE OLD MILL CRAFT
GALLERY
Evans Farm Inn
Rt 123
McLean, VA 22101
(703) 893-2736

THE RUSH RIVER COMPANY
P.O. Box 74
Gay St
Washington, VA 22747
(703) 675-1136

VISTA FINE CRAFTS GALLERY
5 W Washington St
P.O. Box 2034
Middleburg, VA 22117
(703) 687-3317

WHISTLE WALK CRAFTS
GALLERY
7 S King St
Leesburg, VA 22075
(703) 777-4017

YORKTOWN ARTS
FOUNDATION
121 Alexander Hamilton
P.O. Box 244
Yorktown, VA 23690
(804) 898-3076

Gallery Resources

• Washington

AMERICAN ART GALLERY
1126 Broadway
Tacoma, WA 98402
(206) 272-4327

ARTWORKS GALLERY
155 S Main St
Seattle, WA 98104
(206) 625-0932

CARNEGIE ART CENTER, INC
109 S Palouse St
Walla Walla, WA 99362
(509) 525-4270

CORPORATE ART WEST, INC
1600 124th Ave NE
Bellevue, WA 98005
(206) 454-2595

CREATIONS GALLERY
524 First St
Seattle, WA 98104
(206) 624-5578

EARTHENWORKS
1015 Water St
Port Townsend, WA 98368
(206) 385-0328

EARTHENWORKS
713 First St
P.O. Box 702
La Conner, WA 98257
(206) 466-4422

ELEMENTS GALLERY
113 Seafirst Bldg
10500 NE Eighth St
Bellevue, WA 98004
(206) 454-8242

ELLENBURG COMMUNITY GALLERY
408 1/2 N Pearl St
Ellensburg, WA 98926
(509) 925-2670

EMERALD CITY GALLERY
17508 Vashon HWY SW
Vashon Island, WA 98070
(206) 292-8932

FIRE WORKS GALLERIES
210 First Ave S
Seattle, WA 98104
(206) 682-8707

FLYING SHUTTLE GALLERY
607 First Ave
Seattle, WA 98104
(206) 343-9762

FOLK ART GALLERY
La Tienda
4138 University Way NE
Seattle, WA 98105
(206) 634-1795

FOSTER WHITE GALLERY
311 1/2 Occidental Ave S
Seattle, WA 98104-2839
(206) 622-2833

FRANK DUNYA GALLERY
3418 Fremont Ave N
Seattle, WA 98103
(206) 547-6760

FRIESEN GALLERY
1210 Second Ave
Seattle, WA 98101-2926
(206) 628-9502

GARDENS OF ART
2900 Sylvan St
Bellingham, WA 98226
(206) 671-1069

GLASS EYE GALLERY
1902 Post Alley
Seattle, WA 98101
(206) 441-3221

GLASSHOUSE ART GLASS
Pioneer Square
311 Occidental Ave S
Seattle, WA 98104
(206) 682-9939

JANET HUSTON GALLERY
P.O. Box 845
La Conner, WA 98257-0845
(206) 466-5001

LYNN MCALLISTER GALLERY
416 University St.
Seattle, WA 98101
(206) 624-6864
GUILD Artist: Patricia Weyer, see page 196.

MIA GALLERY
536 First Ave S
Seattle, WA 98104-2804
(206) 467-8283
GUILD Artist: Carl T. Chew, see page 163.

MANDARIN GLASS STUDIO GALLERY
8821 Bridgeport Way SW
Tacoma, WA 98499
(206) 582-3355

MESOLINI & AMICI
77 1/2 S. Main St
Seattle, WA 98104
(206) 587-0275
GUILD Artist: Mesolini Glass Studio, see page 192.

NORTHWEST DISCOVERY
142 Bellevue Sq
Bellevue, WA 98004
(206) 454-1676

NORTHWEST GALLERY OF FINE WOODWORKING
317 NW Gilman Blvd
Issaquah, WA 98027
(206) 391-4221

NORTHWEST GALLERY OF FINE WOODWORKING
202 First Ave S
Seattle, WA 98104
(206) 625-0542
GUILD Artist: Thomas Hugh Strangeland, see page 126.

PASSPORTS GALLERY
123 Pine St
Seattle, WA 98101
(206) 628-3793

PETERSON ART FURNITURE GALLERY
122 Central Way
Kirkland, WA 98033
(206) 827-8053
GUILD Artist: Thomas Hugh Strangeland, see page 126.

PHOENIX RISING GALLERY
2030 Western Ave
Seattle, WA 98121
(206) 728-2332

SCANDIA JEWELERS
1011 First Ave
Seattle, WA 98104
(206) 682-7464

STONINGTON GALLERY
2030 First Ave
Seattle, WA 98121
(206) 443-1108

THE COLLECTION
118 S Washington
Pioneer Square
Seattle, WA 98104
(206) 682-6184
GUILD Artist: Frank Colson, see page 80.

THE PANACA GALLERY
133 Bellevue Square
Bellevue, WA 98004
(206) 454-0234

THE WOOD MERCHANT
707 S First St
La Conner, WA 98257
(206) 466-4741

TOPPERS
1260 Carillon Pt
Kirkland, WA 98033
(206) 889-9311

WILKEY FINE ARTS GALLERY
108 Occidental Ave S
Seattle, WA 98104
(206) 343-9070

WILLIAM TRAVER GALLERY
110 Union St
Seattle, WA 98101
(206) 448-4234

• West Virginia

QUILTS UNLIMITED
203 E Washington St
Lewisburg, WV 24901
(304) 647-4208

SANGUINE GRYPHON GALLERY
P.O. Box 3120
Shepherdstown, WV 25443
(304) 876-6569

THE ART STORE
1013 Bridge Rd
Charleston, WV 25314
(304) 345-1038

THE SHOP
The Cultural Center
Charleston, WV 25305
(304) 348-0690

• Wisconsin

A HOUERBOCKEN GALLERY
230 W Wells St #202
Milwaukee, WI 53203
(414) 276-6002
GUILD Artists: Joyce Marquess Carey, see page 35. Bruce Siegel, see page 159.

ART INDEPENDENT GALLERY
623 Main St
Lake Geneva, WI 53147
(414) 248-3612

ARTSPACE
608 New York Ave
P.O. Box 489
Sheboygan, WI 53082
(414) 458-6144

ARTISTRY STUDIO GALLERY
833 E Center St
Milwaukee, WI 53212
(414) 372-3372

AVENUE ART
10 W College Ave
Appleton, WI 54911
(414) 734-7710

BERGSTROM MAHLER MUSEUM
165 N Perk Ave
Neenah, WI 54956
(414) 751-4658

BRODEN GALLERY, LTD
114 State St
Madison, WI 53703
(608) 256-6100

CEDAR CREEK POTTERY
N70 W6340 Bridge Rd
Cedarburg, WI 53012
(414) 375-1226

CONCEPTS IN ART
2605 Kennedy
Janesville, WI 53545
(608) 756-0333
**GUILD Artist: Joyce Marquess
Carey, see page 35.**

DELIND FINE ART
801 N Jefferson St
Milwaukee, WI 53202
(414) 271-8525

EDGEWOOD ORCHARD
GALLERIES
W 4140 Peninsula Players Rd
Fish Creek, WI 54212
(414) 868-3579

FANNY GARVER GALLERY
230 State St
Madison, WI 53703
(608) 256-6755

FANNY GARVER GALLERY
7432 Mineral Point Road
Madison, WI 53717
(608) 833-8000

GALLERY 323 AT RUBINS
323 E Wilson St
Madison, WI 53703
(608) 255-8998

GALLERY OF WISCONSIN ART
931 E Ogden Ave
Milwaukee, WI 53202
(414) 278-8088
**GUILD Artist: Bruce Siegel, see
page 159.**

J M KOHLER ART CENTER
608 New York Ave
Sheboygan, WI 53081-4507
(414) 458-6144

JOHNSTON GALLERY
245 High St
Mineral Point, WI 53565
(608) 987-3787

JURA SILVERMAN GALLERY
143 S Washington St
Spring Green, WI 53588
(608) 588-7049

KATIE GINGRASS GALLERY
241 N Broadway
Milwaukee, WI 53202-5819
(414) 289-0855
**GUILD Artist: Nancy Moore Bess,
see page 199.**

METRO ONE GALLERY
7821 Egg Harbor Rd
Egg Harbor, WI 54209
(414) 868-3399

MINKOFF FINE ART, LTD
10004 N Kirkland Ct
Mequon, WI 53092
(414) 242-5900

MOYER GALLERY
900 Cedar St
Green Bay, WI 54301
(414) 435-3388

NEW VISIONS GALLERY, INC
1000 N Oak Ave
Marshfield, WI 54449
(715) 387-5562

STONE POTTERY & TILEWORKS
105 Commerce St
Mineral Point, WI 53565
(608) 987-2903

STONEHILL CRAFTS
10326 N Hwy 42
Ephraim, WI 54211
(414) 854-4749

THE HANG UP GALLERY
204 W Wisconsin Ave
Neenah, WI 54956
(414) 722-0481

THE POSNER GALLERY
207 N Milwaukee St
Milwaukee, WI 53202
(414) 273-3097

THE PUMP HOUSE
Regional Center for the Arts
119 King St
La Crosse, WI 54601
(608) 785-1434

THE RED BALLOON GALLERY
Hwy 35
P.O. Box 606
Stockholm, WI 54769
(715) 442-2504

THE WOODLOT GALLERY
5215 Evergreen Dr
Sheboygan, WI 53081
(414) 458-4798

TORY FOLLIARD GALLERY
233 N Milwaukee St
Milwaukee, WI 53202
(414) 273-7311

VALPARINE GALLERY
1719 Monroe St
Madison, WI 53711
(608) 256-4040

WISCONSIN ARTISAN
GALLERY
6858 Paoli Rd
Belleville, WI 53508
(608) 845-6600

• Wyoming

ART WEST GALLERY
P.O. Box 1248
Jackson, WY 83001
(307) 733-6379

• Canada

A SHOW OF HANDS GALLERY
1947 Avenue Rd
Toronto, Ontario
Canada M5M 4AZ
(416) 782-1696

CABBAGES & KING
710 Ninth St
Canmore, Alberta
Canada T0L 0M0
(403) 678-6915

DUNES STUDIO GALLERY
Brackley Beach, RR #1
Prince Edward Island
Canada C0A 2H0
(902) 672-2586

INUIT GALLERY
345 Water St
Vancouver, BC
Canada V6B 1B8
(608) 688-7323

MOUNTAIN AVENS GALLERY
709 Eighth St, P.O. Box 47
Canmore, Alberta
Canada T0L 0M0
(403) 678-4471

NIJINSKA'S GALLERY
Cairbou St
Banff, Alberta
Canada T0L 0C0
(403) 762-5006

SANDRA AINSLEY GALLERY
2 First Canadian Plaza
Toronto, Quebec
Canada M5X 168
**GUILD Artist: Cohn-Stone Studios,
see page 185.**

SUSAN WHITNEY GALLERY
2220 Lorne St
Regina, Saskatchewan
Canada S4P 2M7
(306) 569-9279

THE ART GLASS GALLERY
21 Hazleton Ave
Toronto, Ontario
Canada M5R 2E1
(416) 968-1823

THE PRIME GALLERY
52 McCaul St
Toronto, Ontario
Canada M5T 1V9
(416) 593-5750

THE QUEST
105 Banff Ave
Banff, Alberta
Canada T0L 0C0
(403) 762-2722

National Organizations and Associations

AMERICAN CRAFT COUNCIL
72 Spring Street
New York, NY 10012-4006
(212) 274-0630
Carol Sedestrom Ross

The American Craft Council is a national, nonprofit educational organization founded in 1943 to encourage craftspeople and to foster appreciation of their work. Membership is open to all. The programs of the Council include:

1. A.C.E. Marketing – addressing the marketing needs of American craftspeople through wholesale and retail juried fairs held across the country;

2. American Craft Association – providing a variety of support services for professional craftspeople and other craft businesses;

3. American Craft Publishing – promoting knowledge and appreciation of craft through publication of the bimonthly magazine *AMERICAN CRAFT*;

4. American Craft Information Center – serving the informational needs of members and the public through maintenance of unique reference collections on 20th-century American craft.

The American Craft Museum located at 40 West 53 Street, New York, NY 10019 is an affiliate of the Council.

AMERICAN ASSOCIATION OF WOODTURNERS
667 Harriet Avenue
Shoreview, MN 55126-4085
(612) 484-9094
FAX: (612) 484-1724
Mary Redig, Administrator

The American Association of Woodturners (AAW) is a non-profit corporation dedicated to the advancement of woodturning. Its fundamental purposes are to provide education, information, and organization for those interested in woodturning. Members include hobbyists, professionals, gallery owners, collectors and wood and equipment suppliers.

AMERICAN SOCIETY OF FURNITURE ARTISTS
P.O. Box 270188
Houston, TX 77277-0188
(713) 660-8855
Adam St. John, President/Executive Director

The American Society of Furniture Artists (ASOFA) is a non-profit organization dedicated exclusively to the field of "art furniture" and to the artists who create it. Organized in 1989, ASOFA is the only national organization of such artists.

The Society's nationwide scope and juried membership procedures promote the highest professional standards and provide its members with significant avenues for continued artistic and professional development.

AMERICAN TAPESTRY ALLIANCE
Route 1, Box 79-A
Goshen, VA 24439
(703) 997-5104
Jim Brown, Director

The American Tapestry Alliance was founded in 1982 to: (1) promote an awareness of and appreciation for tapestries designed and woven in America; (2) establish, perpetuate and recognize superior quality tapestries by American tapestry artists; (3) encourage greater use of tapestries by corporate and private collectors; (4) educate the public about tapestry (its history and technique), and to encourage them to recognize high-quality work by local and national contemporary tapestry artists; (5) coordinate national and international juried tapestry shows, exhibiting the finest quality American-made works.

ARCHITECTURAL WOODWORK INSTITUTE
P.O. Box 1550
13924 Braddock Road, Suite 100
Centreville, VA 22020
(703) 222-1100
FAX: (703) 222-2499
H. Keith Judkins, Executive Vice President

Setting the standard of excellent performance for finish carpentry and architectural woodwork for over 30 years, the Architectural Woodwork Institute (AWI) serves the construction industry as a voluntary association of professional woodworkers. The institute promotes the use of fine woodwork through programs of value; through the establishment of quality standards; through education; through publications; through certification; and through governmental and environmental awareness. AWI promotes integrity, quality, and value among customers, design professionals, suppliers and members.

ARTIST-BLACKSMITHS' ASSOCIATION OF NORTH AMERICA
P.O. Box 1181
Nashville, Indiana 47448
(812) 988-6919
Janelle Franklin, Executive Secretary

Artist-Blacksmiths' Association of North America (ABANA) is a non-profit organization devoted to promoting the art of blacksmithing. ABANA serves to help educate blacksmiths, acts as a central resource for information about blacksmithing, and publishes *Anvil's Ring* a quarterly technical journal for blacksmiths.

INTERART CENTER
167 Spring Street
New York, NY 10012
Birgit Spears, Executive Director

The InterArt Center is an independent non-profit art center focusing on interdisciplinary fiber arts. CTA provides a resource library and artists' slide file, educational programming, and thematic group and solo exhibitions.

EMBROIDERERS' GUILD OF AMERICA, INC.
335 W. Broadway, Suite 100
Louisville, KY 40202
(502) 589-6956
Judy Jeroy, President

The Embroiderers' Guild of America's (EGA) purpose is to set and maintain high standards of design, color and workmanship in all kinds of embroidery and canvaswork. EGA sponsors lectures, exhibitions, competitions and field trips; offers examinations for teaching certification; and serves as an information source for needlework in the U.S. EGA also maintains a comprehensive embroidery book and reference library for research and study, and publishes *Needle Arts,* quarterly.

GLASS ART SOCIETY
1305 4th Avenue, Suite 711
Seattle, WA 98101
(206) 382-1305
FAX: (206) 382-2630
Alice Rooney, Executive Director

The Glass Art Society (GAS) is an international non-profit organization founded in 1971 to encourage excellence and to advance the appreciation, understanding and development of the glass arts worldwide. The Society holds an annual conference and publishes the *Glass Art Society Journal* and semi-annual newsletters as well as a roster of the membership each year.

HANDWEAVERS GUILD OF AMERICA, INC.
120 Mountain Avenue, B101
Bloomfield, CT 06002
(203) 242-3577
FAX: (203) 243-3982
Janet Hutson, Development Director

The Handweavers Guild of America is dedicated to upholding excellence, promoting textile arts and preserving textile heritage. It accomplishes this by providing a forum for education, inspiration and encouragement of handweavers, handspinners and related fiber artists.

INTERNATIONAL SCULPTURE CENTER
1050 17th St. NW, Ste. 250
Washington, DC 20036
(202) 785-1144
FAX: (202) 785-0810
Milari Madison

The International Sculpture Center (ISC) is a non-profit membership organiztion devoted to the advancement of contemporary sculpture. The ISC publishes *Sculpture* magazine, *Maquette,* and *InSite.* Activities include conferences; workshops; Sculpture Source - a computerized referral service and registry; exhibitions; and various other member benefits.

INTERNATIONAL TAPESTRY NETWORK

P.O. Box 203228
Anchorage, AK 99520-3228
(907) 346-2392
FAX: (907) 346-2392
Helga Berry, President

International Tapestry Network (ITNET) is a not-for-profit global network of tapestry artists, teachers, curators and collectors. ITNET works to develop greater awareness of contemporary tapestry as an art form by sponsoring international tapestry exhibitions, educating the public about tapestry, and encouraging dialogue on an international level between people involved with tapestry. ITNET publishes a quarterly newsletter distributed worldwide. Newsletter correspondents and advisory board members search for and share news of exhibitions, educational opportunities and other tapestry events.

NATIONAL COUNCIL ON EDUCATION FOR THE CERAMIC ARTS

P.O. Box 1677
Bandon, OR 97411
(503) 347-4394
Regina Brown, Executive Secretary

The National Council on Education for the Ceramic Arts (NCECA) is a professional organization of individuals whose interests, talents, or careers are primarily focused on the ceramic arts.

Its purposes are to stimulate, promote and improve education in the ceramic arts, to gather and disseminate information and ideas that are vital and stimulating to the teachers, studio artists and to everyone throughout the creative studies community.

NATIONAL ORNAMENTAL & MISCELLANEOUS METALS ASSOCIATION

804-10 Main St., Suite E
Forest Park, GA 30050
(404) 363-4009
Barbara Cook, Executive Director

The National Ornamental & Miscellaneous Metals Association (NOMMA) is the trade organization for those who produce ornamental gates, railings, furniture, sculpture and other fabricated metal products. NOMMA publishes a professional "glossy" magazine, newsletter, plus various sales aids. The association also holds an annual awards competition, trade show and convention. During the convention, NOMMA provides an intensive education program. NOMMA has six chapters, one regional association, and 20 committees.

NATIONAL WOODCARVERS ASSOCIATION

7424 Miami Avenue
Cincinnati, OH 45243
(513) 561-0627
Edward F. Gallenstein, President

The National Woodcarvers Association's (NWCA) aims are to promote woodcarving; fellowship among its members; encourage exhibitions and area get-to-gethers; list tool and wood suppliers; find markets for those who sell their work.

Many distinguished professional woodcarvers in the United States and abroad share their know-how with fellow members. NWCA proudly lists several internationally famous authors of carving books on its roster.

SOCIETY OF AMERICAN SILVERSMITHS

P.O. Box 3599
Cranston, RI 02910-0599
(401) 461-3156
Jeffrey Herman, Director

The Society of American Silversmiths (SAS) was founded in April 1989 to preserve the art and history of handcrafted holloware and flatware, and to provide its artisan members with support, networking and greater access to the market. SAS also educates the public in demystifing silversmithing techniques and the aesthetic and investment value of this art form through its free consulting service. Another aim of SAS is to assist those students who have a strong interest in becoming silver craftsmen, through supplier discounts and workshops throughout the school year. In addition to an outstanding benefits package, all members have access to SAS's technical and marketing expertise, artisan archives and a referral service that commissions work from its artisans.

SOCIETY OF NORTH AMERICAN GOLDSMITHS

5009 Londonderry Drive
Tampa, FL 33647
(813) 977-5326
FAX: (813) 977-8462
Bob Mitchell, Business Manager

The Society of North American Goldsmiths (SNAG) was founded in 1970 to promote contemporary metalwork and jewelry. Through its publications, services and advocacy, the Society serves the fine art and jewelry communities with publications and conferences for members, practitioners and teachers of metalwork. Professional metalsmiths, students, collectors, gallery owners and enthusiasts form the dynamic mix of the Society.

SURFACE DESIGN ASSOCIATION

P.O. Box 20799
Oakland, CA 94620
(415) 567-1992
Charles S. Talley, Editor and Administrator

The purpose of the Surface Design Association (SDA) is to stimulate, promote, and improve education in the area of surface design; to encourage the surface designer as an individual artist; to educate the public with regard to surface design as an art form; to improve communication and distribution of technical information among artists, designers, educators, and with industry; to disseminate information concerning professional opportunities in surface design through galleries, studios, workshops, small businesses, industry, and education; to provide opportunities for surface designers to exhibit their work, and to provide a forum for exchange of ideas through conferences and publications.

In addition to sponsorship of local, regional and national workshop conferences, the SDA produces the *Surface Design Journal,* a 52-page full-color quarterly magazine, and the *SDA News,* a 12-page quarterly newsletter. The SDA also sponsors the annual Betty Park Award in critical writing and makes available limited scholarship assistance to promising students.

WOODWORKING ASSOCIATION OF NORTH AMERICA

Box 667
Falmouth, MA 02541-0667
(508) 548-2555
Steve Chalmers, Managing Director

The Woodworking Association of North America (WANA) serves individuals and companies engaged in woodworking and promotes woodworking as an artform. WANA issues a member bonus packet with plans and special offers. The association also sponsors the Woodworking World Shows with seminars, workshops, and exhibits.

Price Index

Page	Artist	Item/Location/Price
9	Karen Adachi	top, $1,100; bottom, $1,400
10	Martha Chatelain	$800 - $5,000
12	Susana England	*Azul*, left, $300; *Unquilted*, right, $900
13	Joseph Gallo	Monoprint, top left, $700; Monoprint, top right, $350; Monoprint, bottom right, $650; Monoprint, bottom left, $350
14	Susan Gardels	$500 - $1,800
15	Lenore Hughes	$300 - $5,000
16	Joan Kopchik	*Cascade*, top, $800; *Hanging Garden*, bottom, $800
17	Cal Ling	*Fall Rice Fields - Part I*, top, $1,600; *Purple Sky Over Rice Fields*, bottom, $3,150
18	Marjorie Tomchuk	*Red Lake*, top, $3,600; *Sunrise Valley I*, bottom, $3,600
19	Ellen Zahorec	*The Triangular Edge*, top, $2,000; *Guardians of the Holy Virgins*, bottom right, $800; *Sixty Year Shroud #2*, bottom left, $3,500
21	Rebecca Bluestone	*New Sounds*, top, $2,950; *Silk Journey*, bottom right, $1,500; *Hexagram*, bottom left, $2,250
22	Linda Denier	*Do You Know the Way*, top, $1,150; *Oz*, bottom, $2,400
23	Alexandra Friedman	$150 sq. ft. - $225 sq. ft.
24	Irene R. de Gair	*Lillies*, top, $1,500; *Coral Panels*, middle, $70 ft., *Triangles*, bottom left, $75 ft.; *Landscape*, bottom right, $85 ft.
25	Victor Jacoby	*Warner Mountain Landscape*, bottom, $1,200; *On the Road Again*, top, $1,800
29	Loretta Mossman	*Vestido en Magica*, bottom, $5,000; *Arches of Dawn*, top right, $2,500; *Red Sand*, top left, $4,500
30	Deann Rubin	$300 sq. ft. - $350 sq. ft.
31	Efrem Weitzman	$120 sq. ft. - $400 sq. ft.
33	B.J. Adams	*Isolated Permanence*, top, $1,000; *Ten Views of Milford Sound*, bottom, $2,300
34	Barbara Cade	*Pansy*, top, $1,500; *Lily*, bottom, $2,900
35	Joyce Marquess Carey	*Building Blocks*, top, $130 sq. ft.; *Ribbon Candy*, bottom, $170 sq. ft.
36	Gloria E. Crouse	*Creme-de-la-Creme*, top, $150 sq. ft.; *Diverse-Directions*, bottom, $12,000
38	Layne Goldsmith	Modular Wall-Relief Hangings, starting at $100 sq. ft.
39	Ruth Gowell	*Tropical Patterns*, top, $2,500; From *Series IV*, bottom, $240 - $300
42, 43	Marie-Laure Ilie	Pg. 42, Ancient Art, $100 sq. ft. - $120 sq. ft. retail; Pg. 43, *Sailing Red and Blue*, top, $2,600 retail, *Beyond Memories*, bottom, $3,500 retail
45	M.A. Klien	*Twilight in the Hills*, left, $2,500; *Blue Grotto*, right, $3,500
46, 47	Joyce Lopez Studio	Sculpture, top, $8,000; Sculpture, bottom, $6,200; Sculpture, opposite, $6,400
48	Bonnie Lhotka	*Southwest Sign*, left, $900; *Phone Home*, right, $3,900
49	Dottie Moore	*Dreams*, $1,800
50	Karen Perrine	*Still Water*, top, $5,375
51	Joan Schulze	*East Wall*, top, $2,500; *South Wall*, bottom, $2,500

Page	Artist	Item/Location/Price
54	Joan Stubbins	*The Dawn Series: Revelations I*, bottom, $2,000
79	George Alexander	*Harvest Mirror*, top, $3,700; *Harvest Bowl*, top, $1,000; *Corn Pilasters*, bottom right, $8,500; *Bough Mirror*, bottom left, $5,000; *Harvest Vases*, bottom left, $1,500
80	Frank Colson	Multiface Units, $225 each
81	Jamie Fine	$100 sq. ft. - $110 sq. ft. wholesale
82	Loraine A. Fischer	*The Verdict is Wrong*, top, $980; *Sky Watcher*, bottom, $650
84, 85	Elizabeth MacDonald	Tilework, $250 sq. ft.
86	Richard Thomas Keit Studio	Hand-Glazed Tile Carpets, $180 sq. ft. - $240 sq. ft.
87	William C. Richards	25" Ceramic Plate, top left, $600; Bottles and Bowl, top right, bottles: $250; bowls $350; Six-piece Ceramic Panels, bottom, $1950
89	Alan Steinberg	*Kauai*, top, $975; *Acadia*, bottom, $550
90	David Westmeier	*Ancient Koan*, top, $900; *Primordial Vestiges*, bottom, $1,200
93	John P. Ashley	Serpentine Table, top, $8,000; Sofa Table, top, $6,900; *Soaring*, bottom, $5,280
95	Bruce R. Bleach	Paintings, top, $5,000, bottom, $15,000
96	Lucinda Carlstrom	starting at $100 sq. ft.
97	Beth Cunningham	*Genesis*, top, $500; *Catharsis*, bottom, $750
98	Jeffrey Cooper	Mural, $3,750
105	Trena McNabb	Reynolds Tobacco Company, top left, $20,000; Midcon Corporation, top right, $9,000; Knight Foundation, bottom, $5,000
106	Ervin Somogyi	*Quilted Maple Shield*, top right, $475; *Japanesque Rosette*, bottom right, $1,000; *Celtic Design*, bottom left, $1,100
108	Vincent Tolpo and Carolyn L. Tolpo	$100 sq. ft. - $250 sq. ft.
112	Carter Blocksma	Wall Unit, top, $11,000; Game Table, middle, $4,000; Game Table Chairs, middle, $1,700; Wave Wall Cabinet, bottom, $5,500
114	Donald M. De Witt	Canopy Bed, top right, $1,500; Sofa, bottom right, $1,500; Panel Bed, $1,200, bottom left
116	Kevin Earley	Club Chairs, top, $3,200 each; Reception Desk, bottom, $24,000
118	Murray P. Gates	Sofa Table, top, $1,200; Display Cabinet, bottom, $3,600
119	Glen Grant	*Geese at Rest*, top, $1,150; *Night on the Town*, bottom, $12,500
121	Steve Holman	Ariodante Chair, top, $975; Sideboard, bottom, $7,995
122	Peter Maynard	Pembroke Table, top, $4,000; English Dining Chair, top, $2,000 each, set of ten, Chinese Console Table, bottom right, $13,000; English Dining Table, bottom left, $15,000
123	Ronald C. Puckett	*Bench-a-sarus*, top left, $5,500; *Chaps Chest*, top right, $11,000; *O/M Cocktail Table*, bottom, $7,000
124	David M. Schiller and Bernice Schiller	*Cactus Floor Mirror*, left, $2,300; *Neo/Petro Bench*, bottom right, $2,000; *Feather Table*, top right, $900
125	Anne Shutan	Walnut Bench, top, $6,000; Walnut Dining Table, bottom, $5,000
126	Thomas Hugh Stangeland	Greene & Greene Style Chair, top, $3,000 each, four or more $2,700 each; Buffet, bottom, $4,500

Price Index

Page	Artist	Item/Location/Price
127	Tiger Mountain Woodworks	Oak Trestle Table and lamp, middle right, Table: $2,400 Lamp: $650; Mountain Laurel Desk, bottom right, $2,400; Mountain Laurel Demilune Counsole, left, $1,800
131	George Gradzki	*Flamingo*, bottom, $6,750; Coffee Table, top, $2,650
132	John Kennedy Studios	*Meditation*, top left, $3,800; *Friendship Bench*, top right, $15,000; *Sun Girl*, bottom right, $3,800; *Tranquility II*, middle left, $7,000; *Dancers*, bottom left, $8,500
133	Marsha Lega	*Table F*, top right, $850; *Sculpture #101*, top right, $750; Tables, bottom, $750 - $990; Sculptures, bottom, $650 - $950; Mirror, bottom, $420
137	Larry Benjamin	Glass End Table, top, $1,800; Glass Cocktail Table, bottom, $2,800
138	John Blazy	*The Orient Goes Modern*, top, $1,200; *Crimson Tunnel Syndrome*, bottom, $3,500
142	Johanna Okovic Goodman	*Marie Antoinette*, top left, $1,250; *Toga*, bottom right, $800; *Gold Tux*, bottom left, $1,000
143	Greg Sheres Studio	$1,800 - $20,000
144	Joan Irving	Spiral Circle Accent Table, top, $990; Console Table, bottom, $2,800
145	Slateworks	Egyptian Figure, top, $1,000; Coffee Table Inlay, bottom, $4,000
148	Susan J. Brasch	$1,500 - $5,000
154	Bob Brown and Judy Dykstra-Brown	Floor Lamp, top left, $1,200; Vase, top right, $350; Floor/Table Lamp, bottom right, $1,200; Table Lamp, bottom middle, $600; Vase, Floor Lamp, bottom left, vase: $450, lamp: $1,500
155	Christopher Thomson Ironworks	Spiral Candlesticks, top right, $100 each; Fireplace Tool Set, top right, $328, Log Holder, top right, $201; tables, bottom, $402 - $745 (without glass); Lamps and Shades, bottom, $210 - $350
157	Brian McNally	Leaded Glass Lamp, top, $5,000; Leaded Glass Screen, bottom, $6,500
158	Cathy Richardson	Cylindrical Lamps, left, $800, right, $1,600
159	Bruce Siegel	$250 - $2,000
160	Angelika Traylor	Lamp, top, $6,500; Panel, bottom, $4,000
163	Carl T. Chew	*Zena Sees a Hoopoe*, top, $5,500; *Koi 8*, bottom, $9,975
166	Sue Harmon	starting at $600
167	Helio Graphics	Canvas Pillows, top right, $95 - $120; *Dolphin and Moons*, bottom right, $475, *Going Bananas*, left, $165
169	Boots Culbertson	*Starburst*, top, $500; Group of Fountains, bottom, $500 - $800
170	Linda Dixon and Drew Krouse	*Lizard Temple*, top, $800; Platter, bottom, $200; Bowl, $50, bottom; Teapot, bottom, $65; Large Vase, bottom, $350
171	Edith A. Ehrlich	*Lucifer I*, top left, $400; *Lucifer II*, top right, $400; *Broom Sprouting*, bottom, $300
173	Claudia Hollister	*Enchanted Evening*, top right, $500; *Still Life Stamps*, top left, $250; *Still Life Tea Pot*, Vase, Pitcher, bottom, tea pot: $350; vase: $400; pitcher: $300
174	Tom Neugebauer	*Lifedance II*, top left, $4,200; *At the Center is Strength*, right, $2,500; *The Appeal II*, bottom left, $2,200
175	Charles Pearson and Tim Roeder	starting at $475
176	Betsy Ross	Mini-Vessels, top, $60 - $70; Black/Bronzed Vessel with Handle, bottom, $790; Lidded Vessel, bottom, $1,200; Pedestal Vessel, bottom, $650

Price Index

Page	Artist	Item/Location/Price
177	Linda Bruce Salomon	Ceramic Figurine on Jar, top, $200; Ceramic Dolls and Accessories, bottom, $280 each
181	David Westmeier	Charger, $450; Lamp, $475, Vessel, $425
185	Cohn-Stone Studios	Sand Blown Vessels, top right, $900 - $1,500; Reflecting Bowl Series, middle right, $850 - $1,200; Nest with Eggs, bottom right, $1,200; Tortoise Shell Series, bottom left, $160 - $1,200
186	Dale R. Eggert	Two-Piece Screen, left, $5,800; Sculpture, top right, $2,600; Sculpture, bottom, $2,800
188	J.C. Homola	Fused Dichronic Glass, top right, $420; Fused Dichronic Glass, top left, $380
189	Christine E. McEwan	$25 - $180
190	David Jaworski	*Quest*, top, $8,000; *Cirrus*, bottom, $45,000
193	Orient & Flume Art Glass	*Winter*, top left, $950; Assorted Work, top right, $60 - $1,150; Assorted Fruit, bottom right, $40 - $50; *Square 1*, bottom left, $350
195	Wendy Saxon Brown	*Wash Day*, top, $1,600; *Flat Boxes*, bottom left, $1,100; *Stairs*, bottom right, $1,700
196	Patricia Weyer	*Portal*, top left, $2,000; *Threshhold*, top right, $2,400; *Free of the Freize*, bottom, $5,000 each torso
197	Jonathan Winfisky	Cast Design Bowl, Vase, Perfume Vial, top, bowl, vase: $400 - $500 vial: $90; Bud Vase, Ming Vase, top, bud vase: $120; Ming vase: $350 - $400; Sculptural Design Series Bowl and Vase, bottom, $400 - $500 each; Fluted Bud Vase, Perfume Vial, bottom, vase: $100, vial: $70; Tapered Bud Vase, bottom, $80
201	E.S. Walsh	$80 - $1,000
203	Robert Hargrave	Life Size Standing Figure, right, $1,500; Triple Mirror with Shelf, left, $600
205	Carol Kropnick	$750 - $2,000
206	Anne Mayer Meier	*Old Souls*, top, $75; *Ancestor*, $150; bottom right, *Clan of Wisdom*, bottom left, $575
207	Susan M. Oaks	Fiber Vessels, top right, $350, bottom right, $175, left, $300
208	Lori A. Paladino	Wall Mirror, top, $2,000; Clock, bottom left, $300; Hand Mirrors, bottom right, $150
210	Judy Stone	Bowl, top, $185; Light Switch Cover, bottom, $125
211	S.M. Warren	$800 - $4,000
212	Nancy Young and Allen Young	Handcast Paper Vessels, top left, $35 - $300; Free Standing Sculptures, right, $1,000 - $3,000; Wall Pieces, right, $300 - $700; Wall Shield, bottom left, $900
214	Joseph L. Brandom	Torso, top right, $10,000; Pewter Vessel, bottom, $1,700
215	David M Bowman Studio	Etched, Patinaed Vase, top, $350; Patinaed Round Vases, bottom, $60 - $130
216	Don Drumm	*Stallion*, top, $225; *Chief Joseph's Last Ride*, bottom, $225
219	Andrew Moritz	*Ndovu*, $14,000
220	Martin Sturman	*Adam and Eve*, right, $2,750; Firescreen, bottom left, $1,800; *Dancers*, top left, $975
221	Wasserman Studios	Single Axis Mobile, top right, $1,500; Stabile, top left, $5,000; Multi Axis Mobile, bottom, $10,000

Index of Artists and Companies

Index of Artists and Companies

State-by-State Index of Artists